"*True Worship* is a forthright challe. ....
·tians—whether in evangelical, charismatic, ᴏᵣ .....
tions—to consider a life-changing way to worship the Father,
Son, and Holy Spirit. It is a clear call to local gatherings to
engage in God-exalting transformation and provides practical
instructions to that end. Hustad's well-informed, thoroughly
biblical, and deeply compassionate viewpoint will most certainly help heal our contemporary shortsightedness."

—**William Lock,** *professor of church music, Biola University*

"This book is a fresh voice crying in the wilderness of too many
misguided worship practices in America. It provides a succinct
history of the recent movements in American worship which
have led many churches astray. Hustad emphasizes the historical, biblical, theological, musical, sociological, and practical
undertandings which too often have been forgotten or abandoned in the search to be "with it" for the younger generations.

True Worship is a clarion call to remember and relearn what
true worship is and how music can be helpful in blended,
thematic, participatory, theocentric, and emotionally moving
worship. This is a practical handbook for every minister and
church musician to study together and share with their church
leaders. Most highly recommended!"

—**Austin C. Lovelace,** *author and composer*

"In *True Worship* Hustad in effect is asking, 'Does the church
have a song?' Amid the destructive iconoclasm that characterizes much evangelical worship today, Hustad seeks to
answer this question with the authenticity of one thoroughly
knowledgeable in Scripture, with the integrity of a church
musician with sixty years of experience, and with the discernment of a prophet in a vast wilderness of cultural profanity.

Although he speaks from a *sola scriptura* orientation, Hustad
has thorough command of the traditions that have shaped the
church's worship. You may not always agree with his analysis,

but if you consider it carefully, you will move in the direction of worshiping the Creator 'in spirit and truth.' "

—**C. Michael Hawn,** *professor of church music,*
Perkins School of Theology

"This book enables you to study the important subject of worship through three lenses: biblical theology, church history, and the personal, practical experience of a man whose credentials are impeccable. No 'generation bashing' here and no jeremiads. Just solid theology, historical perspective, and wise counsel from a gifted musician/educator who knows—and cares."

—**Warren W. Wiersbe,** *author and conference speaker*

TRUE WORSHIP

RECLAIMING THE

Wonder &
Majesty

Donald P. Hustad

Harold Shaw Publishers
Wheaton, Illinois

Hope Publishing Company
CAROL STREAM IL 60188

All Scripture quotations, unless otherwise indicated, are taken from the *New Revised Standard Version* of the Bible, copyright © 1989 by the Division of Christian Education of the National Council of the Churches of Christ in the United States of America. Used by permission. All rights reserved.

Scripture quotations marked *NIV* are taken from the HOLY BIBLE, NEW INTERNATIONAL VERSION®. NIV®. Copyright © 1973, 1978, 1984 International Bible Society. Used by permission of Zondervan Publishing House. All rights reserved.

Scriptures marked *KJV* are taken from the King James Version.

Grateful acknowledgment is made to the following for permission to reprint lyrics, poetry, and stories:

"Before the World Began" by John Bell and Graham Maule, pages 75–76. From *Iona Community Wild Goose Songs* © 1987 by Wild Goose Publications, Pearce Institute, 840 Wovan Road, Glasgow G51 3UT, Scotland. Distributed in the United States by GIA Publications, Inc., 7404 S. Mason Ave., Chicago, IL 60638. Used by permission.

"Holy Ground" by Geron Davis, page 100. © 1983 by Meadowgreen Music Company/Songchannel Music Co. All rights reserved. Used by permission.

"The Old Woman in the Cave" by Jane Yolen, pages 189–190. Text copyright © 1986 by Jane Yolen. First appeared in *Favorite Folktales from Around the World*, edited by Jane Yolen and published by Putnam Books, a division of Random House. Used by permission of Curtis Brown, Ltd.

"Prayer for Those Who Make Music," pages 213–214. Copyright by Bryan Jeffery Leech. Used by permission.

Shaw Publishers ISBN 0-87788-838-8
Hope Publishing Code No. 8050

Cover design by David LaPlaca
Cover photo © 1998 by D. Jeanene Tiner

Library of Congress Cataloging-in-Publication Data

Hustad, Donald
    True worship : reclaiming the wonder and majesty / by Donald Hustad
      p.   cm.
    Includes bibliographical references (p.   ).
    ISBN 0-87788-838-8
1. Church music Protestant churches.   2. Evangelicalism.
  I. Title.
  ML3100.H89   1998
  264'.2—dc21   98-23744

---

03 02 01 00 99 98

10 9 8 7 6 5 4 3 2 1

Contents

9 Worshiping God in Educational Truth

in a Strange Land of Intellectual Ambivalence 248

Foreword

History takes curious twists and turns. There have been times when a Baptist and a Lutheran would not have been talking to each other. At such times I would certainly not have been asked to write a foreword for one of Don Hustad's books! But we live in a different ethos. As Hustad says, our current disputes are in-tramural, not *between* denominations or various confessional orientations but *within* them, especially within individual con-gregations. I have sometimes described the scene as sectarian tents peopled with a few combatants who come out long enough to shoot across the aisle at their brothers and sisters be-fore they retreat again into their preserves of private opinion. Martin Marty has described it as "firers of heavy cannon" aimed at each other from atop two mesas, with unwitting noncombat-ants taking cover as best they can in the valley below.[1]

However you describe it, as Hustad says, all communions except the Orthodox "are arguing bitterly" about worship's form and style. This suggests that a Roman Catholic, a Presby-terian, an Episcopalian, a Methodist, a Lutheran, a Mennonite, a representative from the United Church of Christ, or one from any number of other perspectives could have written this book. Each of us would have written it somewhat differently. We wouldn't have said exactly what Hustad has said, nor would we have said it the way he says it, as Marva Dawn's *Reaching Out without Dumbing Down* illustrates.[2] But we would all agree that serious matters lie behind the superficial rhetoric we often hear. We need to thank Don Hustad for having the courage to articulate the serious matters from his perspective. We can all learn something from him.

Though Hustad suggests his "evangelical" tradition may lose its way at the moment more easily than "liturgical" ones, the lure of commercial success and treating people badly is not limited by denominational configurations, confessional positions, or worship patterns. He may be pointing to the reality that historic liturgical forms do protect us from our attempts to foist ephemeral idiosyncrasies on one another, but all of us need to attend to what Hustad has to say. In the present cultural context, those of us in communions with more historic liturgical practices are as tempted to ignore our deepest insights and histories as everybody else is.

Twenty years ago Erik Routley noted "the shocking spectacle of churches feeling obligated to run two services on a Sunday morning, one popular or modern, the other traditional, thus effectively dividing their congregations into two parties which find it convenient not to meet."[3] Some Roman Catholics who began this procedure after Vatican II have more recently called it into question, while Protestants who were slower to begin it have now vigorously imitated their sisters and brothers without learning from their mistakes. This is the phenomenon Hustad addresses: two styles of worship along with an iconoclastic mindset that rejects "classic" hymnic, musical, and liturgical traditions.

Hustad is extremely concerned to be open to the Holy Spirit's renewing power. He wants proper change, recognizes its place, and finds it difficult to criticize what may seem to him ill-advised because it may be more than meets his singular gaze. He bends over backwards therefore to be fair to what he is seeing, and he exhibits compassion and respect for those who disagree with him. But he can't avoid some basic Christian affirmations which he is compelled to recapitulate in the terms of our age. He finds himself forced to look at the history of how we got where we are and then to say some things which he constructively develops. Here's a taste of a few of them:

- Human beings have brains which are not to be disengaged when matters of worship and faith come into view.
- There are biblical themes which cannot be avoided if we are to be faithful.
- We ought to know what theological factors undergird our respective traditions' musical practices and patterns of worship.

- Musical style can become an idol.
- Be wary of triumphalist claims.
- Integrity in our worship is not to be taken lightly.
- There is a difference between entertainment and worship.

In the process we get reflections on the Old and New Testaments; thoughts about instruments and solos; the temptations and dangers of loudness, handclapping, and tokenism; the importance of the congregation's singing, not simply the appearance thereof; the meaning of psalms, hymns, and spiritual songs; and discussions of the church, individualism, ecumenism, secularism, the media, electronic developments, quality, church growth, aesthetics, and education. True to his moderately Calvinist posture, Hustad includes a Service of Word and Table in the Genevan tradition, cognizant of biblical roots and ecumenical points of contact.

What Hustad is doing points to the curious situation which now pertains, namely, that church musicians like him are the most prophetic voices among us. They are far more prophetic than many preachers who have collapsed their message into that of the culture on the premise that it will sell and attract the most customers. Musicians in such situations get used as the church's version of commercial manipulators of the public.

Hustad is unwilling to collapse the Christian message into the cultural envelope of our time and place or into a single theme such as "praise." He is also unwilling to use music as a manipulative tool. Such a position is what makes him and church musicians like him prophetic. They and the rich heritage of the church's music point to a God whose grace is not identifiable with one time, one place, or one theme. Grace finds its locus in the person of Christ and the whole story of God's faithfulness from creation to consummation. Christ tented among us in the flesh at one time and place, to be sure, but he is also the Alpha and Omega of all time and all space. Hustad suggests a certain humility in such a presence might be appropriate. He would have our worship and its music point to God in Christ, not to our manipulative uses that highlight our own egos and power plays.

To get some perspective on the topic of this book, imagine a child who was born as Hustad was writing it. By the year 2020 Hustad and many of the rest of us may well be dead. The child will be twenty-two years old. What will we have left that child now become an adult? What will we have left the rest of our children? Will we have left a spiritual ecosystem parallel to the physical one we have polluted so badly? Will we have left a truncated part of the Christian story? Will we have left none of it? Will our children have to jump over our generation to earlier ones to find the Christian message again, or will we have celebrated its fullness in such a way that they can remember from our worship what transcended our understanding but will touch theirs?

If we leave our children without the fullness of the story, we will not be the first generation to do so. Fortunately God has graciously rescued the church in the past and promises to do so in the future. Let that reality remind us that our delusions of statistics and growth are like the grass that fades and withers in the evening. Let us learn from the "weak" oases of worship God raises up in every community which shame the "strong" and mighty whom, as Mary reminded us in the *Magnificat,* God puts down. Such oases are not characterized by any single denominational or confessional label, but in them the multi-textured heritage of the church's song resounds around Font, Word, and Table, nerved by the power of the Holy Spirit. In them commitments are made to real people in real neighbor-hoods with real needs, not to mighty statistical tabulations. In them the gospel is enfleshed in song. They provide the conti-nuity and ballast of the church for us and for those who follow us. It is such faithfulness and evangelical commitment to which Hustad points. We do well to listen to him.

Paul Westermeyer
Luther Seminary
St. Paul, Minnesota

Introduction and Acknowledgments

In my previous books, *Jubilate!* and *Jubilate II*, I began with a short record of my pilgrimage as a "schizophrenic musician." The research and writing for those volumes helped me to make sense of the anomalies and paradoxes with which I have wrestled since beginning my church music ministry.

In beginning this book, I am haunted with a new perplexity. How could the hopes for better church music—which have sustained me for more than fifty years—suddenly be threatened with extinction? Church music and worship have been dynamic arts during those years, with regular challenges and changes that I believed were healthy for the church. How is it then that many congregations are tending to reject much of their central heritage of music—hymns and gospel songs, and organ and choral music? And how could this insistence on iconoclastic change sweep across the country and around the world almost overnight?

I notice also that I am not alone in my confusion. Though changes in culture call for *proper* changes in worship and its arts, the rationale underlying today's new forms and practices often is faulty. Church growth specialists give advice about worship planning without considering biblical teachings or liturgical principles; church leaders follow their advice for purely pragmatic, often political reasons. Worship planners copy Willow Creek Community Church's "seeker event" paradigm for worship services, even though founder-pastor Bill Hybels warns them not to do so. Non-charismatics often borrow their worship style and congregational song materials from the charismatic renewal movement, without recognizing that the new forms and practices do not reflect or support their own theological heritage.

I am aware that, though we are experiencing more radical change than ever before in my lifetime, this is not the first worship/music revolution in church history. Notably in periods of renewal—the Reformation, the Pietist movements, the Camp Meetings and later American revivals—the church has abandoned worthy church music forms in favor of simpler, sometimes conspicuously inferior, styles. So as I have asked before: Is this another one of God's painful but promising revival times in the life of the church? Only in the last few months—watching the rise of renewal movements—have I begun to answer that maybe it is. I've watched the rise of renewal movements. The prominence of confession of sin in the recent Promise Keepers rallies and the acceptance of the movement by the media and the general public are encouraging. Also, though those "men only" stadium gatherings cannot be expected to model typical worship for local churches, their use of congregational song is more thoughtful, and therefore more exemplary, than most contemporary patterns.

This book is written principally for nonliturgical evangelicals, partly because Marva Dawn's monumental work, *Reaching Out without Dumbing Down,* is directed to her own heritage—the liturgical community—and partly because our temptations are more threatening than theirs. For many Lutherans, Episcopalians, and Catholics, being "contemporary" means changing the arts, especially music, without ravaging liturgical words and actions. Even so, I believe a church loses something important when it decides that all its music must be modern, that is, less than twenty-five years old. But it loses much more when it eliminates biblically authorized practices and words, and increasingly fails to recognize the difference between worship and contemporary entertainment!

I addressed many of these church music issues in *Jubilate II.* Having had more time for reflection, I reexamine them here at greater length. Because my pilgrimage has caused me to wrestle increasingly with questions about evangelical worship, that subject gets a new, central emphasis.

This is a book for study, not for casual reading. It is basically a primer of historical worship concepts but because evangelicals have just begun thinking about the subject, it requires careful perusal. Above all, *read all the Scripture passages completely.* As in all areas of life, the Bible is our best instructor in worship. What the Bible says for itself may be both more interesting and more significant to hear than what anyone says to explain it.

In our day of changing language that evokes strong opinions pro and con, it is difficult to write anything without offending someone. My own word choices will reflect my convictions about proper gender language, both for human beings and for God. However, a number of quotations will include gender-inclusive words such as "man" and "mankind" which I would not use in my own writing.

If the writing sounds at all prophetic, I hope it comes across as "weeping" rather than "thundering." None of us has any excuse for arrogance, especially when we remember our own failures to think straight and to act accordingly. My wife, Ruth, is often uncomfortable when I describe our wedding more than fifty years ago as "relatively pagan." The service included organ music, love songs, no congregational hymns, no reading of Scripture, no sermon, and scant prayer. But it was no different from any other nonliturgical wedding of that time and culture; to have added those other components would have seemed very strange to our families and friends. "Besides," says Ruth, "we didn't know better." "Yes, Darling," I reply, "but now we do!" Today, our weddings are often better liturgy—Thanks be to God!—but I fear our regular worship services are poorer. And that is a matter more for tears than for anger.

Many people have helped me write this book. Most of all, Paul Richardson has given generously of his time and wisdom. His musical and biblical-theological insights are matched by his skills in language and writing. Some sentences in the finished copy come verbatim from his red-ink comments on my original manuscript. Kerchal Armstrong also has helped immensely, by his encouragement, by sending me copies of the books and articles he reads, and by conducting discussions of the individual chapters with working church musicians in central Indiana.

Arnie Hustad, a Minnesota cousin, was instrumental in getting me off on the right foot biblically, especially in chapters 1, 3, and 4; it's good to know that there is a bona fide theologian and Bible scholar in the family! Calvin Johannson checked on the material pertaining to Pentecostal and charismatic renewal life. Wes Ramsey and Carol McClure were helpful in evaluating present-day commercial religious music. Students at Southern Baptist Theological Seminary worked with two preliminary drafts of the material, helping me find and strengthen the weak spots.

Through the years, George Shorney of Hope Publishing Company has been more generous than most publishers, probably because he considers friendship and shared goals to be germane to business success. The management and editors of Harold Shaw Publishers have also been very helpful.

Finally, thanks to my family who have contributed much to my thinking in always lively, sometimes heated discussions. Mark, Donna, Sondra, and Marcia have also read the manuscript and offered helpful comments. My wife, Ruth, with her encouragement, has kept me going when I was ready to quit, thinking at times that the battle was already lost, and at other times that I didn't have the necessary weapons to join the fray! To her, my love, this book is dedicated with love.

Apart from these credits, *Soli Deo gloria*—to God alone be glory.

Donald P. Hustad
Louisville, Kentucky

Prologue

Singing the Lord's Song
in a Strange Land

By the rivers of Babylon,
    there we sat down, yea, we wept,
    when we remembered Zion.
We hanged our harps upon the willows
    in the midst thereof.
For there they that carried us away captive
    required of us a song;
    and they that wasted us
    required of us mirth, saying,
    Sing us one of the songs of Zion.
How shall we sing the LORD's song
    in a strange land? (Psalm 137:1-3, KJV)

This is the Word of the Lord. *Thanks be to God.*

So begins a classic Hebrew "blues" song that contains some of the bitterest language in all the psalms of lament. Like all blues songs, it is also a ballad, a poignant narrative of personal experience. The singer—possibly a returning "son of Asaph," a Levitical temple musician—recalls the time when the forces of King Nebuchadnezzar overran the kingdom of Judah, sacked the city of Jerusalem and its temple, and carried him away with other Jewish survivors as servants to Babylon. There, tormenting captors derisively challenged them to provide entertainment in song. "Sing us one of your joyful, religious temple songs!" they said. The singer skillfully weaves into the lyrics images of agonizing sadness—the sitting posture (like Job on the ash heap), the silent harps hung in the "weeping" willows, and the final convulsive sob: "How shall we sing the LORD's song in a strange [foreign] land?"

For Jews, full worship occurred only in the beloved temple at Jerusalem, where sacrifices were offered regularly morning and evening, and the Levitical choir sang psalms and canticles from the two sides of the great altar. Some scholars believe that synagogue worship began during the Babylonian exile and that, for those services of Scripture reading, discussion, and prayer, priestly choir singers were pressed into service to chant the liturgy. If so, the experience narrated in Psalm 137 may have occurred outside the synagogue, where Jews would have felt it inappropriate to sing their sacred words and melodies, especially for entertainment purposes! Singing songs of worship on command, to please pagan listeners, would have secularized what to them had been holy. It could only have increased their feeling of hopelessness in dehumanizing captivity in a strange land.

The Strange Land of Modern Culture

In our own day as well, worship musicians find themselves in something of a "strange land" when singing the Lord's song. Many are involved in some degree of conflict because of opposing ideas about the style and content of worship. During the last several years, many churches have become convinced that the worship order they had always followed, and especially the music they used, was suddenly out of date! Almost overnight, often without careful study and discussion, both order and materials were changed radically, or a "contemporary" service was added to the schedule to accommodate the *stile moderno,* the *nuovo musicae.* Just as quickly, the church organized itself into opposing camps—or at the least, aggressive debating societies. One group justified the radical replacement of worship traditions as necessary in order to attract a certain group in society. The other faction contended that what was really happening was an unacceptable secularizing of everybody's worship experience. Sometimes the conflict literally tore the church in two!

In this book, I try to explain why the revolution occurred and to help thoughtful people prepare for the postrevolutionary future. I believe that the unfolding of events was a predictable evolution, which began in the historic practices of Christians known as "evangelicals." In a sense, given their history and mindset, plus post-World War II developments in modern popular culture, the revolution was as inevitable as it was troubling.

Setting the Stage Historically

American evangelicals (those who proclaim the "evangel" or "gospel" in terms of personal salvation) have taken the lead in evangelism and Christian missions for more than two hundred years. In frontier life, entire communities welcomed the itinerant evangelists and their accompanying musicians. The church's faithful rejoiced because people of God were coming to dispense divine grace, while the "unwashed" found the visitors' preaching and singing to be fully as entertaining as the traveling medicine man show.

To the present day, many evangelicals have exulted so much in their "free," nonliturgical identity, that few of their scholars have paid attention to the theology and practice of corporate worship. In their more mundane, year-round worship life, Sunday services have resembled evangelistic crusades or Bible study gatherings. One of their acknowledged tools of evangelism was the gospel song, whose words presented the basic gospel of sin-judgment-grace coupled with an invitation to "come to Jesus" or a testimony to the "born again" life in Christ. The music of the first gospel songs resembled that of Stephen Foster's ballads of the mid-nineteenth century. Like its secular model, gospel song music became popular with the masses; it provided the staple musical fare for Sunday services, was featured in occasional sacred concerts, and was distributed widely, thanks to typically American commerce. Critics of early revivalists called them "religious enthusiasts" because their services abounded in what the culture viewed as extravagant emotion, expressed in both the preaching and the music.

Evangelical life, with its limited range of worship styles and its folk-like, performance centered music, changed very little in the early twentieth century. A new communication device called radio appeared in the 1920s and was welcomed as a new medium for spreading the gospel.

The "big bang" which set off the present revolution in church music came at the close of World War II. All the pent-up dreams and hopes for the church, suppressed during those war years, suddenly began to be fulfilled. Evangelicals rose to the challenge of the new opportunities with their historic zeal for evangelism, an increased willingness to unite in ecumenical parachurch activity, and a new awareness of Madison Avenue promotional techniques. Further, they added a new element which almost guaranteed success—modern technology.

In the late 1940s, urban evangelicals presented Saturday night Youth for Christ (YFC) meetings—with a pleasant mix of entertainment, some elements of worship, a new brand of music that emphasized "choruses," and powerful preaching— to reach a specific age group. Billy Graham began his ministry as a YFC evangelist. When he moved on to conduct the largest evangelistic crusades in history, his service format became a new worship model for churches to copy. Of course, Billy never presumed that evangelistic meetings were full worship. He grew up in the psalm-singing Associate Reformed Presbyterian Church in Charlotte, North Carolina. Though he was ordained a Southern Baptist minister in 1939, he has probably occupied a church pew most frequently in the company of his wife, Ruth, who remains a committed Presbyterian.

Evangelicalism was becoming the dominant force in American church life, and one of its hallmarks was its distinctive parroting of each successive secular pop music style. "Sacred concerts" and recordings proliferated in that electronic age with the help of booming sound systems and high-fidelity recording. When television was added to the scene in the 1950s, the door was opened for several new megabusinesses that profited from the interrelated activities of religious radio, television, concerts, recordings, and music publishing. Though their purported goal was to serve the church, their inherent tendency was to dominate the scene with their own musical offerings and to mold the church into their own success-oriented, personality-centered, show business images.

At the same time, some evangelical leaders became aware of the twentieth-century liturgical movement in mainline churches, and they too moved toward serious consideration of public, corporate worship, often for the first time. New service orders were developed to meet the needs of God-centeredness and full congregational participation. Talented young musicians, with diplomas from colleges and universities, pushed for "better performance of better music" in church. Others, trained at Bible colleges and seminaries, developed new concepts of ministry, combining Christian formation with music education. As a result, many congregations learned historic, theologically rich worship hymns for the first time, and evangelical poets began to write new, solid hymnody. Choirs of all ages were organized and trained by musicians who had earned master's degrees and even doctorates in church music.

The early 1960s saw the advent of both the "worship celebration movement" and the charismatic renewal movement, signaling the beginning of the end for the more serious movements of worship thought and action. Worship celebration began in the Anglican Church when Geoffrey Beaumont and other members of the Light Music Group used various popular music styles to reach delinquent baptized members. Almost overnight, a horde of youthful performing groups appeared in British churches, writing and singing their own songs, often in imitation of the Beatles. In our own country, the new, more folkish sounds were soon heard in youth musicals (like *Good News),* while the more brash expressions were propagated by the West Coast "Jesus people" and their imitators.

The neo-Pentecostalist charismatic movement began at the fringe of evangelicalism, but its adherents were soon welcomed into the fold. They developed and propagated a philosophy of worship based on their theology and expressed in simple "praise-and-worship" songs and performance-oriented contemporary Christian music, which they sold quickly and easily to their new evangelical friends. After all, non-charismatics had seldom bothered to work out their own worship/music theology, so they were ready customers for something new to replace their tired gospel songs. Even though the new words and musics tended to ignore evangelical history and to deny its basic theological values, this was hardly noticed. Besides, though they were not as overtly enthusiastic as the charismatics, emotional expression was part of their stock in trade.

Finally, in the 1980s the church growth movement recommended "consumerist" choices in worship in order to reach the Baby Boomers—the remnant of the 1960s dropouts who still retained some interest in things spiritual. Evangelicals took their advice seriously because of the centrality of evangelism in their consciousness—and because they weren't able to identify the theological and liturgical issues at stake. Thus, a logical, almost inescapable progression of historical events set the stage for the current worship revolution, which has been the source of some creative growth and much bruising conflict in today's church.

Changing Paradigms

In our day, church growth experts constantly use the phrase "changing paradigms" in discussions of ministry in the church. Joel Barker says, "A paradigm is a set of rules and regulations (written or unwritten) that does two things: (1) it establishes or defines boundaries; and (2) it tells you how to behave inside the boundaries in order to be successful."[1]

Those buzzwords usually appear in expressions like this: "We live in a day of changing paradigms of how to do church." Such a statement, with its purposely modern, secular ring, is intended to signal a vital message: "Listen now! This is *new truth.* Here's the required formula—the pattern or example for church life, especially for worship and its arts—to which you must conform in order to be 'with it,' to succeed, perhaps even to survive in this revolutionary day." The emphasis is on the word *changing,* so the principal characteristic of the new paradigm is its novelty, its apparent freshness and creativity. The impression given is that the new paradigm is embodied *truth.* The old paradigm is wrong, or at least worn out, and must be discarded.

On this we will all agree: We live in a time of unprecedented cultural change, far beyond what we might expect in the predictable rhythms of history. Mike Regele, in *Death of the Church,* says that our world is experiencing social change that is "unpredictable, discontinuous, chaotic, and transformative," unequaled perhaps since the sixteenth-century Reformation.[2]

Many culture watchers call today's world post-Christian, recognizing that Western culture has not been even nominally Christian since the dawn of the eighteenth-century Enlightenment. However, until very recently our culture has been friendly to, or at least tolerant of, the message of Christ's gospel; but today's society is increasingly hostile to it and to the institutions which promote it. Regele ties this paradigm shift to the emergence of postmodern thought, which in its most radical form says that "no truth is absolutely true, therefore we cannot make any statements about the nature of reality, of right and wrong."[3] He says that the situation is aggravated in the United States by the rise of an increasingly pluralistic society, in terms of both race and religion.

To his credit, Regele does not join the chorus of church growth gurus who prescribe a detailed, iconoclastic approach to worship based on consumer preference. Individuals like George Barna, Doug Murren, Lyle Schaller, and George Hunter insist that the new paradigm of the church is that of a mission field.[4] Just as missionaries adopt the language and culture of a target group for purposes of evangelism, so the church must adopt the music and worship style desired by the unchurched in the neighborhood, in order to reach them. Since, it is said, Baby Boomers and their children (sometimes called "Busters" or "Survivors") don't like traditional, theologically loaded hymns, such hymns should be replaced with simple, repetitious praise-and-worship choruses. Since they don't like choirs, such groups should be disbanded or used only in connection with a visual presentation such as a music drama or a "singing

Christmas tree." Since these Boomers dislike organ sounds, that venerable symbol and tool of Christian worship should be replaced by synthesizers, guitars, and drums. Since they reject traditional historic preaching styles, sermons must be simple, brief, and relevant, narrative in style, and never theological, prophetic, or confrontational. Since they dislike the strictures of formal occasions, protocol, and "dressing up" (except for weddings and the high school prom), everything about worship must be casual.

Unchanging Principles

Why should we question change—or what seems to be something new and creative—in crafting worship forms and arts? Surely the Creator God sets an example for human creatures to follow, with a never-ending supply of new patterns for snowflakes and cloud formations and human faces. Besides, the basic expectation of typical Western art is that it will be new—a fresh expression of beauty that has never been experienced in exactly the same way before.

Without a doubt, each time we encounter God in worship should be a vital, fresh, life-changing experience. However, I believe we must question today's preoccupation with novelty. For one thing, the demands of religious *ritual* seem to be at cross-purposes with those of radically creative worship. In his book *The Magic of Ritual,* Tom Driver points out that the celebration of rites that are agreed to in advance brings an order and serenity to life that is related to, and even contributes to, an underlying cosmic order. Also, ritual tends to unite people emotionally, thus establishing community. Finally, ritual assists in the dynamic process of social as well as personal change through ritual processes of transformation.[5]

So worship artists may need to limit their freedom to be innovative or to make things new by means of novelty and surprise. If individuals in the congregation are expected to be "actors in the worship drama" as Kierkegaard so aptly put it,[6] they must know in advance what the roles demand. Further, the Christian church expresses its historicity, its continuity, and consequently its *authority*, partly by repeating the same actions and words from one generation to another.

At the same time, we dare not tolerate worship presentations that people find to be boring and meaningless, simply "going through the motions." In the theater, where the same words and actions are repeated verbatim night after night, actors use good performance techniques to make each performance come alive as a work of art. Worship leaders must do the same when they participate in repeated services on any given week-end. But, in fact, many of the "new" forms are as rigidly stylized (only in a deceptive way) as any liturgy. On the other hand, all historic worship orders offer alternative forms that follow the pattern of the church year, with changing hymns, canticles and anthems, changing Scripture readings, sermons, and prayers. Evangelical worship planners can offer even more variety, without yielding to the temptation to titillate and surprise would-be worshipers to the point of entertainment.

An ancient Latin motto, *lex orandi, lex credendi* ("the rule of prayer is the rule of faith"), says that the way we worship determines what we believe. Consequently, while we all may agree that the radical changes in modern culture call for changes in the church's response to culture, we must guard the God-truth that is inherent in the church's two-thousand-year, Scripture-based tradition of worship. Why do Barna, Murren, Schaller, Hunter, and other church growth "prophets" presume that the church's principal changes should occur in its expression of worship that determines its character and identity? Dare we allow "seekers" for God and truth to choose the new paradigm for their (and our) worship of God? Should not the music, the sermon, and the prayers for believers' worship be different from that used in a "seeker event"? If we agree that worship form must undergo change in every generation, and especially now, how do we decide what choices to make from the many available varieties of "contemporary" worship? For instance, why use praise-and-worship music rather than Taizé chants or Iona Community songs? This book seeks answers to all these questions.

It seems to me that following the advice of the church growth leaders will sacrifice basic principles that give the church its character and strength and eventually produce the following negative results:

1. Music and other worship arts will be determined on the basis of popular preferences and their superficial emotional appeal, not because of their true worth and their deeper cognitive and emotional meaning.

2. Denominational identities, and the theologies on which they are based, will be forgotten. The full ecumenical creed may then be reduced to "Jesus is Lord" or even "I love Jesus."

3. The church's memory will be lost, especially as it is recorded in songs and in art symbols. Loss of memory means loss of identity.

4. The idea of a local church united in self-sacrificing love will be a thing of the past because individuals will continue to divide into worship groups according to age and aesthetic preference.

5. Arts in worship will be reduced to the least common denominator of congregational taste—determined mostly by commercial interests.

6. Preaching will be brief and simplistic, avoiding the challenge to respond in commitment, or even to think deeply about Christian faith.

7. Worship will be hardly distinguishable from "religious entertainment."

If, for the moment, these characteristics attract attention in the media and encourage some individuals to transfer membership to the "most successful" local megachurch, in the long term I believe they will hasten the demise of the institutional church. Marva Dawn argues that such an approach is "dumbing down" in order to reach out to the unchurched.[7] Instead of countering the evil of today's postmodern culture, it aids and abets it.

Worshiping in Spirit and Truth in the Twenty-first Century

For a response to the modern dilemma, I will examine the most significant New Testament words about Christian worship. These words were spoken by the Lord Jesus himself in an encounter with a Samaritan woman, who was judged by the Jews to be an apostate and by her own people to be a person of loose morals. In today's worship style discussion, she would be called a "seeker."

> So he [Jesus] came to a Samaritan city called Sychar, near the plot of ground that Jacob had given to his son Joseph. Jacob's well was there, and Jesus, tired out by his journey, was sitting by the well. It was about noon.
>
> A Samaritan woman came to draw water, and Jesus said to her, "Give me a drink." (His disciples had gone to the city to buy food.) The Samaritan woman said to him, "How is it that you, a Jew, ask a drink of me, a woman of Samaria?" (Jews do not share things in common with Samaritans.) Jesus answered her, "If you knew the gift of God, and who it is that is saying to you, 'Give me a drink,' you would have asked him, and he would have given you living water." The woman said to him, "Sir, you have no bucket, and the well is deep. Where do you get that living water? Are you greater than our ancestor Jacob, who gave us the well, and with his sons and his flocks drank from it?" Jesus said to her, "Everyone who drinks of this water will be thirsty again, but those who drink of the water that I will give them will never be thirsty. The water that I will give will become in them a spring of water gushing up to eternal life." The woman said to him, "Sir, give me this water, so that I may never be thirsty or have to keep coming here to draw water."
>
> Jesus said to her, "Go, call your husband, and come back." The woman answered him, "I have no husband." Jesus said to her, "You are right in saying, 'I have no husband'; for you have had five husbands, and the one

you have now is not your husband. What you have said is true!" The woman said to him, "Sir, I see that you are a prophet. Our ancestors worshiped on this mountain, but you say that the place where people must worship is in Jerusalem." Jesus said to her, "Woman, believe me, the hour is coming when you will worship the Father neither on this mountain nor in Jerusalem. You worship what you do not know; we worship what we know, for salvation is from the Jews. But the hour is coming, and is now here, when the true worshipers will worship the Father *in spirit and truth,* for the Father seeks such as these to worship him. God is spirit, and those who worship him must worship *in spirit and truth."* The woman said to him, "I know that Messiah is coming" (who is called Christ). "When he comes, he will proclaim all things to us." Jesus said to her, "I am he, the one who is speaking to you." . . . Many Samaritans from that city believed in him because of the woman's testimony. (John 4:5-26, 39, italics added)

This is the gospel of the Lord. *Praise be to you, O Christ.*

As in the past and the future, the church will find answers to today's conflict and confusion about legitimate worship in Jesus' words: "True worshipers will worship the Father in spirit and truth." To worship in spirit means "in God's way" because God is Spirit. This is true worship of the true God by the human spirit; but such "worship of the heart" may be expressed in physical, even aesthetic ways and forms. As William Hull has written:

> To worship *in spirit* does not mean that all holy places and material aids should be abandoned but that the creative, life-giving power of God should infuse whatever human forms are utilized. . . . The Samaritan woman must learn that worship is not validated by a traditional place but by a transcendent power.[8]

I hardly need to say that worshiping God "in truth" means worshiping in *God's* truth. Jesus clarified the issue for the

Samaritan seeker when he said that the Father's truth was given initially to his chosen people, the Jews, and that he (Jesus) was their promised Messiah. In the words "the hour is coming, and is now here," he said also that he—the person who stood talking to her—was the full Truth, in whose name all Christian believers would eventually worship, through the revealing and enabling of God the Holy Spirit.

God's truth is given to us in the Hebrew Scriptures and also in the New Testament documents that bear witness to God's self-revealing and self-giving in Christ. Each of this book's chapters quotes largely from Holy Writ in identifying specific rubrics (directions), as well as examples and principles, of worship. Further, since all truth is God's truth, I dare to deal with issues of cultural truth, aesthetic truth, liturgical truth, and educational truth, as the Holy Spirit has revealed it to the church through the centuries. These arguments also will be based on biblical statements, principles, and examples. I believe they supply helpful answers to today's pressing and perplexing questions.

An Overview of This Book

Each chapter of this book will examine an area of God's truth, in the context of history and of prevailing cultural reality, in order to help readers identify errors in the modern culture-captive church and to point to a way out of our "strange land" dilemma.

Chapter 1, "Worshiping God in Spirit and Truth," defines the ultimate requirement of worship that God seeks and will accept—Trinitarian worship that stems from our love of God and of our neighbors. It also sets that standard against the preoccupation with service forms, techniques, and musical styles found in today's strange land of obsessive formalism. Proper Christian worship orders allow for both discipline and spontaneity, and, above all, conform to the standard "in spirit and truth."

Chapter 2, "Worshiping God in Cognitive and Affective Truth," asserts that God also requires that worship shall conform to *all* biblical-theological truth, especially as expressed to the "left-brain" in rational words. However, truth is also expressed in noncognitive symbols which speak to the "right-brain" through the senses and are called "emotive" or "aesthetic": musical sounds, other symbolic things, and actions. Today's culture tends to admire the emotive/intuitive above the rational and often ignores the meaning of words in worship. This chapter urges church musicians to work for a balance of the cognitive and the affective, in which worship words are given their due, in our culture's "strange land of superficial emotionalism."

Chapter 3, "Worshiping God in Theological Truth," acknowledges that interest in theology is at a low point among evangelicals in our time. Just like the mainline churches, evangelical churches have become ecumenical, with groups joining together in activity and fellowship without properly considering the important theological differences that distinguish them. Today, charismatics have established the model for worship and its music for many noncharismatic groups. The call is for *all* evangelicals to worship according to their *own* doctrines in the "strange land of theological confusion" in which we live.

Chapter 4, "Worshiping God in Biblical Truth," points out that Scripture gives many guidelines to help us devise worship forms and actions, including the use of music and other arts. However, certain contemporary groups are quoting pat answers from the Bible about such things as proper music volume, the use of instruments, handclapping, and congregational song styles; much of this interpretation violates basic principles of biblical exegesis. This chapter urges careful discrimination in determining what the Bible really says about Christian worship and its arts, in today's "strange land of differing interpretations."

Chapter 5 examines the tendency of churches to divide at the worship hour over worship/music styles and asks whether this is not a denial of the unity of Christ's body, the church. I believe that *contemporary traditional* worship—in which worthy new works, styles, and forms are constantly being united with the historic—allows successive generations to worship together as they should. This concept may be included in what some people refer to as "blended worship," but that term is used sometimes to suggest that worship can be blended with entertainment. The chapter title is "Worshiping God as the Community of Faith in a Strange Land of Radical Individualism."

Based on the premise that all truth is God's truth, the remaining chapters examine other categories of reality that are not directly related to the words of Scripture or to specific tenets of theology. "Worshiping God in Cultural Truth" (chapter 6) acknowledges that human society includes many different cultures, and that appropriate cognitive and affective languages must be used for each group. However, an examination of the influence of contemporary pop music on the church shows that we are working and worshiping in a "strange land of pervasive secularism."

Chapter 7 searches for a biblical standard of quality in worship's aesthetic forms. The loss of respect for serious art in today's society leads to the popular hypothesis that any type of art is as good as any other; the only standard of acceptability and excellence is human preference. The chapter is titled: "Worshiping God in Artistic Truth in a Strange Land of Aesthetic Relativism."

Chapter 8 looks at the New Community worship services of Willow Creek Community Church in South Barrington, Illinois. Comparing its contemporary services with traditional services, it seems apparent that most contemporary worship is developed by liturgical "house cleaning"—that is, eliminating many elements that have been meaningful in the church for centuries. My outline for a true standard for both old and new worship (taken from the New Testament epistles and Isaiah 6) is presented in this chapter: "Worshiping God in Liturgical Truth in a Strange Land of Destructive Iconoclasm."

Finally, chapter 9 observes that while churches support many educational programs, *congregations* are rarely trained for their most important work—the worship of God. I suggest many approaches to worship education in church life, especially in the worship service itself. I also examine today's declining interest in music training, both inside and outside the church. Certain groups contend that the singing of trained specialists in solos, choirs, and other groups is a denial of the priesthood of believers; others simply don't want to hear "elitist" music in church. This last chapter, "Worshiping God in Educational Truth," argues that musical training in church choirs and other groups is a response to the call to return our talents and gifts to God in the service of the church, even in today's "strange land of intellectual ambivalence."

1

Worshiping God
in Spirit and Truth

*In a Strange Land
of Obsessive Formalism*

It is the spirit that gives life. —John 6:63

*a*t a recent convention of choral directors in San Diego, delegates were discussing the worship ferment in the churches they served. "Our church offers four different services that feature traditional, praise and worship, country, and jazz music," said one. A not-to-be-outdone Lutheran choir director retorted, "We have *five* different styles of worship, and the pastor changes his outfit for each one!"

What should we think about ever-changing worship styles? In John 4, Jesus had a discussion about worship with the Samaritan woman at Jacob's well in which he said that the *place* of worship doesn't matter. I believe that by inference he was saying also that the *means* of worship are not finally important. "God is spirit, and those who worship him must worship in spirit and truth" (John 4:24), Jesus said, repeating that second phrase for emphasis (see verse 23). He was saying that the reality of worship and the sincerity of the worshiper are more important than a church's location or liturgy. That truth seems to be forgotten in our time when worship forms and styles, especially new modes, are the central concern of many people, to the point of obsession.

Admittedly, today's experimenting began with good motives. Pastors were asking: In a "strange land" of an increasingly secular and hostile culture, how can God's people be the deeply committed, evangelistic church God intended? Certain church growth advocates said that in order to attract secular society to our worship services we must use speech and music languages that allow the unchurched to feel at home immediately. Others pointed out that Christians already are too susceptible to the gods of contemporary culture, especially materialism (love of things), hedonism (love of pleasure), and narcissism (love of self), and that a weakening of the God-message in worship would only hasten the church's spiritual decline. Yet the trend to "popular worship" continued and accelerated.

Southern Baptist leader Charles Willis recently named four worship styles that he said were common in that denomination: liturgical, traditional, seeker, and blended.[1] Robert Webber identifies seven patterns that are used in contemporary worship renewal in the Western world: liturgical, traditional Protestant, creative, charismatic, praise-and-worship, convergence, and seekers' service/believers' worship patterns.[2]

In discussing the aesthetics of worship later in this book, I suggest four possible types of worship music: art music, traditional music, folk music, and popular music. Within these categories, worship leaders may choose psalms, chorales, hymns, gospel songs, praise-and-worship choruses, Taizé chants, Wild Goose songs, or other unnamed forms for the congregation. Choirs may sing motets, anthems, arrangements of hymns, gospel songs, or praise-and-worship music. Soloists may choose traditional solos, gospel ballads, or contemporary Christian music.

This chapter contends that, though making personal choices among many possible forms and styles seems to be most significant to today's church attenders, the primary question is: Are we worshiping *in God's way*, in spirit and truth? In other words, are we experiencing true worship—worship of God as Father, Son, and Holy Spirit?

Ministry to God in Worship

In the maze of changing paradigms, this principle remains unchanging: We are called to a ministry to God in worship, and this must be done in spirit and truth. Most people understand *ministry* to mean "giving service, care, or aid; to attend, as to wants and necessities; to contribute, as to comfort and happiness"—all this for the helping of other human beings. Used in the context of the church, the word refers usually to service, care, or aid to other persons, on behalf of God, in the name of Jesus Christ. However, in the Old Testament, especially in the Authorized and older versions, we find reference to a "ministry to God" in public worship: "And take thou unto thee Aaron thy brother, and his sons with him, from among the children of Israel, that he may minister unto me in the priest's office" (Exod. 28:1, KJV). That same phrase appears word for word ten times in the King James Version of the book of Exodus.

In recent Scripture versions, translators have changed the phrase "minister unto me" to "serve me." Yet, in the first recorded version of a complete communion prayer by Hippolytus (d. A.D. 236), the scriptural words "minister to you" appear: "Remembering therefore his death and resurrection, we offer to you the bread and the cup, giving you thanks because you have held us worthy to stand before you and *minister to you*" (italics added).

In modern Orthodox liturgical worship, that same sentence stands in the middle of what is called the Salutation dialogue ("The Lord be with you"—"and also with you,"), continues with the *Sursum Corda* ("Lift up your hearts"—"We lift them up to the Lord"—"Let us give thanks to the Lord"—"It is right to give God thanks and praise"), and ends with the *Tersanctus* (three "holies"), the song of the angels flying around the throne of God (Isa. 6:3).

I include the entire opening section of the above communion prayer. Its language reveals a vivid and moving picture of the transcendent yet gracious God we worship. Indeed, it seems to give us a glimpse of heaven itself:

It is proper and right to sing to You, bless You, praise You, thank You and worship You in all places of Your dominion; for You are God ineffable, beyond comprehension, invisible, beyond understanding, existing forever and always the same; You and Your only begotten Son and Your Holy Spirit. You brought us into being out of nothing, and when we fell, You raised us up again. You did not cease doing everything until You led us to heaven and granted us Your kingdom to come. For all these things we thank You and Your only begotten Son and Your Holy Spirit: for all things that we know and do not know, for blessings seen and unseen that have been bestowed upon us. *We also thank You for this ministry which You are pleased to accept from our hands* [that is, the "ministry of worship" we are offering through this liturgy] even though You are surrounded by thousands of Archangels and tens of thousands of Angels, by the Cherubim and Seraphim, six-winged, many-eyed, soaring with their wings, singing the victory hymn, proclaiming, crying out, and saying:

> Holy, holy, holy, Lord Sabaoth, heaven and earth are filled with Your glory. Hosanna in the highest. Blessed is He who comes in the name of the Lord. Hosanna to God in the highest. (italics added)[3]

In this book, I will not often refer to worship as ministry to God. I quote it in this beginning chapter to say emphatically that worship is much more than an attitude toward God. *Worship is our active service, our joyful and demanding work for God.*

True Worship

The central question of this chapter is: How do we minister to and worship God in spirit and truth? Jesus gave us an answer as he quoted words from the Torah which every Jew of his time knew from memory: "You shall love the Lord your God with all your heart, and with all your soul, and with all your mind, and with all your strength"; then he added, "You shall love your neighbor as yourself" (Mark 12:30-31). Worshiping God and loving God are not absolutely synonymous, but they are closely related, perhaps like opposite sides of a continuous circle. This great commandment says that true worship is determined not so much by the words "traditional" or "contemporary," but by *relationship*—our relationship with God and our relationship with other persons. Worshiping God begins and ends with loving God more than anything or anyone else in the world. It should be apparent then that no person worships God who does not have a love relationship with God. Further, no person worships God acceptably who is not in loving relationship with other human beings, who are "neighbors."

Worshiping in Spirit

Jesus referred to one of the imponderable mysteries underlying God's relationship with humankind when he said to the Samaritan woman, "True worshipers will worship the Father in spirit and truth, *for the Father seeks such as these to worship him*" (John 4:23, italics added). The perfectly holy, all-powerful, all-knowing, unchanging God, the God who needs nothing, seeks the love, the worship, of us weak, sinful creatures. Whereas today's church growth experts refer to unchurched people as "seekers," an anonymous, nineteenth-century hymn writer insisted that God is the true seeker.

> I sought the Lord, and afterward I knew
>   he moved my soul to seek him, seeking me;
> it was not I that found, O Savior true;
>   no, I was found of thee.

John tells us that God is also the first to love: "We love [both God and our neighbor] because he first loved us" (1 John 4:19). When the Holy Spirit enables us to respond to God with our own love and worship, it is through that part of us which is made in God's image: the human spirit. The place of worship will not finally matter, as Jesus told the woman, whether Mt. Gerizim or Mt. Zion in Jerusalem. In the context of this book, we can say that the music of worship doesn't finally matter, whether it be folk songs of aboriginal cultures or the chorale settings of Johann Sebastian Bach. As the Scottish New Testament scholar William Barclay wrote:

> A man's spirit is the highest part . . . the part which lasts when the physical part . . . has vanished. . . . It is the spirit of a man which is the source and origin of his highest dreams and thoughts and ideals and desires. The true, the genuine worship is when man, through his spirit, attains to friendship and intimacy with God. True and genuine worship is not to come to a certain place; it is not to go through a certain ritual or liturgy; it is not even to bring certain gifts. True worship is when the spirit, the immortal and invisible part of man, speaks to and meets with God, who is immortal and invisible.[4]

It may not be helpful to dissect the human personhood in order to identify differences between "heart, soul, mind, and strength"; mostly, those words express the totality of who we are. However, even though the Hebrew word may have slightly different connotations, I have always thought of the heart as the center of human personality, especially with reference to our affections, our value system, and our commitments. As such, it seems to me to be the *sine qua non* in this list of human attributes, closely associated with the concept of "spirit." We worship with the mind only if we love God with the heart. We worship with physical acts and through artistic sounds and things, only to the degree that our inmost being communes with the living God. This then is worshiping "in spirit."

Therefore, I must remind those who insist on radical revision of worship forms and styles that all the changes are "much ado about nothing" unless congregations are truly worshiping God in spirit. I must also insist that the best performance of traditional liturgy is meaningless unless participating worshipers measure up to the great commandment to love God. For both groups, that includes loving our neighbors as ourselves, even if we cannot agree about proper worship styles and music!

It is not enough that we be believers who are baptized members of a church. On any given occasion, we cannot worship "in spirit" unless *at that moment* we are in loving relationship with God and with our neighbors. For this reason, historical worship orders have always offered the opportunity to repair our relationship with God in the Prayer of Confession and the Assurance of Forgiveness. We may also express and symbolize our good relationship with others in the Kiss of Peace. This done, we can enter the worship service with boldness, confident that we have done all we can to remove those sinful hindrances.

> Therefore, my friends, since we have confidence to enter the sanctuary by the blood of Jesus, by the new and living way that he opened for us through the curtain (that is, through his flesh), and since we have a great priest over the house of God, let us approach with a true heart in full assurance of faith, with our hearts sprinkled clean from an evil conscience and our bodies washed with pure water. (Heb. 10:19-22)

That Scripture raises questions that have not yet been dealt with. What does the "blood of Jesus," "the new and living way that he opened for us," and "a great high priest" have to do with our worship of God?

Worshiping in Truth

The answer is contained in the full phrase, "worship in spirit *and truth*" (italics added). These words follow Jesus' reference to Jewish and Samaritan worship, both of which he was about to judge inadequate. Then he said, in paraphrase, "The hour is coming—in fact, it's here now—when the true worshipers will worship the Father in spirit and truth." Scholars agree that these words refer specifically to *gospel truth*, to God's truth as given in Jesus Christ. In the same encounter Jesus claimed to be the Messiah (John 4:26), and later in John's Gospel we read that he said, "I am the way [to God], and the *truth* [of God], and the life [of God]. No one comes to the Father except through me" (John 14:6). For this reason, Christian worship must be conducted in the name of Jesus. This is why we pray to God the Father "in Jesus' name" or "through Jesus Christ our Lord." Further, since Jesus said, "The Father and I are one" (John 10:30), Jesus himself is to be worshiped as God (but not apart from, or in implied contrast to, God).

David Peterson confirms that Jesus was talking about a new way of worship based on his ministry, which initiated a totally different way of relating to God. He states:

> The expression "in spirit and truth" suggests that Jesus is to be the means by which this new worship is to be inaugurated. The two key words "spirit" and "truth" are closely connected in John's portrait of Christ. No one can see the kingdom of God or experience the blessings of the End time without being born again by the Spirit (John 3:1-8). Thus, in slightly different language, the Father begets true worshipers through the Spirit. But it is Jesus who makes the Spirit available to those who come to him, because of his saving work (John 7:37-39).[5]

Worshiping God in spirit and truth—the expression of loving God with all our heart, soul, mind, and strength—is possible only through the "blood shed," the atoning sacrifice of Christ for our sins, and through the Holy Spirit's work of regeneration in the heart and life of the believer. Jesus spoke of that experience as receiving the water he gives which "will become . . . a spring of water gushing up to eternal life" (John 4:14). Through Jesus' incarnation, life, death, and resurrection he gave us the new and living way to knowing, loving, and worshiping God. Jesus also is our ascended and glorified high priest through whom our worship prayers and gifts are presented acceptably to God.

Trinitarian Worship

Thoughtful readers will have noticed that we cannot describe our relationship to God through Jesus Christ without speaking about the Holy Spirit's work in that relationship, and, consequently, in our worship of God and of Christ. The last quotation from David Peterson suggests that worshiping in spirit is an encounter of the human spirit (small *s*) with God's Spirit (capital *S*). John's gospel contributes much to our knowledge of the Holy Spirit, and, thus, to our understanding of the relationships within the Holy Trinity. In the first chapter John the Baptist speaks about his baptizing Jesus:

> I saw the Spirit descending from heaven like a dove, and it remained on him. I myself did not know him, but the one who sent me to baptize with water said to me, "He on whom you see the Spirit descend and remain is the one who baptizes with the Holy Spirit." And I myself have seen and have testified that this is the Son of God. (John 1:32-34)

In his Upper Room discourse with his disciples, Jesus told them that after his ascension his Father would send "another Advocate," the "Spirit of Truth" (John 14:16-17), who "will testify on my behalf" (John 15:26), "teach you everything" (John 14:26), "guide you into all the truth" (John 16:13), and thus, "glorify me" (John 16:14).

This confirms that the Holy Spirit is "God in action," as suggested in the very first words of the Bible's creation account: "The Spirit of God moved upon the face of the waters" (Gen. 1:2, KJV). Even as the Spirit reveals God in Christ to us and baptizes us into Christ's body, the church, so it is the Spirit who calls and enables us to worship, even speaking to God the agonizing petitions for which we can find no words.

> Likewise the Spirit helps us in our weakness; for we do not know how to pray as we ought, but that very Spirit

intercedes with sighs too deep for words. And God, who searches the heart, knows what is the mind of the Spirit, because the Spirit intercedes for the saints according to the will of God. (Rom. 8:26-27)

Trinitarian worship—worship in spirit and truth—is *worship of God in the name of Jesus Christ, by the power of the Holy Spirit.* That is the only worship acceptable to God. Though we refer properly to worship as our gift *to* God, we may not offer that gift except by the invitation and enabling of the Spirit. So, worship is also the gift *of* God, which also helps us to love our neighbors as ourselves. As Welton Gaddy says in *The Gift of Worship:*

> Worship is a gift of response to the invitation of God, who, from the time of creation, judged it not good for a person to be alone. God provided the possibility of fellowship with each other, then God offered individuals an opportunity for fellowship with Him. Throughout history, God has consistently called people together and joined their communion.[6]

Some readers may wonder why there is so little variety in the metaphors I use for the Holy Trinity. I would like to use other biblical names, such as "Creator, Redeemer, and Guide," and occasionally do so for individual members of the Godhead. "Father, Son, and Holy Spirit" will appear almost exclusively for God, Three-in-One, because they are the terms most frequently used in the Scriptures, and in history. I believe also that such consistency will make the presentation more clear.

Worship Forms and God's Approval

Old Testament Scriptures recount several instances when God's people violated basic rules of worship set forth and based on God's truth in the Jewish Law, such as keeping the Sabbath (Jer. 17:19-27), offering the best-quality sacrifice available to each family (Mal. 1:8), or giving the tithe to God (Mal.

3:8-12). These sins brought words of severe condemnation from God's prophets and the promise of forgiveness and blessing if they were confessed and forsaken. On other occasions, worship actions may have been appropriate, satisfying the legal requirements perfectly, but they were rejected because they were not performed with pure hearts.

> With what shall I come before the LORD,
>   and bow myself before God on high?
> Shall I come before him with burnt offerings,
>   with calves a year old?
> Will the LORD be pleased with thousands of rams,
>   with ten thousands of rivers of oil? . . .
> He has told you, O mortal, what is good;
>   and what does the LORD require of you
> but to do justice, and to love kindness,
>   and to walk humbly with your God?
> (Mic. 6:6, 8)

> I hate, I despise your festivals,
>   and I take no delight in your solemn assemblies.
> Even though you offer me your burnt offerings
>   and grain offerings,
>   I will not accept them;
>   and the offerings of well-being of your fatted animals
>   I will not look upon.
> Take away from me the noise of your songs;
>   I will not listen to the melody of your harps.
> But let justice roll down like waters,
>   and righteousness like an ever-flowing stream.
> (Amos 5:21-24)

> Look, you fast only to quarrel and to fight
>   and to strike with a wicked fist.
> Such fasting as you do today
>   will not make your voice heard on high. . . .
> Is not this the fast that I choose:
>   to loose the bonds of injustice,

> to undo the thongs of the yoke,
> to let the oppressed go free,
>   and to break every yoke?
> Is it not to share your bread with the hungry,
>   and bring the homeless poor into your house;
> when you see the naked, to cover them?
> (Isa. 58:4, 6-7)

At first reading, we might assume that in these instances God is saying, "Quit offering sacrifices. Disband your choirs. Quit fasting." Indeed, certain groups throughout history have insisted that the *only* acceptable means of expressing worship are *spiritual*—"in spirit." Not so! Because we are creatures of body and sense, as well as spirit, we can only express worship in community by saying and singing words, and by performing ritual acts, like giving gifts to God, and fasting.

In all these instances, God is not saying that worship forms and acts should be terminated. God is saying that our best words and actions should be offered in spirit and truth, in conformity to God's truth and commands, and in complete sincerity and commitment because we love God with our whole being. This implies also that such offerings are accompanied by ethical living that incarnates the ideals we proclaim in worship.

A Strange Land of Obsessive Formalism

Despite the truth that authentic worship ultimately springs from the human heart or spirit, most if not all conflict about worship centers in its content and performance. Moreover, human beings tend to evaluate the sincerity of worship according to these secondary, technical matters. Historically, "free" and "liturgical" Christians often have been at sword's point over this, with Baptists and Quakers arguing that people who read prayers from a book cannot really be praying, and Lutherans and Anglicans contending that the simple, improvised prayers of evangelicals reveal little acquaintance with a God of holiness and mystery.

The dictionary defines *formalism* in religion as "excessive attachment to external forms and observances." Free church worshipers have always presumed that this particular idolatry is the besetting sin in liturgical churches. But, since all worship has form, formalism can be the idolatry of evangelicals and charismatics alike. We may be guilty of venerating our so-called informality, especially now that many liturgical churches seem to be jumping on our informal, charismatic bandwagon!

Today most of the warfare is intramural—not between denominations or churches, but within congregations. Individual churches in all communions except the Orthodox are arguing bitterly about worship form and style. New types of congregational song (for example, praise-and-worship music, a contribution of charismatic theology and worship) are competing with traditional forms, and in many instances these have replaced the songs with which older folk grew up. Younger worshipers welcome the new, lively, repetitious, and sometimes "warm, fuzzy" expressions, saying that their music meets their emotional needs and is not as theologically overloaded as dreary eighteenth-century hymns. Older folk argue that contemporary choruses are all rooted in emotion, with little theological content; at least those songs don't contain the theology they want to express.

Church growth experts have addressed the desires of the Boomer, Buster, and Survivor generations by advising radical changes to help those age groups feel at home in church. Some of the recommendations: (1) project spontaneity, not formality; (2) scrap the old symbols of pulpit, robes, organ, hymnals, Sunday dress, and worship bulletins; (3) use contemporary music and casual speech, avoiding "God talk," theological sermons, and so on.

Other observers argue that the would-be reformers have not yet demonstrated their commitment to the church—especially not in financial support—and that the loss of historic symbols and the substitution of new music based on secular pop styles is another means of secularizing the church. Boomers and others retort that refusal to go along with contemporary worship updating shows that the traditionalists are not really interested in evangelism!

It must be acknowledged that not all the truth is on either side of the argument, and that conflict and anxiety bring pain to all parties involved. If the modernity crowd are overly committed to wholesale worship iconoclasm ("house-cleaning"), older generations tend to resist any change in service patterns. Whereas contemporary worship may be inordinately preoccupied with expressing human feelings, yesterday's services often tended to defeat the truth they proclaimed by poor rendition and the virtual absence of healthy emotional expression. In such a "strange land" of conflict among Christians, it's a wonder there's any music at all—music of the heart, that is!

In chapter 5 I discuss the effort of some church renewalists to stop the worship wars by adopting a pluralistic standard in worship, offering two or more styles or forms of services to meet the desires of the congregation. The implication—often the stated philosophy—is that worship form/style doesn't matter so long as people find the experience to be "inspiring" or "satisfying." No doubt proponents of such solutions presume that with such an open attitude they could not possibly be guilty of worship formalism. But are they? What constitutes undue attachment to worship's external forms and observances?

Formalism versus "Spirit and Truth" Form in Worship

I am often surprised how many evangelical ministers believe that Scripture gives us no standards for planning and conducting worship services. Does not the command to worship "in spirit and truth" say anything about worship form and style? I believe that good worship form is that which supports true worship—worship in spirit and truth. In contrast, formalism is commitment to worship forms that do not encourage worship in God's way—in spirit and truth.

We have already noted instances in scriptural history and in recent evangelical life where God's people were guilty of worship formalism. In some instances, that formalism was expressed in an intransigent *insistence on change* in worship forms; in others, it was expressed in a stubborn *refusal to change*. Here are three main examples of formalism.

1. Formalism is expressed in an attachment to forms *for their own sake,* apart from the reality of spirit and truth. Unbelievers may enjoy the aesthetic experience of a well-performed liturgical service or the pleasure and excitement of a contemporary gathering. However, they cannot worship God because they have no conscious relationship with God; theirs is the most obvious example of formalism. Believers may have the same aesthetic or pleasurable experiences in those settings; but if for any reason they fail to meet God fully when in-spirit-and-truth worship is offered, they too are guilty of formalism.

2. Formalism is expressed in an attachment to worship forms that *do not conform to the full truth of God,* as we understand it. "In spirit and truth" forms will express that truth in their words, actions, and symbolism. Obviously, as expressed earlier in this chapter, "full truth" includes all that which is expressed in the Trinity—God the Father, Son, and Holy Spirit. Also, because Jesus promised that after his ascension the Spirit would "guide . . . into all the truth," including "the things that are to come" (John 16:13), worship form should be based on *all God's truth.* In later chapters, I discuss worship in the light of theological truth, biblical truth, ecclesiological truth, cultural truth, aesthetic truth, liturgical truth, and educational truth.

3. Formalism is expressed in attachment to worship forms that are inadequate because they are planned with *wrong objectives,* including:
   a. Principally evangelism. Neither an evangelistic crusade meeting nor a seeker service is full worship, in spirit and truth. Both Billy Graham and Bill Hybels (of Willow Creek Community Church) have articulated this.[7]

b. Principally Bible knowledge, or pastoral ministry, or fellowship. None of these ministry-to-people serendipities of worship should be the central objective; the central focus should be ministry to God—worship in spirit and truth.

c. Political purposes. True worship in spirit and truth should not be compromised simply to satisfy congregational demands or to compete with other churches.

d. Modernity. One of today's seductive invitations to formalism arises from the erroneous idea "new is always better," that radical societal changes generated by modern technology must perforce be matched with comparable changes in worship. Not so, unless the final result is worship in spirit and truth!

e. Tradition. For several reasons, tradition is important in worship, as I have already suggested and will explain in greater detail later in this book. But decisions in service planning should not be held captive to such arguments as "We've always sung the Doxology after the Offertory." I believe that today is a propitious time for every congregation to renew its worship, making healthy changes in order to better achieve worship in spirit and truth.

The Lord Is Truly Here

How do all of us, traditionalists and revisionists alike, ensure that we meet God's ultimate requirement for worship in spirit and truth? First, everyone should agree that if worship is to be with the whole being, worshipers must be aware that God is *really present* with them. That awareness must include more than the conviction that "God is everywhere, and therefore, here," or that "through the Holy Spirit, Christ dwells in each member of his body, the church," and therefore he is with me in the place of worship. This deeper realization stems more from our understanding that we worship in a *purposeful encounter with God,* as mentioned by the Lord Jesus: "Where two or three are gathered in my name, I am there among them"

(Matt. 18:20). The phrase "in my name" acknowledges that Christian worship is possible only because of God's love revealed and given in Christ's incarnation, life, death, resurrection, and continuing intercession to God for us. It means also that Christ gives himself to us each time we meet, speaking to us through his Word and feeding us at his Communion Table, all through the action of the Holy Spirit.

Don Saliers says that our awareness of God's presence in worship must be based on a realization of God's "absence"—not that God is ever "away," but that we are not always conscious of the Eternal Presence.[8] This is why at the beginning of a service a prayer "invokes" God's presence and expresses our hopes for the worship encounter. Its real purpose is to center our attention on God so that God becomes present to us—around, above, behind, under, and within us. This is the God who created the universe, who redeemed us from sin and self-centeredness to a life of mutual receiving and giving love, both with God and with other human beings, and who is ready to reveal and to give more of himself to us. Though such God-consciousness can and should be ours in daily life—in the midst of our work or play or family rituals—this encounter is distinctive. It is an appointment of God's choosing (Heb. 10:25) in which we meet with other believers as the church, the Body of Christ, as Saliers says, "singing, listening, attending to one another, and bringing our lives to the symbols and actions."[9]

If this full awareness were the experience of every worshiper, the spiritual power unleashed would be awesome indeed. Annie Dillard challenges the "clichés and commonplaces of our worship art" with these words:

> On the whole I do not find Christians, outside of the catacombs, sufficiently sensible, aware, of conditions. Does anyone have the foggiest idea what sort of power we so blindly invoke? Or, as I suspect, does no one believe a word of it? The churches are children, playing on the floor with their chemistry sets, mixing up a batch of TNT to kill a Sunday morning. . . . It is madness to wear ladies' straw

hats and velvet hats to church; we should all be wearing crash helmets. Ushers should issue life preservers and signal flares; they should lash us to our pews.[10]

In Christian tradition, this sense of God's presence has been called *transcendence* and has included the awareness of mystery or miracle. I am convinced that a sense of God's transcendence must include awareness of God's *immanence,* as well. The transcendent One-in-Three God, of whose presence we become aware, is our Creator, Redeemer, Sustainer, and Judge, the God beyond our understanding and imagining. But the immanent God, One-in-Three, is also present—our Friend, Lover, Nurturer, Father, and Indweller, closer to us than hands or feet. Perhaps because it is impossible for human reason to reconcile such transcendence with such immanence, human beings have difficulty balancing these concepts of God in their worship. Partly for this reason, in this book I will refer to God as "transcendent-immanent."

In much liturgical worship, the sense of God's transcendence-immanence may center in the Service of the Table, in which Christ is understood to be "truly present" in the bread and wine, given for our spiritual food and drink. In nonliturgical traditions, the transcendent-immanent God may be encountered more in the preaching of, and responding to, God's Holy Word. In modern charismatic worship, God's transcendence-immanence is associated with the miracles of glossalalia, healing, and prophecy, all understood to be spiritual gifts of God the Spirit to the worshiper (1 Cor. 12:9-10).

However, all believers should expect to sense God's presence in other phenomena, as well. We may experience it in the room in which we gather—perhaps in soaring space overhead, or in stained glass windows, or in the worship furnishings—pulpit, communion table, baptistry, or banners. We may encounter it in the sound of the congregation singing, or of the organ and other instruments. We may know it in the greeting and love expressed, in the name of Christ, by our friends and neighbors. We may recognize it best in the words of Scripture or of prayers, because then we may hear the actual word of God and talk to him, as Moses did "face to face" (Exod. 33:11).

In the dedication of Solomon's temple, it seems that music uniquely communicated the presence of God. Following the listing of the hundreds of Levitical singers and instrumentalists, we read:

> It was the duty of the trumpeters and singers to make themselves heard in unison in praise and thanksgiving to the LORD, and when the song was raised, with trumpets and cymbals and other musical instruments, in praise to the LORD,
> "For he is good,
> for his steadfast love endures forever,"
> the house, the house of the LORD, was filled with a cloud, so that the priests could not stand to minister because of the cloud; for the glory of the LORD filled the house of God. (2 Chron. 5:13)

When I began my music ministry many years ago, I was very conscious of my responsibility to help believers become aware of God at the outset of the service. In those days, many churches invariably used a three-line Call to Worship from Habakkuk 2:20, with music by George F. Root. (See next page.)

I remember the temptation to prolong the silence in the rests of those last measures, so that folks would really be gripped by God's presence. On other Sundays, I used a heaven-storming sound like Gounod's "Sanctus" ("Holy, holy, holy," Isa. 6:3), which was that nineteenth-century composer's effort to reproduce the glory expressed by angels in Isaiah's vision of God.

Many Baby Boomers tell me that they don't like that music and want to hear something more modern, either praise-and-worship choruses or contemporary Christian music that resembles the secular music with which they grew up. They don't say that their style of music reveals God to them more clearly, but they may imagine that it does. Of course, I can't be sure that all the people who are comfortable with Root and Gounod

The Lord is in His ho-ly tem-ple, The Lord is in His ho-ly tem-ple; Let all the earth keep si-lence, Let all the earth keep si-lence be-fore Him, Keep si-lence, keep si-lence be-fore Him. A-men.

really experience God's presence through that music, either. Maybe they just like those musical sounds, one soft (plus silence) and one loud! That is another reminder that reality is in "spirit and truth," not in the form or style—or even the emotional experience—of the music.

On Worship as Memorable Experience

In reading the account in the book of Chronicles about the dedication of Solomon's temple, one might get the currently popular idea that a sense of the presence of God is always associated with some overwhelming emotional *experience.* As Davis Duggins wrote:

> Nearly all of us remember times of being overwhelmed by the nearness of God and responding in praise and awe. It might happen alone in prayer, around a campfire with friends, or even at a concert with strangers. Frequently, the experience comes unplanned and takes us by surprise. Something happens that we can't explain fully, something

that transports us into the presence of God and fills us with reverence and joy.

There is only one problem—it doesn't happen very often. The memorable high points of worship seem to come only a few times in life. A lot of us have stopped expecting anything more.[11]

Of course I've had all those same experiences, and I would tend to trust most my judgment about the one which occurred alone in prayer. Around the campfire I might have been responding as much to nature itself, though it could have included the realization that the God of creation, my Savior and Friend, was with me at the moment. At the concert I might have been evaluating more the emotional impact of the music—whether the symphonic sound of Beethoven or the high-decibel impact of Stryper.

I'm not talking about those high moments of emotion that come only a few times in life. I'm presuming that we expect to sense the presence of God *every time we meet in a service* and at any moment through the week when we consciously acknowledge God's presence in life. Worship is not an occasional burst of emotion that sneaks up on us unawares. Worship is not an experience that any person—preacher, music director, or worship leader—can "lead us into." Worship is the conscious, demanding work of the believer,[12] led and enabled by the Holy Spirit alone. Worship is "practicing the presence of God"—the One-in-Three—in an act of the will, by the grace of God. Of course, in our quest and resolve we will be helped or hindered by our surroundings—the architectural setting, symbolic furnishings, actions, speech, and music. But true worship depends more on our inner motivation and persistent effort than on any outside influence. Like all work, it gets easier, more natural, the more we do it.

Holy Protocol

I believe also that it is important for us to recognize and acknowledge God the Trinity in our worship, not because

Father, Son, and Holy Spirit are jealous of their individual identities, but because it is important to us in experiencing God, Three-in-One. Actually, we cannot separate God from God in God's actions. For instance, Scripture says that each person of the Trinity is Creator: that Yahweh "God created the heavens and the earth" (Gen. 1:1), that "All things came into being through him [God the Word]" (John 1:3), and that "the Spirit of God swept over the . . . [creation] waters" (Gen. 1:2). Again, some Christians may imagine that the transcendent God is the God-the-Father we reverently *fear*, while the immanent Lord Jesus is the God we intimately *love*. However, the ancient Jews understood that they were to love God with all their heart/soul/mind/strength, and the book of Revelation pictures Christ as the Judge with a sharp two-edged sword, who has the keys of Death and of Hades (Rev. 2:12; 1:18).

At the same time, we can acknowledge appropriately each member of the Godhead, and also the Trinity, and should do so in worship, if for no other reason than this is the God of the Bible. Someone has said that we commit idolatry when we think and speak of God as so transcendent, so far removed from our daily lives, that we presume he has no claim on us. We are idolatrous also when we think and speak of God as so immanent—so much in our own image—that we suppose we can manipulate him. If we worship the Three-in-One God of Scripture, we will not make those tragic mistakes.

Worship leaders/planners are most responsible for ensuring that proper holy protocol is observed in church services. They must be sure that the congregation is not invited to participate mostly in "Jesus worship," as some evangelicals are accused of doing; that tends to be true of musical worship when gospel songs are the principal fare. We should address our prayers of adoration, thanksgiving, confession, dedication, and petition—whether sung or spoken—to both God and Christ; traditionally, the church has given some precedence to praying to God because Jesus told his disciples to pray, "Our Father," and because all our praying is in his name, *in nomine Jesu Christe*.

Many believers tend to think of the Holy Spirit as only immanent because the Spirit lives in our mortal bodies (Rom.

8:11); but what is more transcendent in God's action than the creation and control of the cosmos! Also, we address the Spirit less frequently in word and song because we identify him as the Spirit of God or the Spirit of Christ, who is involved in our worship of both God-the-Father and God-the-Son. When we do pray to the Spirit, it is usually to request some holy action, as in the ancient Latin hymn, *Veni, sancte Spiritus* ("Come, Holy Spirit"). Note the many action nouns and action adjectives, as well as verbs, in this translation.

> Come, Holy Ghost, our souls inspire,
> and kindle with celestial fire;
>> thou the anointing Spirit art,
>> who dost thy sevenfold gifts impart.
>
> Thy blessed unction from above
> is comfort, life, and fire of love;
>> enable with perpetual light
>> the dullness of our blinded sight.
>
> Anoint and cheer our soiled face
> with the abundance of thy grace;
>> keep far our foes; give peace at home;
>> where thou art guide, no ill can come.
>
> Teach us to know the Father, Son,
> and thee, of both to be but one;
>> that through the ages all along
>> thy praise may be our endless song.
>
> Praise to thy eternal merit,
> Father, Son, and Holy Spirit.
> *(Transl. John Cosin, 1627)*

I have recently learned to identify the Spirit in my personal praying, especially in connection with my efforts to produce this book. Frequently I came up against a formidable chasm in my thinking that stalled the writing and tempted me to give up the project. In time, a solution would dawn on me, the chasm was bridged, and I would be glad that *I* had found a solution. Then I remembered that, on the manuscripts of Johann Sebastian Bach, the initials "J. J." appear frequently (meaning *Jesu, juva;* "Jesus, help me"); without doubt, the maestro experienced similar problems and his prayers were answered. Now, I too say "Thank you, God" or "Thank you, Holy Spirit."

Many people tend to think of the Holy Spirit as God who interrupts or replaces our traditional forms with some startling new experience, as in the wind and fire and strange speech on the first Day of Pentecost. That idea is expressed in the Quaker tradition of speaking in worship "when the Spirit moves," as this old spiritual relates so well:

> I'm gonna sing when the Spirit says "sing," . . . (repeat)
> I'm gonna pray when the Spirit says "pray," . . .
> I'm gonna shout when the Spirit says "shout," . . .
> I'm gonna dance when the Spirit says "dance," . . .
>   and obey the Spirit of the Lord.

Certainly, God acts occasionally in such a spontaneous manner, and it is thrilling to experience. However, if the Holy Spirit is responsible for the movement of the stars and planets that can be predicted hundreds of years in advance, the Spirit helps us in liturgical planning as well as in worship improvising. The Spirit gives us new words for worship, sometimes created on the spot. The Holy Spirit also makes the ancient words of Scripture and the texts and music of historic liturgies become fresh and life-giving in human experience.

Finally, I have noticed recently that the Holy Trinity—Father, Son, and Holy Spirit—is seldom acknowledged in evangelical worship, except in a few hymns and choruses and in baptism ("I baptize you in the name of the Father, the Son, and the Holy Spirit"). Many Lutheran churches begin every service with the ascription "In the name of God the Father, God the Son, and God the Holy Spirit." In the Roman Catholic mass, the Trinity is proclaimed in the *Kyrie,* the *Gloria in excelsis,* the *Credo,* at least three times in the Eucharistic prayer, and in the

Agnus Dei. In the Orthodox liturgy, the Trinity is addressed and venerated more than sixty times, with the congregation making the sign of the cross in each instance.

Time was that most evangelicals ensured that the Holy Trinity would be honored in services by singing both the Doxology ("Praise Father, Son, and Holy Ghost") and the Gloria Patri ("Glory be to the Father and to the Son and to the Holy Ghost"), and in giving a benediction, for example, "May the blessing of God Almighty, the Father, Son, and Holy Spirit, be upon you, and remain with you forever. Amen."

Today, in the interest of being "contemporary," both those musical praises and the spoken blessing have been dropped in most evangelical churches, with no proper substitutes. I am not suggesting that the timeworn Doxology and Gloria Patri should be reinstated; modern worship should use the title "Holy Spirit," not "Holy Ghost," and both Gloria Patri tunes are dated and should be replaced. But it is an unspeakable affront to God not to mention frequently his Three-in-One presence in our worship!

These then are the ABCs of Trinitarian worship. I have included other definitions of worship in appendix I of this book. For those who want additional study, I recommend *Worship, Community and the Triune God of Grace* by James Torrance. Based on the biblical truth that believers are "Christ's body and that we (and our worship) are accepted by God because of Jesus' spotless and obedient life, sacrificial death, resurrection, and continuing work as our Great High Priest," Torrance says,

> Christian worship is, therefore, our participation through the Spirit in the Son's communion with the Father, in his vicarious life of worship and intercession. It is our response to our Father for all that he has done for us in Christ. It is our self-ordering in body, mind and spirit, in response to the one true offering made for us in Christ, our response of gratitude (*eucharistia*) to God's grace (*charis*), our sharing by grace in the heavenly intercession of Christ.[13]

Final Thoughts

In some ways, arguing about what music we enjoy in worship is a little like debating what brand of grape juice (or wine) we prefer for the Lord's Supper. The essence of worship lies in our apprehension of God, not in our fleeting pleasure in sound or the taste of liquid in a Communion cup. In today's "strange land of obsessive formalism," worship must express primarily our love relationship with God, Three-in-One, and with other human beings, as stated in the great commandment (Mark 12:30-31).

The formula for worshiping in this way is simple but challenging. First, we must be sure that our love relationship with God in Christ is contemporary, that is, up-to-date. We must also be "at peace with our neighbors." Then, we must simply purpose to experience God's presence in worship whenever the Holy Spirit invites us to do so!

Carol Doran and Thomas Troeger suggest that long-time worshipers experience the presence of God in one or more of the worship elements that have become particularly "holy" to them: hymns, prayers, actions (like going forward for Communion), and the worship space with the God-reminding symbols it contains.[14] For that reason, these persons feel robbed when "new worship" eliminates those elements. Perhaps that explains why even the slightest change in worship form (like singing a new hymn, or moving the Doxology to another place in the order) or in the worship setting (like the color of the new choir robes) provokes a strong objection by somebody. Of course, we must all examine our responses to be sure they are prompted by discernment and not by self-centered sentimentality.

We should say yes *whenever* the Holy Spirit invites us to "see God," first in the elements that are already holy to us, and increasingly in all the actions, words, music, or things that are used. Worship is, after all, more a matter of intent than of accident. We must remember that those nearby in worship are also God's children, even though the elements that help them "see God" may be less holy or even objectionable to us. We should share what we can of their expression and experience;

this is one way to love our neighbors as ourselves. In between, we should lift our hearts in our own worship prayers—adoration, confession, thanksgiving, and supplication.

In the next chapter I continue the discussion of the last half of the challenge Jesus spoke to the Samaritan woman: True worshipers will worship God *in truth*. And truth is perceived both intellectually and intuitively through a balance of words and other communicating symbols.

2

Worshiping God in Cognitive and Affective Truth

In a Strange Land of Superficial Emotionalism

You will know the truth, and the truth will make you free.
—John 8:32

*Y*ears ago our oldest daughter, Donna, came home from a children's activity at church happily singing a little Bible chorus: "The Word of God is like a hammer; it breaketh the rocks in tway" (for "twain," Jer. 23-29). In an effort to get her to think about what she was singing, I asked her what the song meant. "Don't be silly, Daddy," she said. "It doesn't mean a thing; it's just a song."

With an eight-year-old child, this was cute and it provided a story that helps me get the point of this chapter across. However, when this is the unspoken experience of most adults in church, as I believe it is, it is tragic.

My daughter is now a clinical psychologist and she tells me that her discipline emphasizes that the emotions we feel are caused and/or sustained by conceptual thought. Further, in a healthy, balanced life, our emotions will be appropriate, valid, and "true"—that is, based on rational thinking rather than on distortion of facts.

In this chapter, I will discuss how music and other arts used in connection with words can either *help* or *hinder* full worship in spirit and truth. It is important to know whether our emotional feelings in church are being caused and/or sustained by theological truth or whether they reflect some distortion of truth. From this point on in the book, my definition of "truth" will include *all God's revealed truth*—that is, theological and biblical truth.

Rational Worship

Worshiping in truth implies that we must worship with our "knowing" faculties; the word used by scholars is *epistemology*, that is, pertaining to the science of knowing, or knowledge. The first idea that comes to mind is that we must worship God with the *mind* as well as with the heart, the human spirit. For believers, worshiping God in truth means worshiping *in conformity and agreement with all the message of the Bible*, God's self-revealing in written words. One of my definitions of full worship is "a full self-revelation of God and a full response to God by the human person—in the heart but also with our knowing faculties, which are centered in the brain."

Anglican pastor and author John Stott has said,

> The Christian doctrine of revelation, far from making the human mind unnecessary, actually makes it indispensable and assigns to it its proper place. God has revealed himself in *words* to *minds*. His revelation is a rational revelation to rational creatures. Our duty is to receive his message, to submit to it, to seek to understand it, and to relate it to the world in which we live.[1]

Stott agrees that the human faculties mentioned in the great commandment of Mark 12:30 are not really separable—that the biblical word for "heart" really includes the mind.

> The first characteristic of heart-worship is that it is rational; the mind is fully involved in it. For the "heart" in Scripture is not simply equivalent to the emotions, as it usually is in common parlance today. In biblical thought the "heart" is

the center of the human personality and is often so used that the intellect is more emphasized than the emotions.[2]

No doubt most church attenders presume that mental and intellectual activity goes on in worship. After all, we hear, speak, and sing words that should be commonly understood. But are they? How many folks could recite the central emphasis of the sermon after it is completed? How many could give the central meaning of a typical hymn? How many people follow the language of prayers carefully, so they may say "amen" to them, perhaps audibly, but especially with mind and heart? If the answers to these questions are "too few," we must admit that many people are not fully worshiping in truth. Whether the fault lies in the techniques of preaching, praying, and singing, or in the worshipers' listening and hearing, the result is the same, and it is unacceptable.

Everybody agrees that modern television addiction has tended to make our generation more responsive to the communication of images and less responsive to words. For that reason, many consultants recommend that we make greater use of drama and other visual materials in our worship, and those means are helpful. However, our most explicit revelation of God is couched in the written words of Scripture, and the church cannot allow Christian believers to become less literate. Eventually we must say (as do the business interests who are competing in the world market with the highly literate cultures of Japan and Germany), "Teach American young people to read!"

Intuitive Worship

However, the cognitive-rational-intellectual communication of words is only one part of our activity in knowing God—of receiving God's self-revealing and responding to it; that is the activity of the left-brain. The right-brain part of us—the affective-intuitive-emotional part—"knows" God and responds to God through other symbols, especially the aesthetic, as expressed in sensory experiences of many kinds. Both right and left-brain activity are important in apprehending God and responding to God.

In worship, left-brain knowing and responding happens mostly in understanding words spoken in Scripture lections, prayers, the sermon, baptism, the Lord's Supper and words sung in hymns and other vocal pieces. Right-brain knowing and responding happens through hearing the music which accompanies hymn and vocal texts; through purely instrumental music; through seeing banners, architecture, narrative windows, and sanctuary furniture; through feeling and tasting the bread and wine of Communion; through standing, kneeling, walking, shaking hands, and other physical acts.

We should not minimize the contribution of the right-brain in knowing and worshiping God. Music added to text (for instance, the Swedish folk melody coupled with "How Great Thou Art") not only gives us a means for the whole congregation to pronounce those words in unison, but it can add powerful emotion to underline their cognitive meaning. When an adult experiences baptism, feeling the water adds meaning to hearing the words, "I baptize you in the name of God the Father, God the Son, and God the Holy Spirit"; the congregation shares the meaning in seeing the font (or baptistry) and the actions, and even in hearing the splashing water, as well as in remembering one's own baptism. In prayer, the postures of kneeling or of standing with upraised hands emphasize two different realities, and both are authentic. In the Lord's Supper, right-brain knowing and worshiping is absolutely essential: The words "take and eat" (and drink) must be followed with those actions. The true spiritual meaning is apprehended mostly in lifting the bread from the tray and in tasting the liquid in the cup.

When the Left and Right-Brains Conflict

In the examples given above, the left-brain and right-brain act in complementary fashion. A. S. Herbert insists that the dual action of God's ancient people, in offering sacrifices while the Levitical choir chanted words, was not mere coincidence:

It is important to remember that the utterance of the words, together with appropriate actions, was believed to have power. They are not merely pious reflections, but effective words through which Israel's "soul" was conveyed to God, and his energy in judgment and renewal was released into Israel's soul and through that into the world of nature and man.[3]

However, at times the right-brain and left-brain may act in opposition to, or competition with, each other; when that happens, full cognitive worship may be inhibited.

When the apostle Paul said "I will sing praise with the spirit, but I will sing praise with the mind also" (1 Cor. 14:15), he was talking about these two ways of knowing God and expressing worship. I believe he was referring to two experiences of singing, one in which the right-brain alone was active (uttering unintelligible, glossalalic words with melody), and the other in which the left-brain was dominant (with intelligible words fully understood and affirmed). That entire chapter emphasizes that worship should involve predominantly our rational-cognitive personhood. In this verse, I hear an implication that, though music may add emotional meaning to words, at times there may be *conflict or competition* between the cognitive and the emotive in singing, and in other acts of worship. In concluding his argument, Paul seems to emphasize certain words in the statement: "*but* I will sing praise with the *mind* also" (italics added). The question then is, When should our minds be active and dominant in worship, and when may we worship in a purely intuitive-emotional way? Or, how do we ensure that the intellectual and the emotional are balanced, in worship that combines words with other arts?

Words with Music

I believe we should consider church music basically to be *theological* expression—part of the dialogue between God and worshipers. With few exceptions, music in worship is coupled with important words. For this reason, we should choose literature—for instance, hymns and choir pieces—in which the music "fits" the text. True, good words may be supported and enhanced by a variety of musics. But the music, or dance, or any other art, must be the *servant* of theological truth, not the master. This is an unchanging principle in this day of right-brain, aesthetic-emotional preoccupation in worship: God must be worshiped in full theological truth.

In their classic book *Music and Worship in the Church*, Austin Lovelace and William Rice explain why music (the affective) often may be the master of the text (the cognitive). They contend that music's aesthetic appeal to the emotions is instantaneous; it takes longer for the mind to get into gear to understand the words, and many folk never bother![4]

Many years ago at a dinner party, the wife of a renowned professor of Old Testament studies complained that we musicians didn't really appreciate the good old hymns, such as "In the Garden." When I tested her cognitive understanding of the old gospel song by asking, "What garden?" she replied, with some exasperation: "What difference does it make? It's my favorite song!"[5]

Such incidents illustrate a well-entrenched tradition among evangelicals, who seldom have paid much attention to words in worship, except possibly during the sermon. In the past, we often referred to everything preceding that important feature of the service as preliminaries. Many of our people scorn the precise words of liturgical worship as meaningless ritual, and are most comfortable with prayers that are obviously improvised, saying little that demands careful attention. They also prefer familiar hymns (which really means "favorite tunes") rather than less-known texts that more clearly match the successive worship actions of the service or the emphasis of the sermon.

For many years, this awareness disturbed me greatly, and eventually I realized that it is not easy to understand hymn words, especially while singing them.[6] A hymn is both poetry and theology, and our culture has little interest in either! In singing, we utter one syllable at a time, concentrating on fitting each to its proper pitch; as a result, often we do not identify the meaning of a phrase or a full sentence. Consequently, unless ministers and church musicians study hymnology, they are ill-equipped to choose hymns wisely or to teach their meaning to the congregation. Perhaps this explains why many younger pastors have yielded to the suggestion to drop traditional hymns in favor of the repetitious mini-hymns of praise-and-worship music. At the same time, many older worshipers sense that this is a weakening of worship, even though they too may not understand completely the hymns they love.

Strangely enough, one of our most familiar hymns—"Love Divine, All Loves Excelling" by Charles Wesley—may be the least understood.

> Love divine, all loves excelling,
>   Joy of heaven to earth come down,
> fix in us thy humble dwelling,
>   all thy faithful mercies crown.
> Jesus, thou art all compassion,
>   pure unbounded love thou art;
> visit us with thy salvation,
>   enter every trembling heart.
>
> Breathe, O breathe thy loving Spirit
>   into every troubled breast;
> let us all in thee inherit,
>   let us find the promised rest.
> Take away the love of sinning,
>   Alpha and Omega be;
> end of faith, as its beginning,
>   set our hearts at liberty.
>
> Come, almighty to deliver,
>   let us all thy life receive;
> suddenly return, and never,
>   nevermore thy temples leave.
> Thee we would be always blessing,
>   serve thee as thy hosts above,
> pray and praise thee without ceasing,
>   glory in thy perfect love.

Finish then thy new creation,
    pure and spotless let us be;
let us see thy great salvation
    perfectly restored in thee:
changed from glory into glory,
    till in heaven we take our place,
till we cast our crowns before thee,
    Lost in wonder, love, and praise.

I find that poetry often becomes more cognitive when I restate it in prose, stanza by stanza. Here is my paraphrase of the hymn:

Jesus, "Joy of Heaven," who, as the Incarnation of God's love, came down to earth: grant us your crowning mercy by entering our hearts, bringing us your salvation.

Lord Jesus, breathe your Holy Spirit into each of us. Be the end (the Omega), the completion, of our salvation as well as the beginning (the Alpha). So, take away our love of sinning, and let us enter into the spiritual liberty or rest God has promised us (Heb. 4:1-11).

Almighty One, as you came to us and gave us your life in the experience of new birth, come to us again in sanctifying grace, and never leave us. We want to praise you and serve you constantly, as the angels do in heaven.

O Christ, in all of life, continue your work of our sanctification, day by day and year by year creating us anew, making us more in your image. For this we will love and praise you, now and through all eternity.

Obviously, this song is not primarily an expression of praise. It is rather a hymn of invocation, in which we petition God in Christ to accomplish a spiritual work in our hearts through the Holy Spirit; as such, it is just as appropriate in beginning the service as a spoken invocation.

Even so, we need to explain the "suddenly return" phrase in stanza three. Many modern Wesleyans believe (as Charles Wesley did) that God comes to people in two works of grace which can be instantaneous—regeneration and entire sanctification (thus, *suddenly* return).

Fortunately, most hymns are not as obscure in meaning as this favorite. I suggest that, at least on some occasion when it is sung, each stanza be followed by the spoken translation given above. (For such a purpose, there is no copyright restriction.)

Other Means of Emotive Worship

In worship, certain short musical selections appear without words, like short instrumental works played as a Prelude, Offertory, or Postlude, or possibly even a period of instrumental praise in the middle of a service. We can find worship meaning in this experience as well—perhaps a unique opportunity to sense the presence of God.

If the music is commonly associated with a text that worshipers know, like Luther's chorale "A Mighty Fortress Is Our God" or Jack Hayford's chorus "Majesty," hearing it can bring those words to mind, and the worship experience can be both emotive and cognitive. Reproducing the words of one stanza in the service order or on an overhead screen, or even citing the hymnal number in the worship guide, would help to jog the memory. At other times, the music style (whether wordbased or not) can be identified as "familiar to my experience in church" and can remind worshipers of other times when they have met God in the company of those sounds, encouraging them to renew and repeat that experience.

In the same way, other works of art—the architecture of the room and the furnishings (pulpit, organ, baptismal facility, communion table, cross, candles, and banners) become reminders that can move us from a sense of God's absence to a realization of his very presence. On the other hand, these right-brain, artistic means of worship could become mere entertaining interludes, or even distracting "idols," if they are not sanctified (made holy) by words that explain their "God meaning."

Worship Arts and Superficial Emotionalism

Today, evangelical churches are giving more attention to the arts than at any time in my memory. Many congregations welcome the use of banners, of drama, and even of dance (expressive movement). This is good news! For too long evangelicals have tried to worship meaningfully using little more than words and music.

At the same time, and possibly because of these changes, churches often give more attention to the style of their music than to the words the music carries. Much contemporary Christian music acknowledges this by limiting the text of a song to one or two phrases, repeated over and over again. Now we hear that Busters (the children of the Baby Boomers) would prefer church music *without words!*

Today's lack of concern for verbal truth becomes apparent in typical nonliturgical services whenever words are combined with music. An anthem or a solo will be performed, without supplying the text in print. Whatever the choice, few worshipers will know the words from memory. But they do not complain, though the resulting experience is largely or completely intuitive-aesthetic, not cognitive. If you asked them if they understood the words, they would probably say "of course"; to say otherwise would be to criticize the musicians' diction! They should say that they identified occasional words like "God" and "grace" and perhaps a repeated refrain. But no listener gets the full message of an unfamiliar song unless the full text can be followed in print.

Words as rational symbols are losing out to other aesthetic-intuitive symbols, as well. Evangelicals have always been reticent to use sufficient words to give meaning to Communion. Usually, someone offers a prayer of thanksgiving for the elements that remind us of Christ's suffering and death for our salvation, and the pastor repeats the words of Institution that are our authorization for the observance: "The Lord Jesus on the night when he was betrayed took a loaf of bread. . . ." (1 Cor. 11:23-26). Recently, some of my students participated in a service in a charismatic Pentecostal church. At the close of a long season of prayer including glossalalia, bread and wine were distributed and the leader simply raised the chalice (like a wine glass at a wedding reception), saying "To your health"—nothing more. On another occasion, I played for the wedding of the son of a prominent evangelical minister, in which the Lord's Supper elements were served, but only to the bride and groom, *with no spoken words whatsoever.* Such an occurrence should be cause for theological scandal among evangelicals, but no one even mentioned it![7]

Each of these instances gives evidence that cognitive words of biblical truth are not sufficiently important to modern pastors or to congregations, who are content with worship that is more superficially affective than rational.

The Danger of Idolatry

False worship can always be identified as *idolatry,* the substituting of a false god for the true God of biblical revelation. In chapter 1, I suggested that worship form and style are the preoccupation of many churches today and that these could be false idols which are substituted for worshiping God in spirit, with the whole heart. Similarly, symbols in worship can become idols. I believe that happens when we fail to make them "holy," that is, spiritually meaningful, with sufficient biblical-theological words. When we insist on a certain style of music for hymns, choral pieces, or solos—whether high art or pop art—without giving careful attention to the words sung, we tend to make a god of the music style.

Recently, our church presented a group of young girls in interpretive movement, accompanying the recorded singing of a contemporary Christian song. The dance was modest and beautiful, and carefully coordinated to express the meaning of thoroughly biblical words. However, many in the congregation didn't know the song, couldn't identify its words from the performance, and had no printed text to follow. So, our worship opportunity was limited to right-brain interpretation of human bodies in movement—hardly qualifying as worship "in truth." Later, when this was mentioned in a workshop, one person asked, "Isn't it possible to worship God with praise, simply because of the beauty of the human form in motion?" My answer: "Possibly, for an individual believer who attends a classical ballet, but not in the burlesque theater, and not in church!"

Bodily movement can be an emotionally moving and authentic means of perceiving God when it is the servant (not the master) of theological truth. I remember vividly a Maundy Thursday service which presented the Latin mass sung to music by Guillaume de Machaut (ca.1300–1377) and reverently danced by an individual. Even for trained musicians, fourteenth-century music is difficult to experience as worship. But I knew from memory the English language meaning of every Latin phrase—which also was included in the service order, and the interpretive movement did for me what the music could not do by itself. It made the thoroughly scriptural truth in the *Kyrie* (Lord, have mercy), *Gloria* (Glory to God in the highest), *Credo* (I believe in God the Father Almighty), *Sanctus* and *Benedictus* (Holy, holy, holy, Lord God of hosts), and *Agnus Dei* (Lamb of God, who takes away the sins of the world) come alive—and I worshiped.[8]

When words appear with some other art—whether music or action or artifact (object)—two complementary things happen: *The words explain the art, and the art gives added meaning to the words.* However, symbolic art that is not associated directly with the liturgy should also be explained verbally. Our church in Louisville, Kentucky, enjoys three magnificent windows that are placed at the two sides and front of the sanctuary: One depicts Creation, one Calvary, and one the Holy Spirit in Ministry.[9] In the course of worship, our pastor refers frequently to features of the windows, which helps to ensure that they will communicate truth to the congregation, rather than becoming idols in which we take selfish pride but find little spiritual meaning.

God Talk and Other Language Issues in Worship

Since words are so important in the dialogue with God in worship, we must consider also their quality and characteristics. The contemporary church has examined and changed certain traditional worship language, to ensure that it is understandable and not offensive to any worshipers. We began by replacing the seventeenth-century intimate pronouns "thee-thine" (in speaking to God) with the twentieth-century intimate forms "you-yours." The change created problems only in the historic songs that worship scholars believed we should retain in the church's memory; in those examples, word changes were made, with varying degrees of success. In the long run, most hymnal editors agreed that we can keep "thee-thine" language in certain hymns and anthems, until common usage replaces them with newer works, all of which will be in the "you-yours" version.

Many evangelical ministers agree also that they must refrain from using the terms "man" and "mankind" as gender-inclusive when speaking of both women and men, and composers do the same in writing hymns and other church music. However, many retain the biblical masculine names (like "Father" and "King") for God. Occasional pronouns are also used, though I have discovered that many hymns are strengthened by replacing the too frequently used "he" or "him" with a repetition of the word "God." Contemporary hymn writers like Thomas Troeger and Brian Wren have demonstrated how many other images for God can enrich our worship language.[10] In fact, the search for adequate words to identify our God, Three-in-One, has occupied devout Christians throughout the church's history, as shown in this thirteenth-century prayer of praise.

> O burning Mountain, O chosen Sun,
>   O perfect Moon, O fathomless Well,
> O unattainable Height, O Clearness beyond measure,
>   O Wisdom without end, O Mercy without limit,

O Strength beyond resistance, O Crown beyond all
    majesty:
The humblest thing you created sings your praise.
Amen.
(Mechtild of Magdeburg)

Finally, all hymnal editors acknowledge the need to be sensitive to the possibility of offending persons outside the white
European heritage that has dominated evangelical church
song, such as foreign nationals (in phrases like "heathen
tribes"), African-Americans (using "black" as a symbol of sin),
and handicapped persons (in words like "blind," "lame," "deaf,"
and "dumb").

Church growth specialists have reminded us that certain
individuals reject all traditional hymns because they are "theologically loaded." They say also that we should be cautious in
our use of God talk in *all* worship words, including preaching
and praying. The re-symbolizing of worship speech began by
changing the opening biblical greeting—"The Lord be with you
. . . and also with you"—to "Good morning" (which originally
meant "God's morning"). Eventually, the fear of using worship
jargon led to wholesale house-cleaning of important worship
elements. Such word-worship actions as calls to worship, in-
vocations, prayers of all kinds, and benedictions are being
discarded, evidently because they are believed to be meaningless to certain age groups.

For years I have taught a course in historical worship, and
my students have noticed that traditional liturgies contain
much more God talk than they hear in a typical evangelical
worship service. This includes repeated reference to our redemption through Christ, our "bent to sinning" and our need
of God's constant forgiveness and cleansing, and our mor-
tality and the inevitability of God's judgment. I have noticed
also that some preachers meet the challenge to be "seeker
sensitive" by romanticizing their language in such a way that
it sounds vaguely religious, but nobody knows exactly what
has been said.

I believe that such restrictions and solutions are absolutely unacceptable, even though they may give less offense to prospective attenders. How can we worship God without expressing theology—the words and thought about God? Instead of bypassing or romanticizing God talk, we should interpret the meaning of biblical words in the context of the worship service itself.

I heard recently of a church, which years ago I would have identified as "narrow fundamentalist," that includes secular songs (like "White Christmas" and "Rudolf, the Red-Nosed Reindeer") in its new Christmas presentations. Unbelievers do come to church at Christmas time, thus giving us an opportunity to speak the Good News to them, but it won't be done in that sort of secularizing. We communicate the gospel best, not even in idyllic, pastoral carols like "Away in a Manger" and "O Little Town of Bethlehem," but in those that speak of Christ's *kenosis* (self-humbling), incarnation, and eventual suffering and death for our redemption (like "Hark, the Herald Angels Sing," the original text of "What Child Is This," and several of the annual Christmas songs written by Timothy Dudley-Smith).

Every generation in my memory has had its own problems in worship with excessive anthropomorphism, which the dictionary defines as "ascribing human form or attributes to a being or thing not human, especially to a deity." Possibly because men and women do possess some of the attributes of God (we are made "in the image of God," Gen. 1:27), modern irreverence is expressed by seeming to address God as an equal. This spirit underlies evangelicals' traditional preoccupation with subjective congregational song. Whereas objective hymnody proclaims "God Is Love, Let Heaven Adore Him," the gospel song says "O How I Love Jesus." (And the modern substitute might well be "O how I love loving Jesus.")

In chapter 1, I spoke about the need to experience God as both immanent and transcendent. Ruth Duck, in her book *Finding Words for Worship*, says, "A relational understanding of worship makes room for reverence and for intimacy, since this loving, powerful, and wise God seeks to be in a covenant relationship with us. An appropriate theology of worship, then, calls for language reflecting *reverent intimacy*" (italics added).[11]

In certain forms of praise-and-worship music, singers speak to God directly in endearing terms that are common in human relationships, for example, "I Love You, Lord"; "Father, I Adore You"; "The Greatest Thing in All My Life Is Knowing You"; and "You Are My All in All." I believe those choruses may be used in an appropriate context, but only in moderation. As the Psalms demonstrate, those immanent, personal words should be balanced with other texts which speak of the holiness, the "other-ness," of God ("We Worship You, Almighty God," or "Immortal, Invisible, God Only Wise") and also with third person language ("He Is Lovely, He Is Holy," or "Praise to the Lord the Almighty"). Remember that John Wesley felt that his brother Charles's hymn, "Jesus, Lover of My Soul," was appropriate for private reading, but too personal for corporate worship!

Words for "Informal Worship"

Does all the above discussion imply that we should not use the typical speech of today's informal worship, that is, contemporary, nontheological language that is supposedly free from clichés or jargon? Well, that depends. Certainly modern worship should communicate utter *honesty* in all its talk, and we may stretch our language resources to the limit in saying that the gospel of Jesus Christ meets every need of life. Homilies should convey biblical truth in as convincing and gripping a style as possible, so long as the truth is not overwhelmed by the art of speech! Perhaps a sermon should be entertain*ing* (that is, holding the attention agreeably) but not entertain*ment* (that is, diversion or amusement). After all, speaking and hearing the truth of God is serious business.

However, in considering the entire service, we must ask: Do our words make us aware that the eternal, holy, and finally incomprehensible God is truly present? If any style makes us more conscious of the gifts and personalities of worship leaders than we are aware of God, we must reject it. In our hymns, Scripture reading, and prayers—words from God or words to God—do we express the reverent intimacy that is necessary, because the living God is participating in the conversation? Such questions should convince us that we cannot completely rid our services of jargon or God talk, which is our only means of expressing "God truth." Every area of life has and needs its jargon. Do we really believe that the ultimate world of God's domain must limit its conversation to words understood by those who have not yet become part of God's family?

Making Words Understandable in Worship

Since words are the primary means of rational communication, they should be the central concern of those who plan and conduct worship. First, they should be audible to everyone in the worship room because of both good diction and good acoustics (assisted by a public address system if necessary). Second, good rhetorical techniques should enhance the meaning of words, so they become as meaningful as possible; this includes proper inflection, accentuation, and pacing. If persons from the congregation are used in service leadership, they should receive coaching, possibly with a rehearsal in the worship room.

The following additional suggestions are offered to worship planners and leaders for making words understandable in various worship components.

In congregational song.

1. Choose hymns because of their specific textual content, to meet particular needs in various parts of the service. When this is done consistently, worshipers learn the meaning of hymns through their placement and use.

2. Sing the entire hymn, or all that is pertinent to the service involved. A hymn communicates a complete idea in its total structure; to thoughtlessly omit stanzas distorts the content. Singing medleys of hymns, using one stanza of each, ensures

that only the most general meaning will be conveyed; such a practice has merit when that is the objective but it should be the exception, not the rule. In this connection, I must say also that typical praise-and-worship singing is more a sensual than a rational experience.

3. Identify the function of hymns with appropriate titles in the worship guide: Hymn of Praise or Thanksgiving, Confession, Petition, Challenge, or Dedication; or Hymn of Invocation or Response or Benediction. Above all, be sure the hymn text conforms to its title.

4. If possible, introduce the hymn with a clue as to its meaning; or, place a brief note in the bulletin following the hymn's listing. In the case of "Love Divine, All Loves Excelling," discussed earlier in this chapter, this sentence could be printed or spoken: "The hymn, addressed to Jesus Christ, prays that the Holy Spirit will accomplish God's sanctifying grace in our hearts, day by day and year by year, until we stand 'pure and spotless' in God's eternal presence."

5. Use tunes that enhance the rational meaning of words. Consider using historic texts with both old and new melodies to reach all age groups and to demonstrate that the words are more important than the music.

6. Follow Luther's practice of alternating groups in successive stanzas of hymns, for instance, men and women, or congregation and choir. This directs the attention of each group to the meaning of the text, especially *when they are not singing,* and is especially appropriate for hymns addressed to one another (like "Brethren, We Have Met to Worship").

7. Use modern-language theological hymns rather than choruses that say little or nothing. The Iona Community in Scotland is producing fine examples of congregational music. One of its songs, "Before the World Began," is a paraphrase of the prologue to John's Gospel:

> Before the world began, one Word was there;
>   grounded in God he was, rooted in care;
> by him all things were made, in him was love displayed,
>   through him God spoke, and said, "I AM FOR YOU."

Life found in him its source, death found its end;
   Light found in him its course, darkness its friend.
For neither death nor doubt nor darkness can put out
   the glow of God, the shout, "I AM FOR YOU."

The Word was in the world which from him came;
   unrecognized he was, unknown by name;
one with all humankind, with the unloved aligned,
   convincing sight and mind, "I AM FOR YOU."

All who received the Word by God were blessed;
   sisters and brothers they of earth's fond guest.
So did the Word of Grace proclaim in time and space
   and with a human face, "I AM FOR YOU."[12]

In choral, solo, and other noncongregational music.
   1. Follow the same principles given above in choosing the music.
   2. Take great care in perfecting diction.
   3. Unless the words are known by the congregation (as might be true of Handel's "Hallelujah" chorus), supply the complete text in appropriate form in the worship order. This is an aid both to comprehension and to reference for devotional use. It also will reduce conflict over music preferences; when a "new" style is presented (whether classic or modern), drawing attention to the text will reduce the negative impact of the music. Of course, copyright requirement will need to be met; today's copyright licensing agencies will be helpful in this regard.

In instrumental music.
   1. When the music is associated with a hymn text (whether familiar to the congregation or not), print at least a portion of those words in the bulletin, unless the text will be sung in the same service; or, refer worshipers to that text in the hymnal.
   2. Choose music whose text is related to the service theme.
   3. When the music has no textual association, a psalm verse could be included whose words match the music's expression: for instance, any pastorale could be followed with Psalm 23:1

("The Lord is my shepherd, I shall not want") or Psalm 42:1 ("As a deer longs for flowing streams, so my soul longs for you, O God").

In dance.

1. Use dance with spoken texts or with words plus music that are well-known or easily identified by the congregation. It is impossible to follow both the symbolic movement and an unfamiliar printed text simultaneously.

2. Exotic means of communication, like dance or drama, contribute most to worship when they occur infrequently, with a well-nigh flawless performance.

In Scripture reading.

1. Be sure that Bible passages are read clearly, expressively, and deliberately. For guidance in coaching others who will read, see *Getting the Word Across: Speech Communication for Pastors and Lay Leaders* by Robert Jacks.[13]

2. Set the context of each reading with a brief spoken introduction. For instance, introduce 1 Corinthians 11 by saying: "In this part of Paul's letter to the church at Corinth, the apostle talks about problems in community life and in worship."

3. Consider presenting a Scripture reading as a drama, perhaps using Michael Perry's *The Dramatized Old Testament* and *The Dramatized New Testament.*[14]

In praying.

1. Determine the nature of the prayer to be offered on behalf of the congregation and list it accordingly in the service order, whether Invocation (petition for the service), Confession, Dedication, or Thanksgiving and Supplication. Refrain from including all forms in one prayer. If thanksgiving and supplication are joined in one prayer, begin by speaking all the words of gratitude, follow with all the petitions, and perhaps close with thanksgiving that "God hears and answers our prayers."

2. Write out the prayer completely and read it expressively many times. Then, if you want to deliver it spontaneously,

prepare an outline on a card to remind you of the prayer subjects.

3. Avoid the practice of asking the organist to play a musical background to the prayer. Presumably, this is done to help worshipers (or the worship leader) sense the presence of God or to cover any lapses in the improvising of words. This sort of "mood creating" prevents folks from hearing what is prayed because their attention is drawn to the musical sounds and perhaps to the song texts with which they are associated.

In preaching (with apologies to the experts!).

1. Don't try to communicate too much in a single service. There was a time when homileticians suggested that folks might remember "three points" of a sermon, summarized by a hymn or poem. Today, they may recommend that a narrative style be used, emphasizing just *one* central thought. A musical follow-up in a hymn, anthem, or solo provides an opportunity for both contemplation and response.

2. Earlier, I suggested that simplicity and clarity should be the principal objectives in communication. Creative language that stimulates the imagination is desirable, so long as it holds the attention and communicates clearly. In this regard, the line between success and failure is extremely narrow. Many preachers are helped by a congregational discussion of the sermon (immediately following the service, or some evening); thus they can be sure folks are hearing what they intended to say!

In conducting the Lord's Supper and other special actions.

1. In general, evangelical groups have used few words in celebrating the sacraments (ordinances): I am convinced that this reduces the meaning of these actions. For example, the Lord's Supper should include: (1) the central idea and expression of thanksgiving; (2) telling the story of redemption through God's revealing in creation, in history, and especially through Jesus' incarnation, life, death, and resurrection; (3) the anticipation of Christ's return, when we will celebrate the marriage supper of the Lamb for all eternity; (4) a prayer that

God the Holy Spirit will accomplish his spiritual purposes in our lives, especially that we might experience true communion with God and with each other; and (5) a closing doxology to the Trinity, with a congregational "Amen."

2. The same goal of fuller expression in words should be pursued in baptism, dedication of children, and in any other special worship action.

On the Other Hand . . .

As I reread the last few pages of this chapter, I realize that they might seem to encourage a basically didactic, rationalistic approach to worship, and that would be wrong. Words themselves speak emotionally as well as cognitively. Music and other arts add important meaning to the words with which they are associated. Further, it is impossible for individuals to be fully cognitive every moment of a service; when our rational self slips out of gear momentarily, or even longer, the intuitive takes over, and some familiar, holy action, sound, or thing reminds us that God is still present! Also, God sometimes uses that holy nonword evocatively—to get our attention, and then leads us from the music or action or thing to the words. For this reason, I believe that we must make all words available and understandable for worshipers, so that they can worship cognitively whenever the Spirit helps them focus on word meaning.

Final Thoughts

J. D. Crichton reminds us that, whereas aboriginal worshipers primarily use actions to acknowledge their deities, God's people in both Old and New Covenants depend on words: "because faith comes by hearing . . . and because response in words is the specifically human way by which man makes known to himself and to others that he has received the word."[15]

When I attended church as a boy, words were almost the only means of worship expression we had. Of course, we used music with words, but the music was simple, not sophisticated. Yet I doubt that the adults in those services gave full attention to the texts—though I can repeat them today, word for word! We also used simple actions and words associated with baptism and the Lord's Supper. But we had no time or place for other symbolic actions or things—and no desire to include them. Rather, we criticized the churches we identified as *liturgical,* convinced that they substituted those symbolic "irrelevancies" for sound preaching of the Word and praying. Perhaps they even worshiped their symbols and traditions instead of God, we thought.

Today, a wide range of the arts are available to us and are being welcomed into our services. But we evangelical, nonliturgical believers are now remiss, as liturgical churches never were, in not using sufficient *words* with these actions and things to make them meaningful, cognitively as well as intuitively. We also allow our pleasure in music styles to dull our minds to the meaning of important texts. I believe this may be the outstanding fault of evangelical worship in today's "strange land" of superficial emotionalism.

3

Worshiping God in Theological Truth

In a Strange Land of Theological Confusion

A religion without dogma is like a parcel tied up without string.
—Christine Longford (from *The Quotable Soul*)

*F*rom my years of working with the Billy Graham crusade team I remember with love and gratitude Grady Wilson, one of Billy's boyhood friends and a longtime preaching associate. Grady was converted to faith in Christ in the same service as Billy. He used to say that he had an agreement with God: If the Lord would keep Billy true to his calling, he (Grady) would keep Billy humble. To that end, he often told stories about Billy's occasional gaffes in his early days of ministry. But he told even more deprecatory tales about himself.

Grady often regaled us with accounts of his annual preaching commitment at a camp meeting for cowhands and other ranch workers in Texas. On one occasion, he told us, a wizened old cowboy said, "Brother Grady, we just love your preaching. You don't give us no doctrine, or nothin'!"

To be sure, Grady could sound like a Southern revivalist preacher when he wanted to. But his sermons were always true to his understanding of biblical theology, which was very similar to that of Billy Graham. If some Christians are ambivalent about theology and theologians, secular culture thoroughly disparages them. The eighteenth-century skeptic Thomas Paine said, "The study of theology . . . is the study of nothing; it is founded on nothing; it rests on no principles; it proceeds by no authorities; it has no data; it can demonstrate nothing; and it admits of no conclusion."

But theology has to be the noblest of sciences. The dictionary calls it "the field of study, thought, and analysis which treats of God, his attributes, and his relations to the universe." Martin Luther had it right: "Theology should be empress, and philosophy and the other arts merely her servants." This chapter continues our discussion of worshiping in truth in terms of theology, our systematized understanding of the truth of God.

Worshiping God in Theological Truth

Worshiping God in truth means that worship words will be theological expressions—words of faith, words about God. The ancient song of Moses and Miriam—actually, the first recorded biblical song, in Exodus 15—proclaimed that God had become Israel's salvation by throwing Pharaoh and his army into the Red Sea. A first-century hymn clarified and amplified that Old Testament theology by declaring that Jesus Christ is God our Savior:

> There is one God;
>   there is also one mediator
>   between God and humankind,
> Christ Jesus, himself human,
>   who gave himself a ransom for all. (1 Tim. 2:5-6)

In the third-century church, opposing theological groups voiced their debates about Christ's equality with God the Father in songs; history records that their competitive outdoor musical processions often ended in fights with fists and clubs. In the sixteenth century, Martin Luther proclaimed the new Reformation understanding of faith in his chorales. Two hundred years later, Charles Wesley gave hymnic form to the theology of England's Great Awakening that birthed Methodism.

While religious leaders normally try to guard the theology

expressed in their worship music, they also have borrowed hymns freely across confessional and denominational lines, so long as the text conformed to their own doctrinal convictions. Trinitarian American evangelicals long have claimed Sarah F. Adams' "Nearer, My God, to Thee," though its writer was a Unitarian. "Faith of Our Fathers," written by Catholic Frederick W. Faber, has been revised to conform to *Protestant* faith. As a result, Faber's reference to Roman Catholic "fathers, chained in prisons dark" by sixteenth-century Protestants may be thought by some to refer to Protestants persecuted by Catholics!

Sometimes mistakes are made in choosing hymns, and congregations wind up singing things they don't really believe. In chapter 2, I pointed out that many congregations sing Wesley's "Love Divine, All Loves Excelling" without identifying the distinctive Methodist doctrine it teaches. It is said that "Rock of Ages, Cleft for Me" (by Augustus M. Toplady) was written to refute that particular Wesleyan theology, but few hymnists today could tell you how it does so. Many groups sing "Come, Ye Thankful People, Come" (by Henry Alford) as a Harvest-Thanksgiving hymn without realizing that its principal theme is Christ's second coming and the final judgment. Finally, many evangelical choirs have sung the Latin hymn *Ave, verum corpus* ("Hail, True Body"), usually to music by Mozart, even though the text expresses reverence of communion bread as the "true (actual, physical) body" of Christ.

In today's church life, doctrinal confusion in worship words and actions may occur because theological issues are much less significant than they were even fifty years ago. Individuals reared and educated as Methodists or Presbyterians or Disciples of Christ often will attend and join what was once a competing group. The uniting of churches in ecumenical fellowship and action also encourages this kind of "theological homogenization." In earlier times, ecumenism was characteristic of more liberal, mainline churches. Today, it is equally a hallmark of evangelical groups, so that frequently members of the Church of the Nazarene will become Baptists, and vice versa, and both those denominations establish churches whose affiliation and theology are hidden under a neutral name such as "Community Church" or "Christian Fellowship Church."

I am convinced that we should cultivate as broad a fellowship as possible within Christian groups. At the same time, I believe that a church's doctrinal distinctives should not be lost. I was present at the Congress on World Evangelization in Lausanne, Switzerland, in 1974 when evangelicals and Pentecostals, and some of the new charismatics, joined their hands and hearts in fellowship, after years of mutual suspicion and conflict. Since that time, charismatics have taken the lead in worship thought and action. Many of their unique ideas and worship procedures have been copied widely by non-charismatics and have become the dominant model for today's worship revolution. Though their *basic* worship ideas are sound, some aspects of their specific theology and practice do not conform to historic evangelical truth. I believe it is dangerous to confuse theological issues in this way in the name of "Christian community." All Christians should understand their own theology and express it as fully as possible in their worship.

In this chapter I will trace briefly the history, theology, and worship both of classic Pentecostalism and of the new charismatic renewal movement, pointing out that many concepts that are called "creative" in contemporary worship are really second-hand, warmed-over ideas from the charismatic tradition. Certainly, charismatics have the right and the responsibility to develop their worship to conform to their doctrines. However, non-charismatics should reject copycat worship; if they are truly creative, they will devise their forms within the boundaries of their own theology, based on their own understanding of Scripture.

The Classic Pentecostal Churches

The modern Pentecostal movement originated in the United States in the first decade of the twentieth century and is generally associated with the 1906 founding of the biracial Apostolic Faith Gospel Mission on Azusa Street in Los Angeles. According to *The New Dictionary of the Christian Church*, the first Pentecostalists came from Wesleyan holiness theological roots, and in their renewal awakening they emphasized "Spirit baptism" as an experience subsequent to conversion and evidenced by speaking in tongues. They preached also the inspiration of the Bible, salvation by conversion and revival, instantaneous sanctification, and divine healing, claiming to be a restoration of original "Day of Pentecost" Christianity, as described in Acts 2:1-13. The movement quickly became international, as Pentecostal revivals occurred in Scandinavia, Great Britain, India, and Latin America. In the United States, it evolved into largely segregated denominational groups like the Assemblies of God, the Church of God in Christ, the Church of God (Cleveland, Tenn.), the Church of God of Prophecy, the International Church of the Foursquare Gospel, and the United Pentecostal Church International.[1]

Pentecostalism grew slowly during the first half of the twentieth century. By 1950, in some of its larger white denominational churches worship had become more disciplined and sophisticated, hardly differing from that of non-Pentecostal Baptists. Although Pentecostal fellowships were not acknowledged by early fundamentalistic groups (for example, the American Council of Christian Churches), some were admitted as charter members of the National Association of Evangelicals in 1942. After World War II, and especially with the television appearances of such figures as Oral Roberts, segments of Pentecostalism regained their primal fervor and experienced tremendous growth, especially in Third World countries.[2]

One of Pentecostalism's most gifted and widely recognized leaders—Jack Hayford, pastor of the Church on the Way in Los Angeles (associated with the International Church of the Foursquare Gospel)—has developed a thoughtful approach to congregational worship and has written hymns in both traditional ("We Lift Our Voice Rejoicing," 1962) and contemporary ("Majesty," 1981) styles. Classic Pentecostalism also was influenced profoundly (some would say, "renewed") by the emergence of the competitive, neo-Pentecostal development—the charismatic renewal movement.

The Charismatic Renewal Movement

The charismatic renewal movement differs from historic Pentecostalism in its relationship to other churches and groups, mainline, liturgical, and evangelical. In the 1950s the Full Gospel Business Men's Fellowship International was formed to witness to non-Pentecostals, and the evangelical journal *Christian Life* began to publish items that presented the "Spirit baptism" point of view. On April 3, 1960, Dennis Bennett, pastor of St. Mark's Episcopal Church of Van Nuys, California, announced to his congregation "how he had been led to receive the power and the fullness of the Holy Spirit, and how this had included the 'gift of unknown tongues.'"[3] Shortly thereafter, articles in *Time* and *Newsweek* brought the resultant conflict in that parish to national attention.[4] This one event is often referred to as the beginning of the charismatic renewal movement. Similar happenings were reported by many traditional groups—Roman Catholic, Eastern Orthodox, Lutheran, Mennonite, Methodist, Presbyterian, and Baptist—in the United States and throughout the world. Also, new groups dedicated to charismatic renewal principles and practices were formed, such as the Vineyard Fellowship churches led by John Wimber.

Why has this movement affected the whole church so profoundly and so quickly? For one thing, many of its adherents have been leaders in the religious media. Contemporary Christian music recording artists are successors of the Jesus Movement musicians of the 1970s; for the last twenty-five years, Christian pop music has been dominated by young singers who write and sing songs bearing the charismatic renewal message. Television's religious talk show host Pat Robertson has become both a religious and a political spokesman for many evangelical Christians. Recently, Robertson has muted his identity with charismatic renewal, insisting that he is really a "mainline evangelical"; that is in keeping with the group's idea that the movement is not a renewal of Pentecostalism—it is a renewal of the whole church. Finally, a number of historically evangelical colleges and seminaries have contributed to the current theological confusion by adding Pentecostal and charismatic teachers to their religion faculties.[5]

What is the theology of charismatic renewal? Since the movement includes such disparate groups as Roman Catholics, Lutherans, and Methodists, it does not speak with one voice on many of the cardinal doctrines of the faith. Peter Hocken lists nine essential elements in charismatic renewal. I have chosen a few key sentences from his discussion.

1. *Focus on Jesus.* The Charismatic Renewal Movement is everywhere marked by a focus on Jesus Christ. Witnesses to baptism in the Spirit constantly refer to an encounter with Jesus, a deeper yielding to Jesus, and a fuller acceptance of Jesus as Lord. . . .

2. *Praise.* The first result of the coming of the Holy Spirit in the baptism in the Spirit is a flow of praise [of God and of his Son, Jesus Christ] from within the believer, a verification of John 7:38. . . .

3. *Love of the Bible.* The Charismatic Renewal Movement has been consistently marked by a great love and thirst for the Scriptures. . . .

4. *God Speaks Today.* People baptized in the Spirit . . . experience a directness of communication and guidance from the Lord in a way that shocks or puzzles, attracts or repels other Christians. . . .

5. *Evangelism.* Just as Christians baptized in the Spirit have a new capacity to speak freely to God in praise, so they have a new capacity and freedom to speak to others about the Lord. . . .

6. *Awareness of Evil.* This awareness has caused deliverance and exorcism to acquire new relevance and usage in the Charismatic Renewal Movement. . . .

7. *Spiritual Gifts.* The features most readily identifiable as characteristic of the Charismatic Renewal Movement are the spiritual gifts listed in 1 Corinthians 12:8-10. . . . The gifts that are most prominent and most discussed are glossalalia, prophecy, and healing. . . .

8. *Eschatological Expectation.* The Charismatic Re-

newal Movement is generally accompanied by an increased expectancy and longing for the Parousia [the Second Coming]. . . .

9. *Spiritual Power.* The spiritual power that accompanies the baptism in the Holy Spirit is manifest in the capacity to praise, in the capacity to evangelize, in all ministries of deliverance and the overcoming of evil, and in the exercise of the spiritual gifts. [6]

Many of these faith elements are normal expectations and experiences of Christian believers, but in a continuing life of sanctification by the Holy Spirit, not through a single, instantaneous "Spirit baptism." However, while the statement about praise (item 2) conforms to biblical truth, it seems to me that the charismatic approach in praise-and-worship music is distorted; I will discuss that in this chapter and the next. Noncharismatic theologians differ most with charismatics in relation to "spiritual gifts" (items 4 and 7). Those beliefs influence and tend to determine all the activities of charismatic worship, many of which have been copied by non-charismatics without an understanding of the theological positions behind them.

A Personal Note

For many years I was thoroughly puzzled—sometimes attracted but more disturbed—by certain activities of the movements discussed in this chapter. What does it mean that this flamboyant, less rational expression of Christian faith has become the fastest growing worship in the world and that in some Latin American countries charismatics soon may become the largest religious group? How do I explain that the largest Christian congregation in the world (in Seoul, South Korea) has 200,000 Pentecostal members, and that the sometimes controversial theologian Harvey Cox associates this evidence with the changing of religion in this century?

In his book *Fire from Heaven,* Cox says that three aspects of Pentecostal-charismatic life are "recovery of primal spirituality": (1) glossalalia is the recovery of *primal speech;* (2) such phenomena as trance, vision, healing, dreams, dance, and other archetypal religious expressions constitute the recovery of *primal piety;* and (3) Pentecostalism's millennial outlook based on its eschatology is a recovery of *primal hope.*[7] Primal spirituality has to do with "early, or primeval worship" and carries the assumption that expressions of spirituality have changed through the millennia, for better or for worse.

Cox makes it clear that he understands this to include all human spirituality, Christian and otherwise. Remember, for instance, that "speaking in tongues" happens among Hasidic Jews, Muslims, and even animists, a fact that is freely admitted and discussed without animus in the *Dictionary of Pentecostal and Charismatic Movements.*[8] Again, the biblical writer describes Saul's primal experience of prophesying at Gibeah-elohim (1 Sam. 10:1-13; 19:18-24) as a "dancing frenzy, in which Saul was turned into a different person," a demonstration which may have been comparable to some of today's expressions of "primal piety."

Cox also links Pentecostalism's recovery of primal spirituality to the emergence of postmodern philosophy (in which there is no such assumption as the existence of absolute truth) and the current preoccupations with "spirituality" fads:

> The reemergence of this primal spirituality came—perhaps not surprisingly—at just the point in history when both the rationalistic assumptions of modernity and the strategies religions had used to oppose them (or to accommodate to them) were all coming unraveled. . . .
>
> Long before primal scream therapy, dream journals, liturgical dance, psychodrama, or futurology made their appearances at elite conference centers and expensive weekend workshops, the early Pentecostals were spreading their own versions of all of them.[9]

This explanation of Pentecostal phenomena was confirmed for me at the 1974 conference in Lausanne. One of the speakers—who later became head of one of America's leading mission organizations—testified that he had prayed for the gift of tongues, and that it was given to him. However, he found that it was not helpful, because what he needed more was the "gift of a sound mind." When I asked him privately to explain, he said that it was his understanding that speaking in tongues is a quite normal, lingual-psychic experience available to all human beings. On the other hand, when Pentecostals and charismatics experience speaking in tongues, "it is widely and distinctively (but not universally) viewed as the certifying consequence of the baptism in the Holy Spirit."[10]

When I was young, I heard some preachers say that speaking in tongues was an evidence of the baptism in the Holy Spirit and was required of every Christian, while others insisted that it was "of the devil." Which is true? Russell Spittler indicates that, in different situations, possibly both could be true: "Whatever its origin, glossalalia is a human phenomenon, not limited to Christianity nor even to religious behavior among humankind."[11]

I do not believe God wants me to seek for the gifts of glossalalia or any other forms of primal piety. However, I do believe that, in this postmodern, less-literate day, the church should expect to increase the level of affective expression in worship in response to the perceptual problems of large groups in Western culture; this includes using additional arts and new forms of the traditional art of music. At the same time, we must resist the temptation to abandon theological-biblical content in order to "reach the culture." *Christianity cannot survive unless its eternal truth is taught by its ministers, understood by its believers, and expressed in its worship.* Further, because I believe our culture is less literate today, the emphasis on teaching cognitive truth must grow in direct proportion to the increase in the use of arts.

Thanks, but No Thanks!

So, how do I respond to fellow believers in the charismatic renewal movement? First, I must show them full respect and Christian love because they are following Christ as they believe

God has called them to do. Also, I must give thanks to them and to God for what they have taught that is truth about worship and for the new musical forms they have produced. But when I am convinced they are wrong, I must respond with a different opinion. Here are my arguments.

Christian worship is important for itself.

We all should be thankful to charismatics because they have brought worship to the attention of the whole church. For perhaps two hundred years, many traditional evangelicals have offered limited worship opportunities because of their emphasis on revivalism or on pietistic Bible study. Evidently, their central objectives in weekly gatherings were the worship serendipities of evangelism or of increased Bible knowledge. Charismatics believe correctly that worship should not be limited by such purposes; it exists for the glory of God, who is truly present when believers gather in Jesus' name.

While I say "amen" to charismatics' statement of the primary significance of Christian worship, I cannot agree that their particular expectations for that worship are normative for the church. Also, at times, I am convinced they do not measure up to their own announced standards. Charismatics believe that all Christians are called to experience a baptism in the Holy Spirit and that speaking in ecstatic (unknown) tongues is a required sign of that baptism; they also emphasize the importance of "prophecy" (an immediate and completely authoritative word from God relayed by a single Spirit-baptized believer), and of miraculous healing. They expect that these three gifts will play a large part in their worship services.

Non-charismatic Christians believe that all believers are baptized with (not "baptized in") the Holy Spirit at the time of their new birth and admission into Christ's church ("For in the one Spirit we were all baptized into one body," 1 Cor. 12:13); most believe that no second experience is required in order to be fully Christian. Again, while many non-charismatics agree that some in the early church experienced glossalalia, they point out that the apostle Paul tended to devalue the gift (which he himself practiced, 1 Cor. 14:18) and to impose strict restrictions on its use—restrictions that are largely ignored by modern charismatics.[12] Further, while non-charismatics might agree that it is possible that glossalalia may be used today in worship—by others, if not by them—they insist that no church can survive with half the congregation speaking in tongues and half mute. In such a situation, charismatics' insistence that the experience is normative for all believers creates untenable tension in the church.

Emphasis on praise is central.
Charismatics are correct also in naming praise as our most important response to God in worship, and we must thank them for that. For 150 years, revivalistic, pietistic evangelicals have doted on subjective songs of Christian experience as their principal musical fare in church. They tended also to limit their *spoken* prayer to petitions. Today, everybody is talking about the centrality of praise in worship, perhaps because praise-and-worship singing has become the central feature in many contemporary services.

Charismatic believers identify praise in terms of classic *adoration*—praise that concentrates on the attributes of God's being, often simply repeating the biblical-theological names for God, without proclaiming God's acts on behalf of his people. The idea is expressed in a popular song, "Because of Who You Are," which suggests that such "pure" praise if preferable to that which gives thanks for God's mighty deeds, for example, in creating the world or in sending Jesus Christ to be our Savior. The song is rarely heard anymore, but mainline evangelical pastors frequently repeat the first line of the refrain when beginning a prayer, "God, we praise you because of who you are," giving powerful testimony to the influence of charismatic ideas on the whole body of Christ.

When praise-and-worship music first appeared in our services, I was delighted; for the first time in my life, evangelicals in my tradition showed excitement about singing new objective songs (at least, repeated phrases) of praise. Further, because many of these "tiny hymns" addressed God directly with the pronoun "you," it seemed possible that worshipers might gain a better sense of the true presence of God.

However, a more careful, long-term appraisal of the phenomenon has tended to cool my enthusiasm. Actually, praise-and-worship singing limits a congregation's worship even more than the gospel song tradition did. It offers no opportunity to sing our confession (as in "Search Me, O God"), our holy desires (as in "Draw Me Nearer"), our Christian witness (as in "Blessed Assurance, Jesus Is mine"), our theology of salvation (as in "Grace Greater Than Our Sin"), or our hope of eternal life (as in "Shall We Gather at the River?"). It does not give room even to praise that is thanksgiving because of God's mighty, loving actions on behalf of his creatures, as in the hymn "Praise to the Lord, the Almighty" or in the gospel song "Praise Him! Praise Him! Jesus our Blessed Redeemer."

The narrowly focused approach to worship that is "pure praise" has been the obsessive goal of certain Christians throughout history, especially in the age of medieval mysticism. In such a quest, the individual endeavors to worship God for himself alone, without any reference to his actions in history—in creating the world, in revealing himself to his ancient chosen people, or in sending Jesus Christ to live among us, to die and rise again for our salvation.

In his book *Integrity in Worship* Paul Hoon writes that this concept of the supreme "worthship" of God—his transcendence as shown in his attributes—should *not* be the central motivation in worship. He explains:

> 1. For one thing, the category of value in biblical thought is secondary to the categories of being, decision, and action.
>
> 2. It is not a distinctively Christian idea. Worship defined as the ascription of supreme worth to God can apply to the dance of the sun worshipper or the prayer wheel of the Oriental, to the rites of a mystery cult or the thought of the philosopher, as well as to the prayer of the Christian.
>
> 3. It can also bleach worship of the sense of mystery

and adoration . . . , partly because this category implies that the initiative in worship lies with man. On this view, it is man who "recognizes" and "ascribes" worth, . . . but if any agent is to assign or ascribe worth, it is God who ascribes worth to man rather than man to God.[13]

Hoon makes it clear that true Christian worship centers in God's actions in Jesus Christ for human salvation:

It is precisely the recital of, and engagement with, a particular history bound up with a particular Jew, in a particular land, at a particular time, that is the basis of Christian worship. . . . To the extent that scholars, pastors, and congregations have so critically absorbed ways of thinking bound up with worship understood as "worthship," much Protestant worship has become flabby rather than holy, folksy rather than numinous, hortatory [exhorting] rather than adoring, . . . and one is not surprised that it often appeals to infantile elements in human personality.[14]

Robert Webber speaks to the same issue in a call for fully biblical, Trinitarian worship:

Christian worship is not a reflection on God's essence, but an enactment of God's saving deeds, especially in Jesus Christ, through which God the Father is known and experienced. . . . However, the contemporary praise and worship movement is Father-driven. . . . A worship that overemphasizes the Father runs the danger of not being adequately biblical.[15]

Worship is our work for God.
We also must thank the charismatic renewal movement for reminding us that worship should be the action of the whole congregation. The longtime tradition of nonliturgical, evangelical churches expects pew occupants mostly to observe and listen. Except for the congregational hymns, almost all the

activity is assigned to worship leaders—ministers, the choir, and possibly a few individuals who are invited to lead in prayer or to speak briefly, perhaps giving a "faith witness."

Some observers insist that charismatic worship also is rapidly becoming "spectatorist." But, in the early examples I observed, the entire congregation participated in everything: the singing, the praying, and even the preaching. There was rarely any performance music by soloists or choir; John Calvin's motto, "The congregation is the church's first choir," was followed to the letter—for the most part, it was the church's *only* choir. In times of prayer, each worshiper was expected to speak aloud in chorus—either in recognizable words or in tongues. During the sermon, the congregation was invited to "talk back" to the preacher, in a style that is somewhat comparable to that of African-American churches.

However, this is another instance in which a basically sound concept of worship becomes rigid and distorted in its development. Charismatics believe so strongly that there should be no priest-like performance, that most of their churches have outlawed the choir. To be sure, solo singers are more welcome than choirs, and trained vocalists are invited to participate in the "praise band" that leads (and sometimes drowns out) the congregation in its praise-and-worship singing. I believe that while community singing must be the central music of worship, the biblical and historical tradition of the "priestly choir" still has merit. Choral music provides a *different and valid* experience in worship, allowing talented singers to give to God a special "sacrifice of praise," and offering both singers and listeners an unusual musical vision of the transcendent-immanent God. Many charismatics deny the first proposition categorically, saying that choirs create an elitist priesthood that is contrary to the idea that all believers are equal priests. I believe the Scriptures demonstrate that God's service in worship has room for different levels of talent among "equal priests." I will discuss this matter further in chapter 7.

At the same time, I am convinced that congregational singing itself has suffered under charismatic leadership. Certainly it is less cognitive, partly because of its mantra-like repetition, and partly because there is little variety in subject material. Praise-and-worship choruses invariably consist of pure praise, which possibly should be called *lean praise,* because it does not include our reasons for adoring the triune God. Again, I have observed that such singing often is less participatory than the traditional, even though it may seem to be more inclusive. Partly because the praise-and-worship tradition seldom allows its choruses to become familiar classics, the congregation often is faced with new melodies, even though the words tend to be rehashes of the old. As a result, many charismatic worshipers do more clapping and rhythmic shuffling ("dancing") than singing. The total effect is always "successful" because the trained singers and instrumentalists make it seem so, with the help of high-decibel sound systems.

I believe there is merit in the occasional use of concerted, improvised prayer in worship. We do it occasionally in our Wednesday evening supper/prayer services at church, when someone at each table leads in supplication for the hurting members of the church family. But, when that is the *only* mode of congregational prayer, I fear that the practice encourages radical and unhealthy individualism rather than a mature developing of the church's prayer life. Scripture has given us both directions and models for corporate prayer; a church's united mind and heart will be shaped best when one person "guides" in expressing the entire group's adoration/confession/thanksgiving/supplication, or when the whole congregation speaks together in prepared, printed words.

Also, I am not convinced that charismatics' typical participation in the homily is ideal. Unlike the African-American model (in which the congregation seems to encourage the preacher), as I have witnessed it, the charismatic technique tends to indoctrinate and control the congregation rather than allow free, individual response to what the Holy Spirit may want to say to each person.

Having said all this, the question of congregational participation or spectatorship remains unresolved. Many mainstream evangelicals still contend that liturgical dialogue is too formal and that participation in either the African-American or the charismatic style is too undignified. But spectator worship is not really very different from religious entertainment! If none of the available models of *worship work* is acceptable, a church must devise its own. Being a "pew potato" in church is even worse than being a "couch potato" at home in front of the television set.

Finally, two aspects of charismatic congregational participation bother me greatly. First, leadership seems to act from a desire to manipulate—from requiring everybody to direct attention to an overhead screen, to controlling the singing with overpowering volume, to asking folks to bark back certain phrases from the sermon, to suggesting (even in the job title) that following the example of the worship "leader" will bring them automatically into the true presence of God.

Second and on the other hand, the watchword of that tradition is *freedom*. One is free to sing or not to sing, to raise one's hands or keep them stiffly at the side, or even to shut one's eyes to everything and everyone around and to "worship Jesus" strictly in private.

I fear that neither of these concepts is in keeping with our call to worship God of our own volition as the undivided church, guided by the Holy Spirit alone without undue interference by human leaders. I deal with this topic in more detail in chapter 5.

Worship involves the whole person.

Thanks also to the charismatic renewal movement for reminding us that worship should involve the whole person—body, intellect, and emotions. However, at the outset I must ask whether or not they live up to their own motto—whether the mind is sufficiently engaged in their singing and praying. In the previous section I discussed physical actions that should be normative for believers. Ever since John Calvin defined worship for the Reformed segment of Protestantism, most formal evangelical services (including Calvin's) have appealed mostly to the thinking self. True, emotions have played some part, usually in the congregation's response to especially effective preaching or in musical worship. Even today, however, typical sophisticated evangelical worship consists mostly of "thinking" rather than of "doing" or "feeling." For instance, I have observed that typical southern, county-seat "First Baptist Church" services are usually quite proper, thoughtful, and friendly, but also predictable and rather dull. In contrast, charismatic worship is both much more emotional and more physical. The excitement stems from the repetitious praise-and-worship singing with its loud, highly rhythmic accompaniment and its attendant clapping/dancing, as well as from the Pentecostal acts of tongues, prophecy, and healing.

At the same time, I cannot believe that we must choose between those two extremes simply because few churches have developed an acceptable middle ground. Of course, some music experiences in worship are always more emotive than cognitive, as when one hears instrumental music without words, or participates in a brief song service of chorus or gospel song favorites in preparation for worship. But it is not reasonable to expect that *all* musical experiences will be purely emotional, as it surely is when the chosen material makes no cognitive demands on the congregation.

Even so, while charismatic worship may be more completely emotional than that of mainline evangelicalism, it offers too little variety of emotional expression. Mostly it is exciting, even frenetic,[16] with occasional shifts to an intimate, quiet mood as when singing "I Love You, Lord" or when experiencing some type of "primal spirituality."[17] But it expresses too little joy that is also serenity, no sober contrition in confession of sin, and no anguish in sharing the hurts in the local congregation or throughout the world.

Again, the affective experiences of charismatics are quite stylized and therefore limited. Their gatherings make little use of the arts, except for music and physical movement, both performed by the whole community. There is little use of symbolism in church design or in furnishings, no drama or fully expressive dance, and no choral art that is worthy of Luther's statement: "Music is a fair and glorious gift of God."

Finally, I get the sense that emotion is used not as a means of expression but of manipulation. For example, praise-and-worship singing that seems to be spontaneous actually follows a predictable progression. Often it begins moderately and increases in tempo, rhythm, and volume over a period of perhaps thirty minutes; at that point, usually the music is hushed, when, with quiet singing or in silence, the Holy Spirit "takes over" and worshipers experience the climax of intimacy with God. In a charismatic service, that is the time when supernatural phenomena, especially speaking in tongues, occur. In this progressive experience, the worship leader (the central figure in the praise band) is very important. Apparently, the leader is authorized and expected to lead the entire congregation "into the presence of God." Accordingly, he or she determines how many times each chorus will be repeated and just when each element of the service takes place.

So, how should theologically discriminating evangelicals plan and conduct their worship? First, because God is present throughout the entire service, they must acknowledge that true worshipers may be aware of God's presence at any time, or all the time.

Accordingly, with the help of the Holy Spirit, they should plan their services with a logical sequence of experiences that offer multiple opportunities to meet God—in praise, confession, Scripture reading, sermon, dedication of self and gifts, and petition, as well as in the Lord's Supper, through thanksgiving and remembrance. I discuss this in detail in chapter 8.

They also must conduct each service within its own appropriate emotional context, expecting that, through the ministry of the Holy Spirit, each person present may experience God in one or more—or even in *all*—of the hour's actions. They must not deny the possibility that God the Holy Spirit may take control of a service of worship apart from human planning and expectation—usually with a spirit of confession and submission to God that is so compelling that everyone present will know that something unusual and miraculous has taken place. But they must not imagine that any human being can lead an entire congregation into the presence of God, Pied Piper style, on a regular basis. Rather, that seems to be a presumption based on emotional manipulation.

Worship includes sacramental concepts.
Charismatics believe that things, as well as people, can be holy;
in this they are true successors to historic Pentecostalists, who
often used handkerchiefs that were "blessed" as agents of divine healing. The concept is usually applied to spatial areas, as
expressed in this gospel chorus:

> We are standing on holy ground,
>   and I know that there are angels all around;
> let us praise Jesus now—
>   we are standing in his presence on holy ground.
> *(Geron Davis)*

The belief that things can be holy suggests sacramental concepts. A *sacrament* is commonly defined as "a visible sign
instituted by Christ to symbolize or confer grace." Many Protestants acknowledge two sacraments: baptism and the Lord's
Supper. A *sacramental* (used as a noun) is something less than
a sacrament, but still a "means of grace"; Roman Catholics list
holy water or the sign of the cross as sacramentals, and many
evangelicals speak of the worship service or the act of preaching as a "means of grace."

Traditionally, the nonliturgical tradition has had difficulty
accepting the idea that things can be holy. In this misconcep-
tion they have perpetuated one of the errors of Neoplatonist
thought—that the physical world (including the human body)
is at odds with all things spiritual. For instance, they often
refuse to call a church's principal room a "sanctuary" (holy
place), saying that only people can be holy; instead, they name
it the "worship room" or, even worse, "the preaching place"
or "auditorium" (where congregational worship action is reduced to "hearing").

Charismatic scholars are constantly working to develop their
full theology, and up to now they have made no declaration
about sacraments or sacramentals. For many believers, if not
for their theologians, speaking in tongues and prophesying are
thought to be supernatural. But Pentecostal phenomena are
defined in Scripture as "gifts," and charismatics do not expect

them to be "sanctifying" agents in the life of receiving believers. Nevertheless, the idea of holy space or holy things does exist, and it is often suggested that some charismatics tend to think of the Lord's Supper as a true sacrament.

Once again, while we congratulate the charismatic renewal movement for supporting certain worship concepts that are not understood by many evangelicals, I must take issue with their specific handling of this issue. As stated earlier, charismatics have a limited concept of right-brain communication through symbolic things, all of which could become "sacramentals" through which they would sense God's presence.

Finally, they tend to make praise-and-worship singing something of a sacrament, and I believe this is not warranted. The charismatic theology of praise suggests that "pure praise" (free of thanksgiving) is God's ordained path to worship in the "holy of holies" where the Pentecostal miracles take place. Here are some of the bold, triumphalist claims for such praise: "Praise silences the Devil. Praise is a garment of the Spirit. Praise leads the believer into the triumph of Christ. Praise brings revelation. Praise prepares us for miracles. Praise is the way into God's presence. God inhabits our praises."[18]

While charismatics are correct in saying that praise is our central response to God in worship, I do not believe that it automatically and miraculously brings us into the intimate presence of God. While some folks may experience God's presence through praise, others may do so better through confession of sin, or through declaring their submission to God.

Worship authority is in the Scriptures.
Earlier in this chapter I quoted a Pentecostal scholar who listed "love of the Bible" as one of the essential elements in charismatic renewal. In token of this, their leaders base their rationale for worship practice on Scripture. Of course, this is true also of all historic liturgical churches—Orthodox, Roman, Lutheran, Anglican, and Reformed. Though mainline evangelicals claim to be leaders in Scripture study, biblical research to determine worship practice seems to be at the bottom of their

priority list. We must thank the charismatics for bringing this matter to our attention once again.

However, just as charismatics differ from non-charismatics in their understanding of what the Bible teaches about the gifts of the Spirit, they also do not agree about what Scripture says concerning other worship practices. In many instances, the charismatic renewal movement bases its worship theology and imagery on images and rubrics gleaned from a few passages in the Old Testament. These will be examined in the following chapter that will discuss how we can worship God in biblical truth. Just as we should plan liturgy according to our own theology, so we should worship in keeping with our own interpretation of Scripture.

4

Worshiping God in Biblical Truth

In a Strange Land of Differing Interpretations

Do your best to present yourself to God as one approved by him,
. . . rightly explaining the word of truth. —2 Timothy 2:15

𝔐any years ago I heard a story about a questionable use of Scripture in a sermon. In a Christian community that expected its members to be modest, even plain in dress and in makeup, a minister decided to preach against the current hairstyles, in which women tended to pile up their long hair on the top of their heads. His parishioners wondered where he would find the text for his announced sermon topic: "Top Knot, Come Down." They were amazed on Sunday morning to hear him read these words which Jesus spoke, referring to the cataclysmic end times, "Let him which is on the house*top not come down* to take any thing out of his house" (Matt. 24:17, KJV, italics added).

If the story is not apocryphal, it is certainly an egregious example of taking a text out of context! Interpreting the Bible can be tricky, and Christian groups differ sincerely about what the Scriptures say about worship.

Certain churches believe that when, at the last supper, Jesus took bread and said, "This is my body" (Matt. 26:26), he meant literally *just that,* even though they differ over whether that mystery is associated with transubstantiation, consubstantiation, or "the real presence" of Christ. Many evangelicals believe that Jesus meant only "This bread represents my body." Again, at the same supper, Jesus washed his disciples' feet and said, "You also ought to wash one another's feet" (John 13:14). Certain Mennonites and others believe that footwashing is a true *ordinance* of worship (an essential Christian rite). Perhaps because it is not mentioned in the New Testament epistles, most Christians believe that it is not required as a regular act of worship.

Because people interpret the Bible differently, some folks believe there is no point in attempting to discover what it says and requires of us. But we can't get off the hook so easily! The Bible encourages us to "do our best" to understand and explain God's Word as the Holy Spirit teaches us (2 Tim. 2:15). This is not easy; like worship itself, it is *work* we must do in order to be approved by God, and not ashamed.

In our own day, charismatic Christians have given new biblical interpretations that have radically affected worship practice for a much broader segment of believers. However, some of those explications are based on questionable exegesis of Scripture. In this chapter, I will examine passages that are believed to speak authoritatively about music volume, congregational song, instruments, and physical actions in worship.

Scriptural Direction and Developing Worship

Scholars acknowledge that the Torah gives specific instructions for the sacrificial worship of God's covenant people, the Jews, and for the construction and furnishing of the tabernacle, with all its artistic symbolism. However, the Pentateuch (the books of the law) contains no prescription for the use of sung prayers (as found in the psalms) or for any types of "word worship" (worship through words either spoken or sung), though these eventually developed both in the temple and the synagogue.

From the structure of the ancient Hebrew texts, and from the examples of later practice, we learn that much of poetical Scripture (Psalms, Proverbs, Ecclesiastes, Song of Solomon) and much of the prophets' writings were designed to be chanted or sung. Nevertheless, the prophet Amos (who *sang* his angry denunciation of the unrepentant Jews of his day) criticizes the "noise" of worship songs (Amos 5:23) and castigates those people "who lounge on their couches . . . and sing idle songs to the sound of the harp" (6:4-5). It is apparent from the context that his anger is vented against insincere worship and self-indulgent pleasure rather than against the worship materials and actions themselves.

The New Testament is even more limited in giving direction for worship and its arts in the early Christian era. Jesus did command his disciples to remember him in Lord's Supper observances (Luke 22:19) and to baptize all who became disciples through their preaching (Matt. 28:19). We have also the record of Jesus' statements about worshiping God "in spirit and in truth," as discussed in the first two chapters of this book. In 1 Corinthians 14:26, the apostle Paul outlines what seems to be a spontaneous service of word worship, spoken and sung, (without the Lord's Supper, but including glossalalia): "When you come together, each one has a hymn, a lesson, a revelation, a tongue, or an interpretation. Let all things be done for building up."

The entire chapter of 1 Corinthians 14 deals with problems the church encountered in glossalalic activity and places the emphasis on love (14:1), order (14:33,40), and edifying the church (14:3,5,12,17,26). Otherwise, it seems apparent that the first Christians were left free to develop their worship rites as they saw fit. Accordingly, they adapted the pattern of word worship from the synagogue, later uniting those activities with the remembrance supper initiated by Christ in the upper room. Throughout the New Testament, more elements of that "Service of the Word" are mentioned individually:

- Scripture lections (1 Tim. 4:13; Col. 4:16)
- A homily (Acts 20:7)
- A confession of faith (1 Tim. 6:13)
- Singing of psalms, hymns, and spiritual songs (Eph. 5:19; Col. 3:16)

- Prayers with a congregational "amen" (Acts 2:42; 1 Cor. 14:16; 1 Tim. 2:1-2)
- Gifts given in a "collection" (1 Cor. 16:1-2)
- Physical action (1 Tim. 2:8)

All historic Christian worship contains these elements, plus the Lord's Supper, and we may presume that their association with the New Testament church has elevated them to the status of rubrics for most modern Christians as well.

In contrast to the Old Testament record of the more right-brain, highly symbolic rituals of God's ancient people, the New Testament record of the earliest church's worship seems simpler and more left-brain and rational. True, things and actions were important, as experienced in the rite of baptism, the eating and drinking of bread and wine, sharing a kiss of peace, and lifting hands in prayer. Also, though synagogue rituals had become formalized by that time, with a well-developed lectionary (see Luke 4:16-21), at least some early Christian worship was probably quite free and spontaneous, and sometimes ecstatic (1 Cor. 14:26). Indeed, in the oldest post-scriptural worship order—recorded in Justin Martyr's *Apology* around A.D. 150—it appears that no set liturgical formulas were spoken; the sermon and prayers were improvised "according to the ability" of the leader.

However, two hundred years later, an anonymous writer in *The Apostolic Constitutions* (ca. A.D. 380) recorded a lengthy liturgy that featured several sermons, a full Eucharistic prayer that included many of the set words and actions of high medieval worship, and such symbolic elements as "a splendid vestment," washing of hands, "fencing" the communion table (to forbid participation by those considered unworthy), and making the sign of the cross. Apparently, the developing worship of Christians had grown beyond the comparatively simple forms of apostolic times, adding liturgical symbolism patterned after the ancient Hebrew temple, as well as sacrificial concepts that were attached to the service of the Lord's Table.[1]

The progression to a common liturgy during the missionary expansion of the church occurred partly as a matter of expediency. Pagans were being converted rapidly and churches were formed before newly baptized and "ordained" pastors could be trained to preach and pray correctly, that is, free from heresy. As a result, seasoned, older believers wrote out acceptable service orders, sermons, and prayers, which were distributed for use by others.

At the time of the fourth-century liturgy mentioned above, the Roman emperor Constantine already had decreed that Christianity should be tolerated. When it became the established religion of the empire, it adopted the rich and ornate symbolism of power and authority common to political rulers. Over a period of a thousand years, the liturgy itself developed into an elaborate ritual that was adorned with the best arts of Western culture. Though each element of the complicated service had its proper theological foundation, the medieval mass was overloaded with ceremony and at least tainted with heresy, encouraging superstition as well as true faith, especially among the church's humblest adherents.

Sola Scriptura in the Sixteenth Century

At the time of the sixteenth-century Reformation, all the reformers adopted the *sola Scriptura* concept as their regulative principle; that is, *the Bible is the only source of authority for the church.* By contrast, both Roman Catholic and Orthodox Christians accept Holy Tradition as well. Martin Luther and Thomas Cranmer held that Christian worship could use any worship means that were not expressly forbidden in the New Testament. Accordingly, they revised the Roman mass to conform to the new evangelical theology, while retaining much of the symbolism and art of their predecessors.

John Calvin broke more sharply with medieval traditions when he applied the *sola Scriptura* principle to his teaching about proper Christian worship. He believed that we may not require believers to use forms or actions that are not specifically prescribed in Scripture:

We may not adopt any device [in our worship] which

seems fit to ourselves, but look to the injunctions of him who alone is entitled to prescribe. Therefore, if we would have him approve our worship, this rule, which he everywhere enforces with the utmost strictness, must be carefully observed. . . . God disapproves of all modes of worship not expressly sanctioned by his word.[2]

Calvin's worship order, adopted in Geneva in 1542, was planned to match that of New Testament believers as he deduced it. It included Scripture, prayers, a sermon, psalms sung "in poetic form" (without instruments), and the Lord's Table (with a long admonition about proper participation, and a long prayer of consecration)—nothing more. All liturgical furnishings (including organs and vestments) were removed from French-speaking Protestant churches. The only arts remaining were those of words and speech, of unaccompanied unison psalm tunes, and the architecture of "stripped" worship buildings. Since its adoption by Calvinistic Puritans, this narrow interpretation of the *sola Scriptura* regulative principle has influenced the worship of Reformed groups and others in Europe and America for more than four hundred years, mostly by limiting what is permitted.

It has been argued frequently that the highly symbolic, artistic worship of the Old Testament was an accommodation to the primitive nature of early Hebrew culture and that the "mostly words" worship of early Christians was an indication of the superiority of that culture and that faith. However the later, almost universal use of symbolic things and actions suggests that we must reconsider that judgment. Liturgical scholars remind us that the communication of symbolism crosses generational and cultural boundaries; it speaks to young and old alike, to both the kindergartner and the university graduate.

As I have already mentioned, right-brain meaning is expressed by the symbolic and nonverbal; its proper use can strengthen the left-brain communication of words. Such a judgment seems to be vindicated in the last book of the New Testament, where John the Revelator uses much dramatic and pictorial language in referring to worship symbolism common to the Old Testament (a lampstand, 1:12; a priestly royal robe, 1:13; and so on). If it was helpful to John to see symbolic "things" in his vision, should it not be helpful to other Christians to experience similar symbolic things in true New Testament worship?

Calvin also dropped the historic church calendar, apparently because of the regulative principle. In Galatians 4:10, Paul reproves Christians who followed the Jewish calendar of fast days, new moons, Passover seasons, and sabbatical years—seemingly condemning the observance of a liturgical calendar. But Paul's principal concern was theological, not liturgical—the Christians in Galatia were teaching that believers must follow Jewish ceremonial law in order to please God. Paul himself observed the Jewish Passover after his conversion, and later church leaders adapted the Jewish system of "feasts and fasts" in creating a Christian calendar, celebrating first Easter and Lent, later Epiphany, and later still, Christmas, Advent, and Pentecost—not as a matter of law but as a *means of grace and edification.*

Some evangelicals have insisted that 1 Corinthians 14:26 implies that only "free," nonliturgical worship is pleasing to God. However, Calvin did not think so. His *Institutes* contain instructions and arguments about worship, including two full orders, under the title "The Form of Church Prayers and Hymns with the Manner of Administering the Sacraments and Consecrating Marriage According to the Custom of the Ancient Church" (Strassburg, 1540; Geneva, 1542).[3]

So, was Calvin misinterpreting the customs of the ancient New Testament church? Acts 2:42 reports that believers baptized on the Day of Pentecost "devoted themselves to the apostles' teaching and fellowship, to the breaking of bread and *the prayers"* (probably the liturgical prayers of the synagogue; italics added). We do know that the apostles included a large amount of liturgical material (including hymns and prayers) in their epistles, and we can presume that the young churches in Asia and Europe treasured and used it. Paul asked specifically that his letter to the Colossians be "read also in the church of the Laodiceans" (Col. 4:16).

The Regulative Principle Today

How then do we interpret the regulative principle of *sola Scriptura* in our day? I take it that we must be sure that our worship communicates the theology of New Testament Scripture, without compromise. I believe also that the verbal and physical forms mentioned in Acts and the Epistles should all appear in contemporary worship, and that words from both Old and New Testaments should abound.

Beyond this, I tend to believe that Luther and Cranmer were closer to the *sola Scriptura* truth than Calvin. I do not find many dogmatic, delimiting statements about liturgical practice in the New Testament. And why should we judge that the fledgling expressions of worship in the infant church—a church that was limited by poverty and persecution—should be the unchanging pattern for all time? Certainly, the church's theology and its canon of Scripture was not complete at that time; why should we expect its worship to be? Finally, I believe that aesthetic symbols—both objects and actions—should be welcomed in modern worship, *so long as they strengthen the meaning of liturgical words.*

In our own day, certain Christians have developed new orders and rules of worship based on specific biblical interpretation. Many of these are rooted more in the Old Testament than in the new covenant. In this regard, they have more in common with Roman Catholicism and Orthodoxy than with the evangelical tradition. Nevertheless, through their influence in the "new winds" of worship known as "contemporary" or "alternative," followers of the charismatic renewal movement have influenced the whole church to a remarkable—and, I believe, in many ways regrettable—degree.

This chapter calls into question the scriptural interpretation on which certain aspects of charismatic worship (and especially its music) are based and challenges mainline evangelicals to develop their own worship philosophy and forms in keeping with their own understanding of scriptural standards.

Musical Instruments in Worship

Most liturgical historians agree that the early church rejected the use of musical instruments in worship, since they are not mentioned in the New Testament Gospels or the Epistles.[4] Based on this tradition, many Eastern Orthodox groups have used only vocal music throughout their almost two-thousand-year history. While certain evangelical churches cling tenaciously to this ancient prohibition, others insist that Psalm 150 contains a divine command to use instruments that is still in effect. Yet, it is difficult to see how either position can be supported by the evidence of Scripture plus the full chronicle of history.

As noted earlier, God gave specific instructions regarding the tabernacle, its furnishing, and all the acts of the sacrificial system in the Torah, but there is no rubric concerning worship song. The full vocal and instrumental glory of formal Hebrew worship seemed to develop under the rule of King David, the musician-composer. After the ark was brought to its final resting place, the record says, "David also commanded the chiefs of the Levites to appoint their kindred as the singers to play on musical instruments, on harps and lyres and cymbals, to raise loud sounds of joy" (1 Chron. 15:16).

This is not to say that David had no divine permission or command—only that we do not know their specifics. Some three hundred years later, in connection with Hezekiah's rededication of the temple, Scripture says this about that king, "He stationed the Levites in the house of the Lord with cymbals, harps, and lyres, according to the commandment of David and of Gad the king's seer and of the prophet Nathan, for the commandment was from the LORD through his prophets" (2 Chron. 29:25).

Again, extrabiblical Jewish history tells us that both percussion and wind instruments were gradually eliminated from use during the period of the Second Temple.[5] Because they were associated prominently with the worship of both pagan neighbors and heretical Jewish sects, they were considered to be unclean. By the time of Christ, only stringed instruments were used to accompany voices in temple worship. Further, since instruments were used only in connection with the sacrificial offerings, they had no place in the worship of the synagogue. This may explain why Paul speaks disparagingly about "a noisy gong or a clanging cymbal" (1 Cor. 13:1), which no doubt were comparable to the "clanging cymbals" and "loud clashing cymbals" which are authorized (if not commanded) for worship in Psalm 150:5. Finally, after the destruction of Herod's temple in A.D. 70, Jews ceased the practice of sacrificial worship and banned the use of all instruments. For all these reasons—and perhaps others—first-century Christians evidently decided that instruments could not be functional in their worship acts.

So, how do we develop a hermeneutic regarding the biblical references to the use of instrumental music in worship? Does the Old Testament record God's rubrics for Hebrew worship and the New Testament God's directives for services under the New Covenant? If so, how do we interpret the changing practice in later prophetic times, when Jews (in good faith, and with a purpose of keeping worship pure) chose to ignore what seems to be a command in Psalm 150 to worship God with wind instruments and percussion? Leaders of present-day Churches of Christ are correct in their assertion that the New Testament epistles do not specifically authorize instrumental music in Christian worship. Are we correct in our conviction that this was simply an accident of history based on the practice of the synagogues and the end of temple worship? Presumably our no-instrument friends interpret John the Revelator's references to trumpets and harps as pertaining only to worship in heaven, when instruments will once again have been sanctified!

I am convinced that there is no final scriptural word on the matter. Instruments are neither consistently prescribed nor expressly forbidden. We must use our own aesthetic and liturgical judgment to determine what use is appropriate. However, we may expect that the arguments will continue, as they have for more than 2,500 years in the Judeo-Christian tradition. Whereas *words* can usually be identified readily as either "holy" or "demonic," *sounds* produced by instruments are more ambiguous.

Loud Music

A high dynamic level on modern electronic audio systems is one of the normal stylistic characteristics of much contemporary Christian music. It seems that high volume—which passes the point at which hearing is damaged—is an integral part of its performance practice or its impact. This practice has been carried over to the sound of voices and instruments that lead the congregation in praise-and-worship music.

The key verses quoted at the beginning of both the preceding and following discussions (1 Chron. 15:16; Ps. 47:1) refer with approval to loud musical sounds in worship. Indeed, a number of such references occur in the Old Testament, and they are used to justify modern practice:

> Sing to [God] a new song; play skillfully on the strings, with loud shouts. (Ps. 33:3)

> And the Levites . . . stood up to praise the LORD, the God of Israel, with a very loud voice. (2 Chron. 20:19)

> And the Levites and the priests praised the LORD day by day, accompanied by loud instruments for the LORD. (2 Chron. 30:21)

There are enough instances of this kind to suggest that the normal "performance practice" of ancient Hebrew worship music was indeed loud. But was the dynamic level a cause of God's blessing for that culture? And if so, are Christians called to reproduce high-decibel worship music today?

Remember that all of these Scriptures refer to what was essentially *outdoor* worship. I have had enough experience trying to produce both choral and congregational music outdoors to know that it is difficult to be heard, even when you have a modern acoustical shell and a public address system. In those ancient times, as today, a normal speaking or singing voice would simply be inaudible outdoors; so "shouting" was the normal dynamic level.

Remember also the two incidents in the life of Elijah that refer to worship volume. In the worship contest on Mount Carmel, after the prophets of Baal had called on their god for several hours, with no response, "Elijah mocked them, saying, 'Cry aloud! ["call him louder" in KJV]. Surely he is a god; either he is meditating, or he has wandered away, or he is on a journey, or perhaps he is asleep and must be wakened" (1 Kings 18:27).[6]

The biblical record says that the frenzied yelling and bloody self-mutilation went on all day, but at the time of the evening sacrifice Elijah came near (in order to be heard without shouting) and offered a short, quiet prayer:

> "O LORD, God of Abraham, Isaac, and Israel, let it be known this day that you are God in Israel, that I am your servant, and that I have done all these things at your bidding. Answer me, O LORD, answer me, so that this people may know that you, O LORD, are God, and that you have turned their hearts back." Then the fire of the LORD fell and consumed the burnt offering, the wood, the stones, and the dust, and even licked up the water that was in the trench. (1 Kings 18:36-38)

Obviously, it was Baal who was deaf, not God. When Queen Jezebel heard about Elijah's victory over Baal's prophets, she swore to kill him, so he fled to Mt. Horeb where he pondered his change of fortune, asking God to "take away his life." And God said to him:

> "Go out and stand on the mountain before the LORD, for the LORD is about to pass by." Now there was a great wind, so strong that it was splitting mountains and breaking rocks in pieces before the LORD, but the LORD was not in the wind; and after the wind an earthquake, but the LORD was not in the earthquake; and after the earthquake a fire; and after the fire *a sound of sheer silence.* (1 Kings 19:11-12, italics added)

Several passages of Scripture suggest that the awesome presence of God demands complete silence:

Be still and know that I am God! (Ps. 46:10)

So that the priests could not stand to minister [the Levite musicians became silent] because of the cloud; for the glory of the LORD filled the house of God. (2 Chron. 5:14)

When the Lamb opened the seventh seal, there was silence in heaven for about half an hour. (Rev. 8:1)

I would suppose that if spiritual virtue is attached to loud worship singing it would stem from the fact that the participants are exerting more physical effort, indicating a higher level of spiritual fervor. In leading congregational singing from the organ, my objective is to encourage worshipers to sing out freely and joyfully, without intimidating them with an overpowering sound. My observation of typical praise-and-worship singing is that it doesn't really matter whether the congregation sings or not. The sound produced by the worship team (with help of the sound system) fills the room whether the congregation sings at all—and many do not!

About Handclapping in Worship

For some worship leaders, the practice of clapping in rhythm with the music, and/or of a frequent burst of clapping as expression of "approval" of some worship action, is commanded—or at least, authorized—by only one Scripture verse in Psalm 47:1: "Clap your hands, all you peoples; shout to God with loud songs of joy."

However, when you check all the references to clapping in Scripture, a very different picture emerges. Three other passages speak of clapping as a symbol of approval, one passage in connection with the crowning of the young king Joash (2 Kings 11:12), and two others in which nature is characterized as responding to its Creator with praise (Ps. 98:8; Isa. 55:12—"the mountains and the hills before you shall burst into song, and all the trees of the fields shall clap their hands.")

However, though these four passages characterize clapping as a sign of approval, five others use it to express strong disapproval, even defiance of the living God:

> For thus says the Lord GOD: Because you have clapped your hands and stamped your feet and rejoiced with all the malice within you against the land of Israel, therefore I have stretched out my hand against you. (Ezek. 25:6-7)

> It [the east wind of God's judgment] claps its hands at them, and hisses at them from its place. (Job 27:23)

> For he adds rebellion to his sin; he claps his hands among us, and multiplies his words against God. (Job 34:37)

> All who pass along the way clap their hands at you; they hiss and wag their heads at daughter Jerusalem. (Lam. 2:15)

> All who hear the news about you clap their hands over you. For who has ever escaped your endless cruelty? (Nah. 3:19)

Some authorities quote Psalm 47:1 as God's rubric for today, without explaining the full biblical record of changing cultural practices in ancient Israel. Further, certain individual churches and groups (including the Promise Keepers gatherings for Christian men) are absolutely consistent in resymbolizing this form of expression, as the Scripture suggests is possible. Clapping for them has become a response that is equivalent to saying "Amen." They clap after congregational singing, they clap throughout the sermon, they clap when people respond to an "altar call." I can imagine that eventually they might even clap for prayer, as members of Congress did when the flamboyant evangelist Billy Sunday once prayed at the opening of their session. However, though many groups have borrowed the less than reverent phrase "giving God a hand" as justification for their action, handclapping in a typical worship service makes no sense when it is only a reaction to stirring up the emotions by some type of exciting performance.

As a worship musician, either conducting a choir or playing the organ, when clapping happens after music, I want to say: "We intended the singing and playing to be sacrifices of praise to God, and would have been pleased if you had listened quietly and thankfully, responding to words with your own cognitive 'Amen' and to the music by 'making melody to the Lord in your hearts' [Eph. 5:19] If you had done so, all of us, performers and listeners alike, could have given a gift of praise to God. But your applause, even if well intended, has robbed us both of that opportunity and privilege. Even if only for a few moments, you turned a service into a concert, exchanging worship for entertainment. And, if I 'accept' your applause to be recognized by others [Matt. 6:2, 5, 16], that's all the 'reward' I will ever get for what I intended to be a worship gift to God."

Come to think of it, perhaps this practice of clapping is a carryover from the world of sacred concerts, religious radio and television, all allied with the contemporary Christian businesses of recordings, videos, and published music. In those specialized experiences—combining entertainment with some elements of worship—applause is normal. Is it possible that much of today's contemporary worship is simply Saturday night's concert moved to Sunday morning, with a sermon added?[7]

Other gatherings of believers seem to add confusion without giving answers. Christian conferences like Promise Keepers and even Billy Graham crusade services are unusual occasions that resemble a state fair or a Super Bowl event, and they offer significant but atypical worship experiences. The response on those special occasions of high emotion should not set the standard for typical worship in a local church.

It should be easy to see the temptations inherent in the practice of handclapping after music in church. People respond most vigorously to the music which stimulates them emotionally, and that never includes pieces of moderate tessitura or dynamics, even when they are God's Word sung exquisitely. Soloists and music directors will tend to choose their music on the basis of information received from congregational applause, not for more significant reasons. Even so, many individuals insist that handclapping is their *chosen response*—that, at the very least, they are thanking God for giving talent to the musicians. For me, the argument is not convincing. Such handclapping really says, "You did well and I enjoyed it." Worship is not the place to praise performers on the basis of our personal pleasure or emotional stimulation. Rather, our motto should be that of the great church musician, Johann Sebastian Bach: *Soli Deo gloria*—"To God alone be glory."

Recently my wife, Ruth, and I attended a service in the Basilica of St. Clotilde in Paris where I once studied with organist-composer Jean Langlais. In the course of the mass, a young couple presented their child for baptism, and afterward the congregation applauded. How could we possibly object to such an expression of approval and joy in that decision and action? But, would it not have been better for that expression to have been included as part of the liturgy, using congregational words and possibly song? Even joyful handclapping in rhythm with such a song would be better than applause!

In modern church life, it is sometimes necessary to take action on some item of "social business" on Sunday morning, when the largest number of members are present. Such an occasion might be the recognition of an attending centenarian, or the departure of a member of the church ministry team. During worship, thanks can be given to God for his gift to the congregation of and through that person. At the service close the congregation can be called together for "business." At that time, the acknowledgement of the individual might include the social "thank you" and applause of the congregation. Some will say that such care and distinction is irrelevant in our day. I contend that it may be unusual, but it is not irrelevant. In Romans 1:25, Paul says that idolatry is worshiping and serving "the creature rather than the Creator, who is blessed forever! Amen."

In all this discussion, I have intended to say that it is risky to take some Scripture passages too literally. I find that Psalm 150 urges me to use body movement and many kinds of instruments to praise God, without requiring me to do so in every worship service or to replicate the exact instruments or dance to which the psalmist referred. It does not require me to ignore the changing historical-cultural meanings of certain styles of music or certain types of instruments. For instance, though Gregorian chant is one of the few types of music that is *always* associated with biblical texts, I am not required to use it in my Baptist church. In the same way, Psalm 47:1 does not require me to clap hands in worship in violation of basic theological principles. Both passages say that every act in worship should be "to God," nothing more and nothing less.

Congregational Song

Another area of modern worship needs a carefully conceived interpretation of Scripture: the subject matter of Christian song. The late Paul Wohlgemuth, a lifelong member of the Mennonite Brethren Church, taught for a number of years at Oral Roberts University, one of the places where charismatics developed praise-and-worship exegesis and theology. Wohlgemuth reminded us that these evangelicals have a high view of the authority of Scripture, and that many of their worship practices, discussed already in the previous chapter, are based on Old Testament passages. He observed:

> Worship activities surrounding the Ark of the Covenant, especially after it was placed in the Tabernacle of David, have become the paradigm of worship that accounts for the current emphasis on Praise and Worship. Within the Tabernacle the Ark of the Covenant rested in the Holy of Holies—place of deep, spiritual, intimate communion and fellowship with God. In this place God manifested His Power, Presence, and Glory. It was in the Presence of the Ark of the Covenant that praise was given day and night, that some of David's Psalms were written, that loud sing-

ing and instrumental playing were heard, and that dancing was practiced. Some theologians see the twentieth-century Charismatic Renewal movement as the spiritual restoration of Davidic worship around the Ark of the Covenant, especially through praise singing.[8]

In historic Christian thought, worship is defined as the *overall activity* of believers in their cultic gatherings, and it includes every affirmative response to God: praise, thanksgiving, confession, dedication (submission), and petition. By contrast, in this new definition, thanksgiving, praise, and worship are *different, consecutive experiences* of the community of faith.

This tradition uses an imaginary liturgical procession within the Jerusalem temple to symbolize the progression of believers to the spiritual "Holy of Holies." Preparation for worship begins in the "outer court" where spiritual pilgrims express musical *thanksgiving* for God's mighty deeds in history and in their individual lives. As they move from the outer court into the "holy place," they sing only songs of *praise*—often Scripture choruses that proclaim the attributes of God, mention the names of God, or simply repeat over and over again "we worship . . . we adore . . . we magnify . . . we praise." Terry Law, a leading proponent of these concepts, has characterized this praise experience as "*tehillah*—singing *halals,* that is, to make a show, to boast, to be clamorously foolish, to rave, . . . to sing praises extravagantly, to celebrate with song."[9]

In this interpretation, the progression from thanksgiving to praise is said to be mentioned in Psalm 100:4: "Enter his gates with thanksgiving, and his courts with praise." However, for some unexplained reason, perhaps lack of time to complete the full worship pilgrimage, the songs of thanksgiving rarely occur; further, they are not offered prominently in publishers' tapes nor mentioned in the phrase "Praise and Worship." Typical charismatic singing features a long period of purely praise choruses. Characteristic titles are "Glorify the Lord," "Mighty Is Our God," "Be Exalted, O God," "Blessed Be the Lord God Almighty," "Praise the Name of Jesus," "Lion of Judah," "Behold the Lamb," and "Let There Be Praise."

Finally, in this particular approach, all the exciting, extravagant, repeated songs of praise give way to a hush of awe, and in silence or quiet song, believers may enter the presence of God, the "Holy of Holies," where (according to this unique definition), *worship* finally takes place. In this most intimate experience of relationship with God, believers may express their adoration however the Spirit leads, speaking or singing in corporate tongues (which is called "Spirit-singing"), in prophecy, or otherwise. Terry Law gives his explanation of the human and divine actions involved:

> First we *will* to praise God, then we *sanctify* our minds through the power of the Spirit, then our *emotions take over* and bring us through the veil into the presence of God in worship. When we come to that final act of worship it is the divine invitation of the Lord Himself that draws us within the veil . . . and it is only when our relationship with God is consummated in worship that we truly feel that we are where He is and He is where we are [italics added].[10]

The scriptural authorization for the full progression from thanksgiving to praise to worship is said to be found in Psalm 95. Verses 1 and 2 give a call to thanksgiving and praise, "O come, let us sing to the LORD; let us make a joyful noise to the rock of our salvation! Let us come into his presence with thanksgiving; let us make a joyful noise to him with songs of praise!" Then, in verse 6, the psalmist gives a call to what these interpreters say is a subsequent experience: "O come, let us worship and bow down, let us kneel before the LORD, our Maker!"[11]

Admittedly, this exegesis of Scripture matches in part the practice of charismatics, who sing jubilant, pure-praise songs for a protracted period of time, leading into a hushed "worship" experience in which the expression is one of intimate love and in which "miracles" (tongues, healing, prophecy) take place. However, few if any charismatics are "kneelers." Rather, in the New Testament pattern of 1 Timothy 2:8, they are more comfortable standing with uplifted hands for prayer.

A Strange Land of Differing Interpretations

It would seem to be doubtful wisdom for a non-charismatic to follow this formula unless it is expected to terminate in the "miracle worship" of charismatics. Nevertheless, it is recommended in one song book prepared for use by all Christians, with no mention of Pentecostal experiences. In *Songs for Praise and Worship*, author Ken Barker gives this rationale:

> A song service can be a loosely connected collection of favorite songs, whereas a worship service has a specific goal—to draw near and minister to the Lord. Therefore, the worship service becomes a journey into His presence. "Enter His gates with thanksgiving, and His courts with praise" (Ps. 100:4). Thanksgiving and praise move us into His presence. Worship occurs when we are before Him.
>
> *Thanksgiving* – is simply expressing gratitude to God for what he has done. . . . Songs of thanksgiving are usually fast, lively, loud and joyful.
>
> *Praise* – is acknowledging and celebrating the person of God. Generally we thank God for what he has done and we praise Him for who He is. . . . The personality of praise is one of joyful celebration, exaltation and majestic splendor.
>
> *Worship* – is the expression of our love relationship to God. . . . Worship requires our full focus on God's presence as a child before the Father, as a servant before the King. The character of worship is one of quietness, reverence, tenderness and serenity.[12]

Earlier I mentioned that songs of thanksgiving rarely occur in these settings. In *Songs of Praise and Worship* there is a listing of many songs in the three categories given above; however, songs of thanksgiving are conspicuously fewer than the others. Moreover, they do not provide a comprehensive resource for thanksgiving to match the biblical Psalms, including thanksgiving for God's creative acts (Ps. 19:1), thanksgiving for God's rule over the nations (Ps. 2:1, 4), and thanksgiving for God's providence (Ps. 105:1). Most songs that do mention thanksgiving simply substitute "I will give thanks" for the praise phrases, "I will bless/praise/glorify/magnify/adore/laud/acclaim." Mention of God's deeds is almost always limited to God's actions on behalf of believers in personal salvation.

Undeniably, thanksgiving is a unique and important aspect of full worship; it is the act of giving thanks, that is, grateful acknowledgment of God's benefits or favors, as in 1 Corinthians 15:57: "But thanks be to God, who gives us the victory through our Lord Jesus Christ." However, in many Scriptures, we are called also to *praise* God for the Almighty's specific actions, as in Psalm 139:14: "I praise you, for I am fearfully and wonderfully made. Wonderful are your works; that I know very well."

It seems a bit strange to base a clear-cut progression of service experiences on two verses of Scripture (Ps. 100:4; 95:2). Further, scholars point out that these verses have a parallel construction with two phrases that are basically rhetorical, not sequential. So, the author was simply associating two types of response to God with two different locations in the ancient tabernacle or temple, and might just as easily have written, "Enter his gates with praise, and his courts with thanksgiving." Also, we have no example in the Psalms—or in any period of Jewish or Christian history—in which worship music shows any such discipline as these charismatic leaders have preached. Both Jewish and Christian worship have tended to alternate thanksgiving with praise (sometimes calling the latter "adoration," a word from the Latin Vulgate Bible) without any such distinction—and also to add confession, dedication, supplication, witness, and even lament, all of which are found in the Psalms.

There is considerable confusion among contemporary worship connoisseurs about the word *worship*. Some British Christians use it in speaking about the musical part of a service. Others in various traditions use it to denote everything except the sermon. Charismatics say that it refers only to intimate expressions of love to God, and some insist that glossalalia or prophecy must be part of the experience. The most common

Old Testament passages use the word *worship* (from the Hebrew *shachah*, "bowing down") to speak more of divine majesty and transcendence, and human awe and submission. Some passages call us to worship because of God's mighty actions (so Scripture uses all three words—thanksgiving, praise, and worship—in that connection). For example:

> Ascribe to the LORD the glory due his name;
> bring an offering, and come before him.
> *Worship* the LORD in holy splendor;
> tremble before him, all the earth.
> (1 Chron. 16:29, italics added)

> *Worship* the LORD in holy splendor;
> tremble before him, all the earth.
> (Ps. 96:9, italics added. "Holy splendor" here seems
> to refer to the priestly vestments.)

> You are the LORD, you alone; you have made heaven, the
> heaven of heavens, with all their host, the earth and all
> that is on it, the seas and all that is in them. To all of them
> you give life, and the host of heaven *worships* you.
> (Neh. 9:6, italics added)

More commonly and historically (partly because *all* of a believer's life should be worship), it has been held that every part of a worship order—including the sermon and, perhaps, even the announcements—should be included under the title of worship.

A New Testament Standard for Christian Song

It seems surprising that if God intended the sequence of thanksgiving-praise-worship to be followed by "new covenant" believers that there is no mention of it in the New Testament. However, another worship triad appears twice—*psalms, hymns, and spiritual songs*—and it constitutes a far broader spectrum of worship song than praise-and-worship singing allows.[13] Like all worship elements mentioned in the epistles, I believe this is a proper standard for God's new covenant people for all time.

I have always marveled that Paul went out of his way to differentiate three kinds of song in Ephesians 5:19 and Colossians 3:16. Most scholars agree that the apostle referred to three different poetical-theological genres of texts with tunes. These forms presumably would have been identified by the Ephesians, in what seems to be a discussion of Eucharistic practice (partly from the reference to getting drunk with wine), and by the Colossians, in what may be a postbaptism admonition. It is impossible to prove exactly what Paul meant by these three titles; but we can identify three types of song that were undoubtedly sung in New Testament times, and they seem to match. Further, these song types were perpetuated in the early church and continue to appear in today's worship.

Psalms.
Almost every scholar agrees that early Christians sang the Hebrew psalms and canticles, as well as newer compositions in the same style, for example, the *Benedictus* (Zechariah's song) and *Magnificat* (Mary's song) of Luke 1. The first-century church took its basic pattern of worship from the synagogue, where many passages of Hebrew Scripture were incorporated into the prayers of praise and petition, and from the Upper Room supper, where Jesus and his disciples may have sung at least part of the *Hallel,* Psalms 113–118. Further, the early church understood that they were continuing the above practice in their broad use of Old Testament psalms in the daily office services.[14]

Hymns.
It is impossible to imagine that the early church would not have added "Jesus songs" to their repertory, in order to express and teach their new faith. Many such hymns are found in the

New Testament; even in English translations they retain their poetic cadence:

> The saying is sure:
> If we have died with him, we will also live with him;
> if we endure, we will also reign with him:
> if we deny him, he will also deny us;
> if we are faithless, he remains faithful—
> for he cannot deny himself. (2 Tim. 2:11-13)

Ralph Martin says that messianic psalms were probably sung first in the Jewish-Christian circles of the first century; their purpose was "partly celebratory, but chiefly apologetic." He believes that such "Christ psalms" are mentioned in the words of 1 Corinthians 14:26, "When you come together, each one has a *hymn*" (from the Greek word *psalmos*).

Later in the evolution of Christian worship, "Christ hymns" appeared (for example, Rom. 10:9ff; 1 Cor. 12:3; Eph. 5:14; Phil. 2:6-11; Col. 1:15-20; 2:6; 1 Tim. 3:16). Martin states that all of these are "variations on the creedal motif 'Jesus is Lord.'" He believes that they were written in response to the teachings of the earliest gnostics, who questioned the "lordship of Christ as the sole intermediary between God and the world." He goes on to say:

> It was *in worship* that the decisive step was made of setting the exalted Christ on a level with God as the recipient of the church's praise. Hymnology and Christology thus merged in the worship of one Lord, soon to be hailed after the close of the New Testament canon as worthy of hymns "as to God" (Pliny's report of Bithynian Christians at Sunday worship, A.D. 112).
>
> It was this close drawing together of the persons of the Godhead which laid the foundation for the Trinitarian creeds, and raised a bulwark against classical gnosticism in the late second century. . . . While "messianic psalms" played their role in defining and defending the church's belief in the fulfillment of Old Testament types and pre-

figurements, it required a new species—the "hymn to Christ"—to open fruitful avenues of Christological and soteriological inquiry that set the church from its early days on a course that led eventually to Chalcedon and the *Te Deum:*

> You are the King of Glory, O Christ,
> You are the everlasting Son of the Father.[15]

So it was that the oldest Christian traditions—those of the Eastern churches—began to sing "resurrection troparia" on Sundays and feast days that remain in use to the present day.

Spiritual songs.

The *koiné* Greek phrase for "spiritual songs" is *odais pneumatikais,* and—since the word *pneuma* is used for both "breath" and "spirit"—could refer to "Spirit odes" or "breath odes," or both. Musicologist Egon Wellesz identifies these as "alleluias and other chants of a jubilant or ecstatic character, richly ornamented," commonly found in many cultures of the Middle East.[16] Like an extended vocalise, they were essentially wordless songs of jubilation sung "on the breath," possibly repeating one word like "alleluia." Some scholars believe this type of song was formalized and memorialized in the *jubilus* of the mass, the originally improvised prolongation of the final syllable of the "Alleluia" before the Gospel reading.

Eric Werner states his conviction that these were glossalalic songs:

> In church and synagogue, extended melismatic chant was regarded as an ecstatic praise of God. . . . Such a conception places this type of singing in close proximity to the glossalaly of the Paulinian age. I venture to put forward my own conviction that the whole concept of the pure, wordless, melismatic jubilation should be considered the last, jealously guarded remnant of an organized form of glossalaly.[17]

Modern Pentecostalists and charismatics insist that this spontaneous singing-in-tongues is still experienced in what they call "Spirit singing." I am convinced that this third type of singing in New Testament worship is confirmed by Paul's words in 1 Corinthians 14:15, in the middle of a long discussion of the comparative values of glossalalic and intelligible expression: "I will sing praise [using spiritual songs] with the spirit, but I will sing praise [using psalms and hymns, and possibly others] with the mind also." It is interesting to note that these three early church forms I have described (which may or may not be those mentioned by Paul) create a Trinitarian formula:

- *Psalms* were historical, highly developed, biblical and/or contemporary expressions of prayer directed to God the Father.
- *Hymns* (at the time they were written) were extra-canonical "Jesus songs" intended to express and to teach the basic doctrines of the new faith.
- *Spiritual songs* were highly emotional, spontaneous jubilations which occurred in the overwhelming consciousness of the presence and power of the Holy Spirit.

Throughout history the church has enjoyed representations of these three forms. Beyond doubt, they greatly exceed the resources of typical praise-and-worship singing. Further, psalms (whole psalms, that is) include all the forms of prayer: adoration and praise, of course, but more thanksgiving in recounting God's gracious acts, plus confession, dedication, petition, and even lament. Hymns (as well as certain didactic psalms) express and teach the faith, not only Christology, but all theology. Spiritual songs (with or without glossalalia) express the joy of our experience in Christ through the Holy Spirit; some of the best examples have appeared during the last two centuries bearing the title "spirituals."

Some of the individual praise-and-worship choruses are useful additions to a congregation's song repertoire. But, even if we did not have Paul's formula for New Testament church singing, I would have to question the validity of the typical praise-and-worship experience, as described in this chapter and the last. I believe it is based on manipulation of emotions and does not conform to the cognitive standard suggested by Jesus' words: "God is spirit, and those who worship him must worship in spirit *and truth*" (John 4:24, italics added).

About a "New Song"

Another significant but questionable scriptural interpretation by present-day charismatic leaders stems from the belief that, through their movement, God is doing a new thing, as prophesied in Joel 2:28 and repeated by Peter in his Day of Pentecost sermon, "In the last days it will be, God declares, that I will pour out my Spirit upon all flesh, and your sons and your daughters shall prophesy, and your young men shall see visions, and your old men shall dream dreams" (Acts 2:17).

Charismatics believe that God's "new wine" should not be jeopardized by being placed in old wineskins, so older hymns should be displaced by new forms, as expressed in the psalm phrase, "Sing to the LORD a new song." As a result, many churches reject the idea that their praise-and-worship choruses should become classics. Every so often the old overhead-projector transparencies are thrown out and new materials are presented to the congregation.

Other Christians believe that Peter said that Joel's prophecy was completely fulfilled on that Day of Pentecost and that the Holy Spirit has been working in Christ's church ever since, guiding and shaping the development of historic expressions and forms of worship. Therefore, when we sing the hymns of Ambrose and Luther and Wesley, we are expressing our identity with them as part of the great "cloud of witnesses" to the perpetuity of God's covenant, as well as the continuity of the Spirit's presence with us.

The phrase "sing to the LORD a new song" appears five times in the Psalms (33:3; 96:1; 98:1; 144:9; 149:1) and once in the book of Isaiah (42:10). I am convinced that, in that ancient culture, which cherished traditional words and melodies of worship passed from each generation to the next, the word *new* indicated more "difference" than novelty. The *NIV Study*

Bible comments that all these verses speak of praise songs that celebrate God's saving acts, especially in a time of national deliverance.[18] So a new song was a different song—a song of victory and praise—as compared to the earlier song of defeat and lament. Its paradigm is expressed in personal witness in Psalm 40:1-3:

> I waited patiently for the LORD;
>   he inclined to me and heard my cry.
> He drew me up from the desolate pit,
>   out of the miry bog,
> and set my feet upon a rock,
>   making my steps secure.
> He put a *new song* in my mouth,
>   a song of praise to our God. (italics added)

Of course, we need songs that are newly composed, and some of the new serious hymns of our day are much stronger worship possibilities than the fads which get so much attention. But I believe the Old Testament writers were referring to a fresh experience rather than a new composition.

Final Thoughts

When John Calvin formulated his regulative principle, he was acknowledging the importance of looking to Scripture for answers as we consider every aspect of human life. In that understanding he was correct, even though some of his interpretations may have been wrong—for instance, his objections to extrascriptural hymns and to musical instruments in church.

The Bible does not give us the easy answers some might prefer, as in a direct rubric: "Be sure you always clap your hands in rhythm when you sing 'Holy, Holy, Holy'; and when the song is completed, clap your hands faster and a-rhythmically." It also does not teach us in riddles that remain unsolved for three thousand years until someone discovers their meaning. Rather, God's Word gives principles that human beings must interpret and apply in each generation.

I find such a principle in 1 Corinthians which speaks to the most important issue discussed in this chapter—the nature of congregational song. Almost the entire chapter deals with the Corinthians' obsession with glossalalia. While Paul admits the possibility and desirability of speaking in tongues in his day, he emphasizes the greater significance of words that are clearly understood: "I would rather speak five words with my mind, in order to instruct others also, than ten thousand words in a tongue" (1 Cor. 14:19).

I have said already that in 1 Corinthians 14:15 ("I will sing praise with the spirit, but I will sing praise with the mind also") Paul acknowledges that he did some singing that was not cognitive; but, in the context of the whole chapter, he insists that rational singing is more important. (Incidentally, I believe that these passages also imply that the *music* associated with words should be potentially "understandable" by the congregation which uses it.)

It is on this basis that I must reject the idea that praise-and-worship music should constitute our *only* singing because it is not sufficiently rational. This principle also strengthens my conviction that when we sing intelligible words, we must be sure that the congregation can identify and understand them!

Similar principles gleaned from Scripture are given in each chapter of this book. In the next chapter, I continue to discuss biblical truth, specifically, Scripture's teaching about Christ's body, the church, as it meets together in worship.

5

Worshiping God as the Community of Faith

In a Strange Land of Radical Individualism

"Purity of heart is to will one thing," Kierkegaard said, not one's *own* thing. —Donald Hustad

*R*ecently a modest-sized church in our community announced that it was initiating an "alternative" worship service. The senior pastor had strong convictions about what true worship should be, and he had opposed dividing the congregation in such a way. Soon afterward, the organist-choir director resigned to take another position and I agreed to serve as interim for a few weeks.

Since the alternative service did not use the organ, I arrived at the church Sunday mornings at about the time the first group was dismissing. I remember thinking that the departing worshipers probably wondered who I was. If they identified me at all, I was the musician who had come to assist in "that other service," which they rejected because it featured historic hymns, followed the Geneva Order of worship, used robes for both choir and ministers, and offered thoughtful, theologically rich, prophetic, evangelical preaching.

Choir attendance had suffered, because of both the conflict and the departure of their longtime director. I admired the faithfulness of those who continued to come, but I could read in their faces their heartbreak over their fractured church.

Though I felt a little uncomfortable in the position I had agreed to fill, I knew that the same tragic conflict was being experienced in many other churches across America. Many full-time ministers of music have suffered through such a worship war, and some have given up on their calling because of it.

This chapter continues the discussion of true worship in a consideration of one of the most important New Testament concepts: *ecclesiological truth*—truth about the church, the community of faith. After the apostle Peter's bold confession of Christ, "You are the Messiah, the Son of the living God," Jesus announced: "Blessed are you, Simon son of Jonah! For flesh and blood has not revealed this to you, but my Father in heaven. And I tell you, you are Peter, and on this rock I will build my church [*ekklesia*], and the gates of Hades will not prevail against it" (Matt. 16:16-18).

In our day, it seems that the church may be threatened as much by conflict from within its walls as from without. However, as Jesus said, the real enemy is still the "gates of hell." Marva Dawn has written:

> Battles waged in denominations and congregations, divisions between advocates of "contemporary" worship and "traditionalists" that lead to animosities and fractured relationships, the loss of the gospel that sometimes ensues, the weakening of Christian character and the consequent lack of substantive truth or genuine love in our outreach to the world are all certainly the work of evil powers to tear apart the Church.[1]

The zeal which is exhibited in worship wars may find its nourishment in the "strange land of radical individualism." Independence and individualism are considered to be good American traits but sometimes are a euphemistic cover for one of our culture's prevailing evils. Of course, neither Dawn nor I would associate the "work of evil powers" to one side or the other in the conflict. Radical individualism can be characteristic of worship traditionalists as well as worship modernists.

Having said that, I can hear someone counter: "But doesn't

Dawn's book—and yours—simply perpetuate the war?" For myself I reply: To me, the term *war* implies an unchristian spirit that springs from selfish motives. If that word characterizes my attitude and writing, I hope that nobody buys this book. If not, I pray that it may help individuals understand the issues better, so that eventually the war will end, not with a defeat for truth or even with a hostile truce, but with a reconciliation that heralds God's blessing and true peace.

What Is the Church?

The Greek word for *church* is *ekklesia,* meaning "called out." *Ekklesia* originally referred to "the assembly of citizens, called out from their homes to vote on legislation and transact other public business."[2] New Testament writers used it to speak of "those who are united by a common confession of Jesus as Lord" and are called out by the Holy Spirit to worship as the church. In the same way, they used the word *synagogue* (Greek, *sunagoge*) for the assembly of the Jewish people.[3]

It is evident then that church means something *local,* referring first to the group "called out" or "called together" and, by extension, to their meeting place. It also has a *universal* meaning, in that the church (called "the new humanity" in Ephesians 2:15) includes all who confess Jesus as Lord worldwide, who have received Christ's Spirit as the first Christians did on the day of Pentecost, and who bear witness to their Lord in a fellowship of faith and love. As Paul Jewett says, that fellowship "is visibly present wherever the Word is truly preached and the sacraments (ordinances) rightly administered."[4]

William Barclay has said, "The two things which must characterize any true church are *loyalty to Christ* and *love to people*"[5] (cf. Eph. 1:15, "I have heard of your faith in the Lord Jesus and your love toward all the saints"). In the church, believers are united organically to Christ and to each other, as Paul expressed in the phrase "the body of Christ" (cf. Eph. 1:22-23: Christ is the head of the church, and the church is the body of Christ). Barclay also stated that Christ died in order to bring all things and all people into one family and one unity.

As it stands, this world is a complete disunity. There is disunity between Jew and Gentile, between Greek and barbarian; there is disunity between different men within the same nation; . . . and, above all, there is disunity between man and God. It was Paul's thesis that Jesus died to bring all the discordant elements in this universe into one, to wipe out the breaches and the separations, to reconcile man to man and to reconcile man to God. Jesus Christ was above all things God's instrument of reconciliation.[6]

Despite God's purposes, unity in the community of faith does not happen automatically or even easily. It comes only with (1) a common understanding of God's full purposes for the church; (2) obedience to God's command to be united in supporting those purposes; (3) agreement about how those purposes should be achieved; and (4) the affirmation of diversity in opinion and grace to acknowledge that others may be sincere in their quest for the mind of Christ.

In this chapter, I will discuss how the present conflict about its worship forms and arts is threatening to tear apart the local church and to damage seriously the universal church. Some of that conflict stems from a failure to distinguish between the church's mission in outreach and its duty to worship maturely. No doubt some springs from a failure to understand the difference between our culture's many types of "religious" gatherings (most of which may be quite valid in that they minister to people) and the demands of *ministry to God* that is true worship. However, what rightly can be called "worship wars" are no doubt closely related to the unchristian self-centeredness that characterizes this period of history.

The Church's Call to Unity

Jesus' passion was for unity in his church. In the Upper Room discourse beginning in John 13, Jesus reviews his ministry on earth in the light of his approaching death. Over and over he

comes back to what seems to be his greatest concern, the
mutual love and unity of his followers:

> I give you a new commandment, that you love one an-
> other. Just as I have loved you, you also should love one
> another. By this everyone will know that you are my dis-
> ciples, if you have love for one another. (John 13:34-35)

> As the Father has loved me, so I have loved you: abide in
> my love. If you keep my commandments, you will abide
> in my love, just as I have kept my Father's commandments
> and abide in his love. (John 15:9-10)

> This is my commandment, that you love one another as I
> have loved you. (John 15:12)

> I am giving you these commands so that you may love one
> another. (John 15:17)

> I ask not only on behalf of these, but also on behalf of
> those who will believe in me through their word, that they
> may all be one. . . . The glory that you have given me I
> have given them, so that they may be one, as we are one.
> (John 17:20-22)

> I made your name known to them, and I will make it
> known, so that the love with which you have loved me
> may be in them, and I in them. (John 17:26)

Many leaders in the church have understood that Christ's Upper
Room prayer calls for organizational unity. For a thousand years
Christians were united in a common church structure. That fellowship was broken in 1054, when the Eastern (Orthodox) and
the Western (Roman Catholic) churches finally and formally
separated from each other, because of theological, liturgical, political, and cultural differences. Today, both groups continue to
pray and hope for a recovery of that primal unity.

In the sixteenth-century Reformation, "protest-ants" took actions that resulted in their separation from the Western (Roman Catholic) church. However, because of their own theological, liturgical, political, and cultural differences, they created four new Christian groups—Lutheran, Anglican, Reformed, and Radical Reformed (Anabaptist, Baptist, and Congregationalist). Divisions (in fellowship, if not in organization) continued within each of these groups. For instance, in the nineteenth century, individual Anglican churches were identified as "Anglo-Catholic" (closest to Roman Catholic in theology/worship), "Evangelical" (Presbyterian-Reformed, with a liturgy), and "Broad" (liberal in theology, with strong emphasis on the "social gospel").

In the United States, Southern Baptist churches still admit to wide differences that divide them on theological, liturgical, and cultural grounds.[7] While they proudly proclaim their unity as a voluntary fellowship, organized for purposes of missions and ministry, Baptist individuals and families are free to choose to attend the local church where they feel most "at home," especially in worship style and music. Baptist historians point out that their worship differences were inherited from two groups who settled in the South in the seventeenth and eighteenth centuries. "Charleston Baptists" are identified with First Baptist Church in Charleston, South Carolina (established about 1695), which typified ordered-but-warmly-evangelical worship led by Calvinist-trained ministers. The other group consisted of the "Sandy Creek" Baptists who settled in Sandy Creek, North Carolina, in 1755. They were suspicious of education and produced an emotional, revivalistic, almost charismatic brand of worship meeting.[8]

In the twentieth century, many church leaders have emphasized again the call to Christian unity, whether in an ecumenical, organizational sense (as in the denominational Council on Church Union) or in a broadening of their fellowship (as in the National Association of Evangelicals). In recent years, a blurring of theological and denominational lines also has created something of an informal unity that many have welcomed. Nevertheless, each local church needs to discover its own *worship identity* rather than to imitate the expressions of others.

War in the Community of Faith

Lest anyone think that a loving and harmonious relationship has *ever* come easily to believing Christians, the New Testament reminds us of several conflicts in the early church:

> Now I appeal to you, brothers and sisters, by the name of our Lord Jesus Christ, that all of you be in agreement and that there be no divisions among you, but that you be united in the same mind and the same purpose. For it has been reported to me . . . that there are quarrels among you, my brothers and sisters. (1 Cor. 1:10-11)

> For as long as there is jealousy and quarreling among you, are you not of the flesh, and behaving according to human inclinations? (1 Cor. 3:3)

> For I fear that when I come, I may find you not as I wish, and that you may find me not as you wish; I fear that there may perhaps be quarreling, jealousy, anger, selfishness, slander, gossip, conceit, and disorder. (2 Cor. 12:20)

Conflict in the early church occurred in several areas. In the longer Scripture passages containing the above quotations, we learn that the church in Corinth disagreed about leadership (Should it be Paul, or Apollos, or Peter?), about how to dress for public worship, about Paul's financial support, and about issues of church discipline. Nowhere does the New Testament say explicitly that early Christians differed about worship styles, but Paul's lengthy, blunt arguments about worship decorum (in 1 Cor. 14) suggest that they probably did. Paul's delineation of "psalms and hymns and spiritual songs" (in Eph. 5:19 and Col. 3:16) may also be a hint that congregational singing also was an area of dispute.

Certainly, questions about music and/or worship style have been reasons for argument, anger, and even schism throughout the church's long history. For instance, whether or not musical instruments should be used in worship has been a question from the third century to the present. Should congregations sing only psalms (God's Word) or can they also sing hymns (human words)? This has been debated since at least the sixteenth century. Should choirs consist of men and boys only (because they represent a male priesthood) or should they include women? This question has been asked in Roman Catholic and Anglican churches.

Today's cultural/generational worship war in the church swirls around such questions as: Should we sing traditional hymns, anthems, and other music, or praise-and-worship music and contemporary Christian music literature? Should we sing from hymnals or from an overhead screen? Should we use organs and pianos, or guitars, synthesizers, and drums? Should we dress up or dress down for worship? Should we have a choir or a worship team, or both? Should we clap hands in applause after musical and other performances? Should worship be predictable (and prepared for) or an entertaining "Sunday surprise"?

A New Paradigm: Willow Creek

The current conflict became national after the emergence of some highly visible examples of contemporary services in the 1970s, like those in Willow Creek Community Church. Founder Bill Hybels says that in planning Willow Creek's activities, he was guided by the responses of his own age group in the community to the question, "Why don't you go to church?" The answers were: (1) "The church is irrelevant to daily life"; (2) "Church services are lifeless, boring and predictable"; (3) "Pontificating pastors preach down at parishioners"; and (4) "Churches are always asking for money."[9]

Hybels began his ministry as a youth leader in a traditional evangelical church in Park Ridge, Illinois, where he used rock gospel music to reach teenagers. The youth group soon outgrew the church and met briefly in a theater nearby. Eventually, Hybels and his associates became convinced that God wanted them to enlarge their ministry to include adults, so they bought property in South Barrington. After buildings were erected, the new church grew quickly, and soon some twenty thousand people were gathering on weekends to hear professional-quality performances of contemporary Christian music, to see short dramatic sketches from everyday life that highlighted spiritual needs, and to listen to excellent, dispassionate but convincing messages about the validity of the Christian gospel in meeting those needs. Hybels invited unbelievers to attend and to listen—without expecting them to dress up, to sing in the service, to place money in the offering plate, or to respond immediately in any other way. Of course, it was hoped that eventually they would respond to the Holy Spirit's conviction of sin and revelation of Christ as our God-Man Redeemer.

The Church Growth Movement

Willow Creek's first focus was on Bill Hybels' own age group, the Baby Boomers, many of whom lost touch with the church in the early 1960s in rejection of both their parents' and their community's standards of behavior. Soon a full-blown church growth movement emerged—largely in the form of book-publishing experts who based their arguments on computerized sociological and other research—urging churches to follow Willow Creek's example in conducting services that would reach that "lost" generation and their children.

George Hunter, missiologist and seminary professor, states the case for changes in dramatic terms:

> The Christian movement now faces its greatest opportunity in the Western world in the last three centuries. Today, we find the real future of Christianity modeled in pioneering local churches. The shape of the Church's emerging opportunity looks like this:
>
> Christendom is largely dissolved, and the peoples of Europe and North America are increasingly secular.
>
> The Enlightenment, which provided the worldview for the secular West, is a spent force. Consequently, people are increasingly receptive to, and searching for, a satisfying

worldview. We are, once again, in an Apostolic Age—much like the age that early Christianity engaged.[10]

Hunter gives ten features of "apostolic congregations," nine of which are demanding but not really surprising (for instance, "Apostolic congregations obey the Great Commission.") But one item gets unusual attention and sounds like a discussion of contextual ministry to ethnic groups in far-off lands, even aboriginal cultures: "Apostolic congregations adapt to the language, music, and style of the target population's culture."

In the same article he offers another list of "Ten Pioneering Principles of Outreach in Apostolic Churches," saying these churches "know that secular people who are open to Christianity do not, generally, respond to the faith when it is expressed in Elizabethan, academic, theological, evangelical, ecclesiastical, or 'politically correct' language." He goes on to say that the requirements to be apostolic and culturally relevant are wide-ranging and might even include "the approach to learning, clothing, leadership styles, and when possible, architecture."[11]

This list I've compiled of modern service-style characteristics shows how radical and sweeping the expectations could be, even if they seem to be inconsistent:

- Be natural. Don't "posture."
- Work for exuberant spontaneity, even surprise. Shun dull formality, as expressed in a printed worship order.
- Use contemporary language. Avoid clichés, biblical language, or theological jargon.
- Be professional. Abhor jarring amateurism.
- "Go with the flow." Don't manipulate or confront.
- Use modern show-biz styles, forms (like drama/dance), and symbols.
- Increase performance elements. Don't insist on participation.
- Use pop or light rock music with electronic sounds

and/or amplification. Forget traditional music, vocal techniques, and instrumentation.

As pastors observed the success of the contemporary-style megachurch in their own community, and began to see the movement syphon off their own members, they were quick to consider following the advice of George Hunter and other church growth specialists.

At this point, many faithful church members (those who had an experiential Christian faith and were consistent in their support of the church) became alarmed. They too wanted to reach their unchurched children (or those of their neighbors), but not at the cost of losing everything that was meaningful to them in worship words, actions, and symbols. Besides, they argued, those new music styles were tonal expressions of the rebellion which caused the Boomers to drop out of the church and of disciplined society in the 1960s. How can we evangelize unbelievers and renew the church by secularizing it, so that it is no longer the church?

If by any chance the senior pastor shared the convictions of those skeptical "faithful" members, he soon became the target of pressure by the younger Boomers who remained in the church, especially of those on the ministering staff (except, perhaps, the seminary-trained church musician). "Everybody's doing it and we must follow suit, if we are to survive," they said. "If we don't, we show that we have no commitment to evangelism." As the tension increased, it seemed that many ministers would be forced to either yield or resign. A number of them, especially pastors and ministers of music, did just that. Others were forced from their positions.

Adding Alternative Services

The obvious and seemingly simple answer to the debate was to add a "seeker" service that met at a different hour or place than the "traditional" one. In this format, the traditional service would continue without change, so the older members would not complain. A second, radically different service was planned to achieve Willow Creek's outreach goals and results, and complaining Boomers and others who chose could attend that service, tailored to meet their own preferences.

It didn't seem to matter that almost everybody was misreading the Willow Creek paradigm. The South Barrington leaders understood and announced that their weekend meetings were seeker events, *not worship services for believers.* So they presented short, entertaining, drama-and-music sessions, with no participation expected, climaxing in a well-reasoned presentation of the gospel. Their baptized members were encouraged to attend those services, but only for the purpose of bringing their uncommitted friends and neighbors. For the worship of believer-members (called The New Community), Willow Creek presents one-hundred-minute worship services on Wednesday and Thursday evenings that are half "exaltation" (mostly worship singing) and half serious, expository teaching, with participation expected.[12] However, most of Willow Creek's imitators missed the point and the example completely, announcing that they would conduct seeker worship that was "more entertaining," and expecting that service to meet the worship needs of their members who chose to attend.

Alternative Services in Church History

Christians have always considered the need to reach those who are not yet committed to Christ. The crusades of Billy Graham or Luis Palau are only the latest in a two-thousand-year history of evangelistic meetings held in obedience to Jesus' Great Commission.

The patristic and medieval church divided its Eucharistic service into two parts: the Service of the Catechumens followed by the Service of the Faithful. Those in catechism school (but not yet confessing believers) were allowed to attend the first part, in which praise, thanksgiving, confession, and petition were expressed in word and song, and the Scriptures were read and preached. They were then dismissed, and only the baptized "faithful" remained for additional "Prayers of the

Faithful," plus the Great Thanksgiving and actions of the Lord's Supper.

In the early nineteenth century, certain evangelicals in England and America became convinced that children should be evangelized and receive Christian training in words and modes suited to their intellectual-emotional capacities. Consequently, they developed the Sunday school movement, with sessions that met first on Sunday afternoons. Of course, children were expected to join their parents in the regular worship service on Sunday morning, and eventually segments of that service (for instance, a children's sermon) were planned especially for their participation.

In the late 1940s, a movement to reach teenagers led to special services on Saturday evenings under the banner of Youth for Christ. YFC rallies were a pleasant mishmash of entertainment and challenge to discipleship geared to high schoolers and younger ages. The citywide meetings were supported by many churches, because evangelism was one of the objectives and because those same young people attended regular worship gatherings.

This was a time when much of America engaged in community "sings" that were sometimes broadcast by radio and television, so church folk also began gathering for sing-alongs. I remember times when, after regular Sunday evening services, young people from several churches would meet to sing their own favorite music—choruses and modern gospel songs by John Peterson, Wendell Loveless, and other writers of that period. But none of these added activities detracted from attendance of all age groups at regular worship.

Problems with Divided Worship for Believers

Earlier in this chapter I said that adding alternative services was a seemingly simple answer to the present-day conflict in the church. If such services were properly conceived and executed, would they not constitute a good solution? As a musician associated with evangelism, I can answer yes, if you refer to Willow Creek's true paradigm: an evangelistic event for seekers and a *different* worship service for believers. I answer no, if you refer to the common misinterpretation of Willow Creek: two very different worship services for *believers,* one of which is supposed to be more "seeker friendly" than the other. Today's popular but misconceived answer to the church's challenge contains problems that are not being discussed adequately. Some of these are in the areas of leadership, personnel, differing theologies, and short-sighted planning.

Leadership burnout.
I admire the musicians who agree to take on the responsibility of conducting more than one type of major service on a weekend. Like their pastors, they are challenged by the need to reach out to the unchurched. These music leaders may feel more "at home," aesthetically or spiritually, in one service than in the other, but, like Paul, they are willing to take on the extra workload—to "become all things to all people" that they might "by all means save some" (1 Cor. 9:22).

But can they offer to God a worthy "sacrifice of praise" in each of those services? Worship planners who lead a genuinely creative traditional service every week spend all the time they have available, praying for the Spirit's guidance; finding fresh, appropriate materials; informing the people involved; rehearsing readers, choirs, and instrumentalists; and later, evaluating the service so that the next might be a better offering to God.

Contemporary worship is altogether different in both materials and techniques, so it requires a completely different group of recruited performers. Musicians are expected to sing and play in a more improvisatory style, often requiring a complete rehearsal of the extended "song worship" *just before the service.* Long before that, the sequence of praise-and-worship choruses or other materials must be planned, with careful thought as to the need for modulations in between. Transparencies must be prepared for the overhead projector and parts arranged and possibly scored for the "praise band."

A number of musicians I know have struggled valiantly to lead well with such a challenge, and have finally asked the church to consider returning to a single, blended service model. Of course, a megachurch has no such personnel problem. It simply hires two (and usually many more) persons to handle the varied responsibilities. But, in my view, a megachurch is not a church that I can identify in the New Testament—a church in which worshipers know and are known by the pastor, and one in which they find true spiritual community with more than a handful of people. Only in such a church can the body of Christ be genuinely *experienced.*

Different theologies.
Very few church leaders seem to understand this truth: *Two different services communicate different theologies* as well as different "styles." The historic principle of *lex orandi, lex credendi* (the rule of prayer is the rule of faith) means that our worship experiences teach us our theology. If one service asks folks to sing typical hymns and the other uses only praise choruses, the former expects the experience to be actively cognitive and the latter is expecting folks to be largely emotive. I believe those are two theologically different ways of meeting God in worship. Again, if the elements of one service present a God who is transcendent (holy, beyond our full understanding) as well as immanent (fatherly, loving, a friend), and the other expresses only the latter, two theologically different concepts of God are given.

This "divided mind and heart" was demonstrated recently in a large Presbyterian church that was evidently experimenting with an alternative service on Sunday mornings. The typical morning services exhibited moderately Calvinistic concepts— the majesty and sovereignty of God expressed in reverent, evangelical prayer, theologically rich hymns, a carefully crafted, God-honoring sermon, and magnificently performed music by choir and organ. The gospel was preached, unbelievers were challenged to accept Jesus Christ as Lord and Savior, and the atmosphere was warm and friendly in Christian fellowship, though still carefully reverent.

The alternative service, led by another musician who served as worship leader, was very different. That person evidently took his material from the quasi-charismatic *Songs for Praise and Worship.*[13] Speaking between the praise-and-worship choruses, he challenged the congregation to move past the "gates of thanksgiving" and the "courts of praise" into worship's "Holy of Holies"—without speaking in tongues, of course! Obviously, there was more congregational participation in this service, including clapping and "dancing"—and more sense of immanence than transcendence.

The first service participants seemed to wait quietly and expectantly for the sovereign God to reveal himself; those in the second seemed determined to bang on heaven's gates to be sure they got God's attention, reminding him that they had followed the proper formula for true worship. Two very different theologies were presented under one roof!

No plans for the future.
It is also apparent that even if the present solutions are expedient, the "church-dividing" folk have no clear plan for the future. One would think that such radical action would be accompanied by an announced purpose and plan, either (1) to continue the two services until the older generation dies off and we can all move to contemporary worship; or (2) to continue with contemporary worship until the Boomers have matured in their faith and taste, at which time we will all return to traditional worship; or (3) some other plan.

It seems apparent that temporary, "band-aid" solutions for worship and outreach in today's culture are being offered, which may be followed by more of the same.[14] In fact, some churches are now offering (in multiplex theater style) three different services, with three different liturgies (and I hope three different musician-leaders!).

Meeting wants, not needs.
The truth is, when a church divides, neither group experiences full, healthy worship. All of us need to experience the company of every age group in the church family. The "contemporary" service misses the serenity and wisdom of senior citizens and the "traditional" gathering lacks the dynamism and forward look of younger worshipers.

The body of Christ is not served well by creating unchanging ghettos of worship/music style. Boomers need to be reminded that they did not invent church—Christians have met to worship for two thousand years. For the church, tradition is a strength. Singing modern versions of ancient words, even ancient melodies, reminds us that our God of history will continue to provide for us as he did for our forebears. At the same time, faithful worshipers need to be reminded that time moves on and older members of the church must move with it. A healthy church maintains its ties with the past, but also revises its liturgy and learns new songs on a regular basis.

Paul Hoon agrees that both "living only in the now" and "regressing into the past" are immature, but he believes that "amnesia is a worse sickness than nostalgia":

> As memory is necessary to the sanity of personality, so tradition sustains the collective personality of a people. But most of all, to reject Tradition as we have defined it is to sin against the Holy Spirit as it ever illumines the mind of the Church and invests the Event of Jesus Christ with meaning. The Spirit is as much the source of continuity, of order, and of heritage as it is of newness and freedom.[15]

The Most Important Argument: The Lord's Table

It is apparent to me that dividing the community of faith into groups according to generational, cultural, or aesthetic lines is not the will of God. We cannot (and should not) expect comprehensive unity in the universal church or in any particular group of churches, but we must strive toward it in the local congregation. That is not to say that, according to another tenet of church growth dogma, a congregation should strive to be "pure"—racially, culturally, or economically. It means that, once we have found "our church," we will agree to work and worship together in love and unity, deferring to one another on points of choice that do not violate our consciences.

It should be patently evident that a program of alternate services creates two churches, not one. Consider the possibility that a single Episcopal church would divide into Anglo-Catholics and evangelicals, with separate services, or that a Southern Baptist congregation would purpose to be both "Charleston" and "Sandy Creek" in commonly sponsored but separate worship service styles. Invariably, the historic ill will between those differing camps would be remembered as one group passes the other between services.

But I propose that the strongest argument against dividing the church is both scriptural and theological, based on the most significant New Testament passage that speaks of our most cherished worship action: the observance of the Lord's Supper.

In introducing this subject, the apostle Paul talks about conflict and church division. "Now in the following instructions I do not commend you, because when you come together it is not for the better but for the worse. For, . . . I hear that there are divisions among you; and to some extent I believe it" (1 Cor. 11:17-18). Paul goes on to complain that in the celebrating of the love-feast—an *agape* meal, to which every believer brought something to share—those who were rich ate their own excellent food and even got drunk on their superb wines, refusing to share with the poor, who went home hungry.

William Barclay reminds us that in the ancient world the church offered the only place where people could come together in mutual acceptance of each other. Outside, the culture was divided between free people and slaves, between Greeks and "barbarians" (those who could not speak Greek), Jews and Gentiles, Romans and "lesser breeds," the cultured and the ignorant. Quoting a church historian, Barclay states:

> "Within their own limits they [early Christian congregations] had solved almost by the way the social problem which baffled Rome and baffles Europe still. They had lifted woman to her rightful place, restored the dignity of labor, abolished beggary, and drawn the sting of slavery.

The secret of the revolution is that the selfishness of race and class was forgotten in the Supper of the Lord, and a new basis for society found in love of the visible image of God in men for whom Christ died."

A Church where social and class distinctions exist is no true Church at all. A real Church is a body of men and women united to each other because all are united to Christ.[16]

Paul then delivers the paragraph that is used in virtually every church that observes the Lord's Supper: "For I received from the Lord what I also handed on to you, that the Lord Jesus on the night when he was betrayed took a loaf of bread. . . . For as often as you eat this bread and drink the cup, you proclaim the Lord's death until he comes" (1 Cor. 11:23-26). We call these the Words of Institution, which both command and authenticate our Communion celebrations. What follows these words has been referred to as church discipline that "fences the table" to prevent unworthy eating and drinking, which would bring God's judgment.

Whoever, therefore, eats the bread or drinks the cup of the Lord in an unworthy manner will be answerable for the body and blood of the Lord. Examine yourselves, and only then eat of the bread and drink of the cup. For all who eat and drink without discerning the body, eat and drink judgment against themselves. (1 Cor. 11:27-29)

It seems clear that Paul is referring to the sin that was described in the verses preceding. To eat and drink "without discerning the body" is to do so without acceptance and love of each other as members of the body of Christ.[17]

It is important to me that these words refer to participation together in an act of worship. When is a church the church? Is it when it votes on a budget or agrees on a person to call as pastor? A church is most truly the church when it meets around the Table of the Lord in worship. When members of the same congregation cannot pass the plate of bread to each other, when they cannot share the common cup (or the tray of individual cups), they cease to meet Christ's standard as faithful members of his body.

All of us understand that we have no authority to "add" to Scripture; yet, somehow, I don't believe that the following application to the demanding inclusiveness of Galatians 3:28 is out of place:

> There is no longer Jew or Greek, there is no longer slave or free, there is no longer male and female, [there is no longer rich or poor, there is no longer Boomer or Buster, there is no longer aesthetic snob or cultural slob], for all of you are one in Christ Jesus. (Gal. 3:28, author's paraphrase)

Postmodern Individualism and the Church

It may seem odd that we are calling into question one of the treasured hallmarks of American culture—what President Herbert Hoover called "the American system of rugged individualism." We take pride that we are not bound by class distinctions as are other cultures; we can rise above (or fall below) our group according to our ability, our determination, and our choices. We exult in our democratic institutions, in which we can differ from other persons and can say so emphatically. To be an American is to be free within our laws, as expressed in a song made famous by Frank Sinatra, to "do it my way."

James I. Packer sees this individualistic mindset as a postmodern reaction of disillusionment against the (earlier) modernist habit of mind. It originated with intellectuals but, with the help of the media, has already influenced much of society. In an article in *Crux* magazine, Packer shows how individualism destroys consensus—even makes rational discussion virtually impossible—in the wider community as well as in the local church. Packer compares our vanishing basis for community with nature's anthills, then states the basic mindset of postmodern thought and describes the cynical techniques used to protect it from successful challenge.

What form does the [postmodern] reaction take? In place of the quasi-behaviorist ideal of rational objectivity creating a collectivist community of like-thinking, well-socialized human ants in smoothly functioning anthills, a new ideal of freedom and fulfillment for the individual has emerged. This ideal assumes the technological conveniences of the anthill as a given, *but rejects the notion of universal public truth on questions involving values;* muffles and scrambles all communication, oral or documentary, by a process of deconstruction; debunks other people's absolutes and values by playful or cynical negation; and reduces public disagreements to power plays and power struggles between competing subcultures and manipulators. (italics added)[18]

In the postmodern world, we may expect that such a statement as "Beethoven has contributed more to Western culture than Elvis Presley" will be answered, "Says who?"—even by some folks who know who Beethoven was. Packer goes on to list the ways in which the new radical individualism is expressed in culture.

In postmodernism, individualistic subjectivity is set in a critical relation to all forms of supposedly scientific and consensual objectivity, and the personal "story" of each human being is allowed to stand in judgment over the corporate "stories" of all human groups, both secular and churchly. Spirituality without truth, individuality without constraints, pluralistic pragmatism, whimsy claiming to be wisdom, desire masquerading as morality, and benevolent tolerance of any and every view that does not tell you that you yourself are wrong, thus constitute the essence of postmodern culture.[19]

Radical individualism, of course, is a form of narcissism, in which we love ourselves and scorn all other persons, all other ideas, all other cultures, all other value systems. The body of Christ cannot thrive if dominated by these self-centered concepts. The proper spirit to show in the fellowship is that of Matthew 20:26, "Whoever wishes to be great among you must be your servant"; and of Romans 12:10, "Outdo one another in showing honor."

James Torrance reminds us that true community can never be achieved by secular society, Marxist or capitalist, even if it is based on the principles of Plato's *Republic* or on the older Stoic concepts of natural and moral law. There is only one answer and it is biblical and Christian:

> Is it not rather to return to "the forgotten Trinity"—to an understanding of the Holy Spirit, who delivers us from a narcissistic preoccupation with the self to find our true being in loving communion with God and one another— to hear God's call to us, in our day, to participate through the Spirit in Christ's communion with the Father and his mission from the Father to the world—to create in our day a new humanity of persons who find true fulfillment in other-centered communion and service in the kingdom of God?[20]

Immediately preceding the great "love chapter" of 1 Corinthians 13, Paul uses the metaphor of the church as Christ's body to suggest that dissension causes *a dismembering to Christ's body:*

> For just as the body is one and has many members, and all the members of the body, though many, are one body, so it is with Christ. For in the one Spirit we were all baptized into one body—Jews or Greeks, slaves or free— and we were all made to drink of one Spirit. Indeed, the body does not consist of one member but of many. If the foot would say, "Because I am not a hand, I do not belong to the body," that would not make it any less a part of the body. . . . But God has so arranged the body, . . . that there may be no dissension within the body, but the members may have the same care for one another. (1 Cor. 12:12-15, 24-25)

Doing things "my way" may be the American way, but it is not the Christian way. It is not the way of the Cross.

Personal Spirituality versus Community in Worship

Not all roadblocks to unity in a church are characterized by overt conflict. In fact, a highly desirable aspect of traditional evangelical life—the pursuit of personal spirituality—can pose a threat to true community in worship that is as real as it is surprising.

For one thing, personal worship seven days a week may be so satisfying that there seems to be no need for corporate worship on Sunday, especially when it is more comfortable "to do it my way" rather than to be servant-members of Christ's body.

In addition to the traditional daily Scripture reading and prayer (and why not a hymn or a chorus?), Americans particularly are attracted to personal devotional pursuits by means of television, religious radio, or recorded tapes and videos. Many follow their favorite preacher/teacher regularly, whether Chuck Swindoll, James Dobson, Oliver B. Green, Robert Schuller, or James Kennedy. They also enjoy programs or tapes featuring favorite Christian singers or a preferred style of Christian music. So how could such *good*, even *ideal*, activity be a threat to uniting the church in worship in our fractious, individualistic day?

In the case of television, I know of few instances in which broadcasting worship does not compromise the service in some way. Television is show business which must appeal to the uncentered minds of people I call "channel samplers." I dare say that even the awareness of cameras present in a sanctuary detracts from the worship of some in the congregation. Radio preachers may do better; they may presume that their audience is committed to listening with some care. Also, they have a reasonable amount of broadcast time in which they can deliver a complete, coherent message.

However, listening to radio preaching and teaching does not automatically prepare one for hearing the Word of God in community. In community, Christ speaks his Word to his body, the church, and holds the *entire community* responsible to respond in dialogue, both personally and as a group. In religious television, radio, or tapes, there is really no opportunity to respond—in song, in word, or in physical action—except perhaps to answer the appeal to send a donation. Again, hearing a sermon apart from the context of full worship action simply perpetuates the idea that preaching is the only significant happening and that liturgical structure and action are irrelevant.

Frequently, ads come in the mail promising that listening to a certain tape of praise-and-worship music will "make God's presence real." This repeats the error of nineteenth-century Romanticism in equating personal aesthetic experience with spiritual communication. We all have experiences that border on this but we must avoid deception. It takes both spiritual and aesthetic discipline to distinguish between pleasant sounds heard from a new compact disc and the true presence of God. Hearing one's favorite music by itself, apart from the spoken word of admonition or prayer, tends to encourage us to enjoy music for its own sake, with little awareness of the theological/liturgical significance of the words sung. Further, it tends to limit one's openness to other musical styles that probably should be included and experienced positively, if the church is to worship in community.

I am convinced that a community of faith is most truly the church when it *participates together* in worship. Sitting together in a theater does not build community; neither does spectator worship, old or new. Singing together can do it, if we consciously center our minds on the action and make a significant effort—but that doesn't happen with typical praise-and-worship music or in much traditional hymn singing. But speaking and singing together in liturgical dialogue—our prayers, our commitment, and our dedication to God—is a sure way to encourage and enable the formation of a congregation into the body of Christ. This does not happen—indeed, it may be compromised—in the otherwise desirable activities of personal worship.

Such speaking and singing must communicate also our dedication to each other as believers. Greeting one another is one way to show this community commitment. I know a church in which some members have convinced their pastor that extending the "kiss of peace" to each other is disturbing to the spirit of worship. Besides, its members say, we greet each other in the foyer, both before and after the service (and, I would add, they visit together in the worship room until the service is called to order).

I'm sure some folks have been put off by the exhibitionist example set in some churches, in which people wander throughout the church sharing bear hugs and kisses, and sometimes extraneous, "unholy" conversation. Yet a Christian greeting in worship is a rubric mentioned in several of Paul's epistles. It is *required* in order to demonstrate that we live up to the second half of the great commandment, to love our neighbors as ourselves. Greetings in the vestibule do not qualify in meeting this command. In the worship service, we greet whomever is near us because we are Christians who must speak our acceptance and love of each other. There, members speak to visitors and senior citizens speak to Boomers and to children, and vice versa.

The character of the greeting is important also. We should probably go out of our way to greet folk we don't know well and those from whom we differ. And because this is a holy greeting, not a social expression, "God's peace to you" is more significant than "Good morning." Also, a firm, fervent handshake is a better "holy" expression than an actual embrace because no one will be offended if you kiss or embrace, or feel slighted if you do not!

Solutions for the Church

I am not suggesting that anyone should limit personal worship, unless (for a physically able person) it takes the place of corporate worship in the local church. I do believe that we should be aware of the differences between public and private worship, and should develop proper expectations for each. Above all, worship leaders should be aware of those differences and should be prepared to develop the congregation's full participation in both.

I have already suggested that the alternative services idea is a band-aid solution which attempts to cover a church's previous failures. Of course, every church must develop a strong ministry of evangelism, to reach folk of all ages, with perhaps a special emphasis on "dropouts" in one or more age groups. That program may include social witnessing contacts by individuals, couples, or small groups; special events such as concerts or lectures sponsored by the church; or Bible study groups in homes. It is fine to conduct seeker events as Willow Creek does, so long as they are not billed as "worship" and substituted for full worship participation by regular church members. I propose the following solutions for strengthening community worship.

Stay united.

I say it again: On the basis of Paul's teaching in 1 Corinthians 11, I am convinced that it is wrong for any local church to be divided by worship theology and style. I have witnessed a few situations in recent years in which the conflict had progressed to such a point that the division seemed to be inescapable. When that is true, if it is not feasible to create two separate congregations, I believe that the pastor and people should issue a shared confession of failure, with a stated resolve to work together toward reunion in worship.

Create a contemporary traditional service.

Before that point is reached, when a church judges that it is not using music and speech languages that can communicate to all individuals it should be reaching, it should add worthy examples to a common service order. The result may be what is sometimes called a "blended service," incorporating new elements with the traditional—new types of music, new forms of praying and perhaps preaching. I prefer to call such services "contemporary traditional," partly to unite the two terms which have been used to express our division. Worship must be traditional because it must demonstrate that our God has intersected all of human history. Worship must be contemporary—renewed and updated—because it happens today. That should always be normal for the church.

In implementing such changes, ministers should first communicate their convictions about the need for unity in the congregation, probably in a Sunday morning sermon with a strong biblical foundation. They should express their commitment to developing services that are true worship, not entertainment, adhering to the biblical and theological standards they hold for worship (see chapter 8, "Worshiping in Liturgical Truth"). They should teach the meaning and significance of all actions in worship, as suggested throughout this book, and especially in chapter 9.

Appoint a worship committee.

A worship committee should be appointed to work with service planners/leaders on an ongoing basis, to ensure that the needs of all groups are being met as nearly as possible. Each of the chapters in this book presents additional suggestions which should help them to meet this goal.

Solve conflicts by prayer.

Few evangelicals understand what it means to be "the community of faith in worship." The common idea is that worship is a personal act, and in church we struggle with something of a handicap because we are required to do it corporately. It should be evident that such a notion leads naturally to narcissism and to conflict that is usually "settled" by another aspect of church polity that can be applied in an unchristian manner—the tyranny of the majority vote. Marva Dawn explains how the church—because it is united to Christ—must worship both as individual persons and as Christ's united body. In solving its conflicts, it must do so as the undivided church, guided in its discussion and prayer by the Holy Spirit.

Since the Church is formed by its relationship with Christ, it is not . . . a democracy. The earliest Christians made their decisions through intensive discussion and prayer until they could say, "It has seemed good to the Holy Spirit and to us" (Acts 15:28).

The nondemocratic process of listening together to the Holy Spirit is especially helpful in the worship war between advocates of high culture and those who want the Church's music to match what they hear outside the Church. The commonality of the discussion will preclude elitism, and the guidance of the Holy Spirit will thwart "popular" perversions of the gospel.

The procedure of searching for consensus under the Holy Spirit's guidance will properly incorporate the gifts of the community—as gifts to be shared for the upbuilding of all, rather than for the self-fulfillment of the gifts' possessors. In a common search for the Holy Spirit's purposes concerning worship, for example, those with gifts of wisdom and faith, those who know the Church's heritage and history, and those with theological and musical training will be respected for the necessary insights they bring to the discussion and as gifts given by God to the community to equip it for greater faithfulness.[21]

If the postmodern mind dismisses such an idea as "idealistic and impractical," no doubt Dawn would say: "Of course! It's biblical!"

The next chapter investigates one of the basic questions underlying this entire discussion: Are certain contemporary worship elements so identified with our culture's secular spirit that they cannot contribute to worship in spirit and truth?

6

Worshiping God
in Cultural Truth

*In a Strange Land
of Pervasive Secularism*

Our music for worship should not be the music we worship.
—Donald Hustad

When gospel singer Ira D. Sankey first visited Scotland with evangelist D. L. Moody in 1873, he was afraid that the serious-minded, Calvinistic Scots would react negatively to his performance. Many Scottish Presbyterians sang only unaccompanied psalms in public worship. They had never before heard America's popular gospel songs, sung by a soloist and accompanied by a portable parlor organ. Sankey's anxiety increased when he saw that Horatius Bonar—Scotland's renowned hymn writer and preacher—was sitting close to his little organ on the platform. Later Sankey wrote:

> Of all men in Scotland he was the one man concerning whose decision I was most solicitous. He was, indeed, my ideal hymn-writer, the prince among hymnists of his day and generation. And yet he would not sing one of his own beautiful hymns in his own congregation, . . . because he ministered to a church that believed in the use of the Psalms only. With fear and trembling I announced as a solo the song, "Free from the Law, Oh, Happy Condition."
> . . . Feeling that the singing might prove only an entertainment, and not a spiritual blessing, I requested the whole

congregation to join me in a word of prayer, asking God to bless the truth about to be sung. In the prayer my anxiety was relieved. Believing and rejoicing in the glorious truth contained in the song, I sang it through to the end.

At the end of Mr. Moody's address, Dr. Bonar turned toward me with a smile on his venerable face, and reaching out his hand he said: "Well, Mr. Sankey, you sang the gospel tonight." And thus the way was opened for the mission of sacred song in Scotland.[1]

It is hard to imagine such a happening in a modern concert of contemporary Christian music (CCM) or even in an evangelistic crusade. In fact, most CCM artists have long since forgotten any call to forthright ministry as Sankey knew it. Nowadays they are unashamedly committed to "alternative entertainment."

This chapter will examine the change in our culture's understanding of *worship, ministry,* and *entertainment,* and will ask whether those changes signal that the church and its gospel are being secularized. I begin with a small dose of philosophy.

Cultural Truth

Biblical-theological truth includes much more than we usually associate with that term. I believe, as Arthur Holmes says in a book so titled, that "all truth is God's truth."[2] For instance, the theological category of *humanity* (formerly called the "doctrine of man"), includes discussion of *cultural reality,* cultural truth. Human beings are created by God, so every natural characteristic of humanity is God-related. Jesus spoke theological truth to the Samaritan woman he met at Jacob's well, but he did so in the context of the culture—the history, traditions, and thought patterns—of Samaritans and of Jews, both of which she knew well. Worship must use a verbal language that is known by the worshipers in a given culture—for instance, vernacular, not Latin. It follows then that the *art languages* of music, of gesture, of architecture, of clothing, of artifacts, must be recognized and understood by the worshipers who use them—Occidental or Oriental, Jew or Gentile, rural or urban, young or old, literate or nonliterate.

Holy Things and Ordinary

At the same time, most cultures tend to designate aspects of human life as either *sacred* (holy) or *secular* (ordinary) based on their association with or separation from acts of worship. To the woman at the well, Jesus identified Mt. Gerizim as the sacred shrine for Samaritans, and the temple on Mt. Moriah in Jerusalem as the holy place of worship for Jews. That same sacred-secular distinction lent poignancy to the lament of the ancient captives in Babylon: "How can we sing the LORD's song in a strange [foreign] land?" (Ps. 137:4, KJV).

As God's holy people, "chosen, set apart," (Lev. 11:44), they could worship fully only in God's holy house.[3] The temple was a holy place, where only more holy people (priests) who were set apart by God could enter and serve. Further, the temple's Holy of Holies contained Israel's most sacred worship symbol—the ark of the covenant—which was regarded as a throne-seat above which the Lord was invisibly enthroned (1 Sam. 4:4). Only the holiest person, the high priest, could enter there, and that in peril of losing his life if God did not accept the sacrifice he offered (Exod. 28:35). Of course, the words and music sung in the temple were also holy; it was the *Lord's song,* without which the sacrifice would be invalid.[4] The Israelites must have thought, "How can we sing it in Babylon, this unholy place, for the pleasure (not the worship) of these unholy people, the Babylonians? God might strike us dead for such blasphemy, as he did Uzzah, who violated the sacred ark by touching it" (see 1 Chron. 13:9-10).

In this chapter, I get to the heart of this book's concern. Critics of nonliturgical evangelicals have said that because we do not understand the holiness of symbolic worship things, like words, actions, places, artifacts, and music, we do not have a proper sense of the holiness of God. Some evangelical leaders have responded saying, "In the new (Christian) covenant, only *persons* can be holy." As a result, some churches refuse to call a worship room a "sanctuary" (a sanctified place). I recall an occasion forty years ago when a Texas Baptist minister led me through his "preaching place" while smoking a foul-smelling cigar! Yet, many parents still teach children that they must act differently in church because "God is there." Somehow, they can't forget that Jesus called the temple "my father's house," so their own worship place is also "the house of God."

The idea that only people can be holy can be traced to the ancient pagan philosophy called *Neoplatonism,* which says: Only spirit can be holy; all material things, including the human body, are and always will be ordinary at best, and sinful at worst.[5] The Christian worldview asserts that because God is Creator and sustainer of the universe, in a sense *all things* become holy to the believer who uses them for the glory of God and for his or her personal good. When specific things, actions, places, and times are used appropriately in worship, they share and communicate something of the character of God, becoming *uniquely holy.*

In our day, congregations divide into opposing camps, arguing whether or not contemporary worship has lost its sense of the holy and is thus *secularizing* the church because the church is influenced too much by the secular world of entertainment, commercialism, and mass media. One group welcomes the breezy informality of demeanor and speech that seems to be borrowed from Christian music concerts and televised religion, while the other complains about a lack of reverence. The "contemporary" crowd complains that the former hymns accompanied by the organ were dreary, archaic, and overloaded with theological jargon. The "traditional" group argues that the new praise-and-worship choruses say nothing *ad nauseum,* and that much contemporary Christian music sounds like a return to the Woodstock rock festival dedicated to noise, sex, and drugs.

Church growth advocates encourage the use of modern speech and popular music styles in order to evangelize the unchurched of Boomer age and younger. Traditionalists are convinced that the change is motivated by our culture's consumerist pursuit of novelty and instant gratification of pleasure desires. As a result, they say, modern services are ordinary entertainment rather than holy worship. In this chapter, I will examine the most conspicuous musical forms that are accused of secularizing worship—Christian rock and contemporary Christian music—and seek for answers.

Secular Becoming Sacred, Especially in Music

No thing, whether object, action, or sound, is intrinsically holy, except in the broad sense that everything we experience is a gift of God's creation. However, things do become symbols and thus communicators of holiness when they are *sanctified* ("set apart"), used in Christian worship, and when accepted as holy by both leaders and worshipers. An ordinary basin or tub is used in the home to hold water; in the church, placed and used appropriately, it becomes a sacred baptismal font. A reading desk in a classroom is secular, but a similar piece of furniture holding a Bible for worship reading becomes a sanctified lectern. Through faith, ordinary bread and drink becomes spiritual food in Holy Communion. Two ordinary sticks of wood placed at right angles to each other become a cross, the most eloquent, visible, holy symbol of our faith. I already have discussed the significance of such sacred signs, since the same symbols speak powerfully to both young and old, to both the scholar and the untrained, through our right-brain, affective perception.

In the study of music in culture, we can discern a constantly recurring pattern of ordinary musical forms becoming holy, simply by their association with the worship of God.[6] Biblical scholars agree that Psalm 29, sung with high reverence in the ancient Hebrew worship of Yahweh, is based on a pagan song used by the Canaanites whom Israel was called to drive out of their Promised Land.

In the early thirteenth century, Francis of Assisi (1181–1226) led an itinerant renewal movement in his native Italy, combining his preaching and singing of the gospel with ministry to the sick and poor. His songs, based on the secular, courtly,

French troubadour forms, were called "spiritual praises" *(laude spirituali)*. For six hundred years the *laude* continued to appear in Europe; though they were not authorized for use in official Roman Catholic worship, these songs continued to be resources for extraliturgical devotions. Francis of Assisi's famous "Canticle of the Sun" is the source of a well-known Christian hymn:

> All creatures of our God and King,
>   lift up your voice and with us sing
>   Alleluia, Alleluia!
> Thou burning sun with golden beam,
>   thou silver moon with softer gleam,
>   O praise him, Alleluia!
> *(trans. William H. Draper)*

In the sixteenth-century Reformation, Martin Luther (1483–1546) wrote hymns in the Bar form (AAB) common to the elegant art music of the Meistersinger and Minnesinger traditions. Some of the tunes were completely secular in origin. In the same era, John Calvin (1509–1564) commissioned the best French poets, Clement Marot and Theodore de Beza, to put the entire psalter in poetic form. Louis Bourgeois (ca. 1510–1561), appointed by Calvin as musical editor for the Genevan Psalter, wrote most of the tunes, borrowing many phrases from secular French *chansons*.[7]

In late eighteenth-century America, British settlers began using secular melodies brought from Scotland, Ireland, and England with traditional English-language hymn texts, for instance, Robert Robinson's "Come, Thou Fount of Every Blessing." Those folk tunes also inspired the writing of new hymns, like "What Wondrous Love Is This." The best-known example of this tradition is the singing of "Amazing Grace," by John Newton (1725–1807), to the Scotch-Irish folk melody popularized in recent years by a bagpipe band.[8]

Often a holy borrowing from ordinary material to serve the church is a sort of parody. Such *contrafacta* were written by Heinrich von Laufenberg (d. 1460), who is identified as "one of the first to adapt German sacred words to old secular tunes, . . . a practice which was afterwards so much in vogue at the time of the Reformation."[9] Later, in the Lutheran tradition, "Flora, meine Freude" ("Flora, my joy") was the model for "Jesu, meine Freude" ("Jesus, My Joy"); and "Innsbruck, ich muss dich lassen" ("Innsbruck, I now must leave you") was altered to become the funeral hymn "O Welt, ich muss dich lassen" ("O World, I Now Must Leave You").

The refrain for the gospel song "At the Cross" parodied a nineteenth-century anonymous secular song "Take Me Home" set to music by John H. Hewitt (known as the "bard of the Confederacy") during the Civil War. Following is the original text:

> Take me home to the place where I first saw the light,
>> to the sweet sunny South take me home,
> where the mockingbird sung [sic] me to rest every night.
>> Ah! why was I tempted to roam!

This was Ralph E. Hudson's adaptation of those words, first published in 1885:

> At the cross, at the cross where I first saw the light,
>> and the burden of my heart rolled away,
> It was there by faith I received my sight,
>> and now I am happy all the day!

Hudson used Hewitt's melody, almost intact, and wrote the refrain text to fit it (borrowing a telling phrase in the first line). Then he added four stanzas of Isaac Watts' penitential hymn "Alas! and Did My Savior Bleed," developed a simple melody for those verses, and published the total result as a gospel song that became very popular in early twentieth-century revivalism.[10]

A Short History: Worship, Entertainment, and the Media

Most of the examples used in this discussion have come from the art music or folk music traditions. When they were written, both Stephen Foster's secular songs and Fanny Crosby's gospel songs fit the definition of "popular" art, in that they were commercial and mass-disseminated. With the passage of time, they too have become folk art. More recently, truly pop forms have crossed over from secular to sacred, for example, southern gospel, western gospel, and country gospel. Because these new forms became the featured attraction in live concerts as well as in radio and television, they aggravated the entertainment versus worship tensions that have existed in the Christian community for some time, and which have recently reached a boiling point.

Has such conflict occurred at other times in church history? We know that during the Middle Ages, in ordinary village life, peasants and nobles sang and danced to Christmas and Easter carols that were excluded from official liturgical worship. Was this an example of using sacred words and music for secular entertainment? Actually, it was probably more a matter of unofficial "folk worship" as contrasted with authorized liturgical acts. Roman Catholic bishops have always determined what music could be used for worship. In the Middle Ages it was Gregorian chant and art music taught by the Schola Cantorum. "Folk" forms—for example, carols and *laude spirituali,* and later the hymns in pre-Vatican II novena services—were heard only outside regular masses and office services.

Also, the idea of a "secular" culture was not understood until comparatively recent times. In the Middle Ages, and even in the early Reformation period, all persons were baptized into the "established" faith of the country in which they were born, and church authorities and civic leaders governed community life in what was understood to be a theocracy (the rule of God). Consequently *all of normal life* tended to be viewed as "sacred."

From our vantage point in history we cannot judge the spiritual impact of carols-with-dance on medieval participants. We might guess that it was a joyful, devotional exercise similar to a modern Christmas program that has moments of God-consciousness but lacks the full and complete, awe-inspiring experience of regular worship.

Sacred-secular distinctions.

Some historians believe that the sacred-secular dichotomy in church music developed largely because of the restrictive decisions of the Reformed leader John Calvin. He so distrusted the seductive charm of music that he eliminated it from his first services. Later, he decreed that certain types of choral and instrumental music might be used in the home and school, but that only unison, unaccompanied, versified psalms would be tolerated in church.

The "radical Reformation" groups (like Congregationalists and Anabaptists) tended to be more democratic in church government, encouraging individual pastors and churches to make their own decision about worship, including its music. Also, their idea of freedom in worship led to the possibility of freedom *from* worship and the developing of "secular" families and a secular culture.

During the eighteenth-century Enlightenment, the idea of a secular world developed fully, with a rational and scientific approach to all of life—religious, social, political, economic, and aesthetic. Musical concerts of nonliturgical music had long been available to nobles, and, during the eighteenth century, secular music performed in public concert halls became entertainment for the bourgeois, the middle class. With the nineteenth-century Industrial Revolution and the beginning of society's move to towns and cities, concerts of both art music and popular music became available to the working class as well.

Revivalism.

Most pious Christians in the early nineteenth century shunned the "worldly" theater and music hall. Yet they found acceptable entertainment (mixed with religion) in the regular visits of the itinerant evangelists and musicians who came regularly to their community. The colorful preaching and singing were as welcome in frontier life as were the performances of the minstrel show or the patent medicine salesman.

Parallel to this history is that of publication. When, after the Industrial Revolution, there was money to be made from a mass market, profit came to commercial church music. Beyond doubt, the nature and use of music in revivalism (and in the nonliturgical churches that conduct evangelistic services every Sunday morning) has contributed to the confusion about what constitutes true worship, as differentiated from entertainment. In that brand of quasi-worship, music has frequently been chosen more on the basis of its familiarity and the pleasing contrast that it gives to serious preaching or praying, than on what the words communicate.

I once heard a veteran gospel singer say, "Music is the adornment of the gospel." The decoration? The accompanying pleasure? The lollipop you get for listening to the sermon? John Chrysostom (ca. 347–407) suggested something similar more than fifteen hundred years ago in a rationale which sounds like Mary Poppins's "spoonful of sugar with medicine" remedy: "When God saw that many men were lazy, and gave themselves only with difficulty to spiritual reading, He wished to make it easy for them, and added the melody to the words, that all being rejoiced by the charm of the music, should sing hymns to him with gladness."[11] However, Chrysostom was not saying that the pleasure of the music should reduce the significance of the hymns' words.

Horatius Bonar was right when he commended Ira Sankey in the story that introduced this chapter. Church music, in any and every style, should not be an entertaining adornment of the gospel. It should be the *gospel itself*—God-in-Christ revealing himself to human beings and their responding in joyful faith and commitment!

Enter sacred concerts.

The confusion between holy and ordinary music increased when "sacred concerts" became available to nineteenth-century believers who rejected the offerings of theaters and music halls. In the 1860s, Philip Phillips, "the Singing Pilgrim," traveled across America to present full services of solo religious song. Soon after, at about the same time Moody called Sankey as his assistant, Phillips offered Sankey an opportunity to travel to the Pacific coast, "to assist him in 'sacred' concerts, for which he was offered flattering pecuniary rewards."[12]

In the same pattern, for the next eighty years, evangelical churches offered occasional concerts to their congregations. These were welcome events experienced in strict moderation, perhaps as often as the twice-a-year choir cantatas. I remember from my youth in the 1930s a certain Winifred Larsen, who was called "the Swedish Kate Smith" because of her resemblance to the popular secular singer both in terms of her appearance and her voice quality. Larsen's performances were welcomed, especially in Scandinavian churches, but I doubt that she ever received generous compensation for her work, and there was certainly no applause after her singing. In those days it never entered our minds that we were being entertained!

Enter mass media.
After 1920, mass evangelism declined in America, as its music and message moved to radio, the new mass medium of the gospel. But radio was more attuned to entertainment than to worship. Undoubtedly this further secularized the message of gospel songs while promoting the personalities of its performers, though still modestly. I remember accompanying George Beverly Shea, our era's (and possibly the all-time best) "gospel singer" on his first tour of the West Coast in 1946. Most Californians had never heard Shea except by radio, though he had already been singing full-time for eight years. By then, in Youth for Christ's Saturday night mix of message and pleasure, applause happened. But in contrast to today, there was only moderate interest in buying the 78-rpm recordings of Shea that were available.

The audio revolution.
Such conservatism in musical entertainment-worship disappeared with the advent of high-fidelity recording soon after World War II. Suddenly, a much larger audience worldwide became audiophiles, passionately interested in listening to music of some sort, and increasingly devoted to one style more than another—whether classical, gospel (both white and African-American), country, western, pop, swing, blues, or jazz. A new industry of "Christian recording" was born, giving a

boost to the careers of the best-known singers of the time: George Beverly Shea, Frank Boggs, Helen Barth, Claude Rhea, Ed Lyman, Rose Arzoomanian, Andráe Crouch, and others. Because record sales depend largely on public appearances, many of those singers employed agents to schedule them in concerts, in churches, and increasingly in mainstream secular venues. Music publishing also profited from increased sales of the newly recorded music, still mostly gospel songs or variants thereof.

A new music for youth.
In 1961 I heard a brand new kind of "Christian" music in England, where I was preparing to participate in a Billy Graham crusade. The "Joy Strings"—featuring Captain Joy Anderson and other soldiers of the Salvation Army—were on stage in Central Hall, Westminster in London. They were strumming guitars and singing—all clustered around a set of traps (theater drums), played by a bearded Army private. The music sounded something like the Peter, Paul, and Mary folk music that emerged at that time in history, but even more like the earlier rock 'n' roll. Before long, British evangelical churches were swamped with youthful performing groups who wrote their own music and sang where anyone would listen, all hoping for a "ministry" as professional performers.

Nothing as radical as that appeared in the United States for several years, though about 1966 "folk musicals" became very popular among youth who were part of the postwar baby boom. In the late 1960s and early 1970s, young converts in West Coast Pentecostal and Baptist groups established an aggressive ministry to combat the twin lures of a sex-and-drug culture and Oriental pagan religions. Their simple gospel message that "Jesus is the one way to God," coupled with some unconventional life styles, led folks to call them "Jesus people" or "Jesus freaks."[13] Most important to our story, they developed a new style of music with a secular (basically rock) beat, accompanied by electronic guitars. That was the beginning of what we now identify as "contemporary Christian music," which has become an enormous commercial industry. More significantly, while it is free of control by the organized church, it has exerted a powerful influence on worship music in our day. Indeed, it is possibly the one socio-musical factor most responsible for the modern revolution in the church.

Music as cultural icons becoming idols.
Popular wisdom says that ours is the most musical culture the world has ever known—that is, if a musical culture is created by a passion for *listening to* and not *making* music. Almost all these music lovers attend concerts and/or listen incessantly to recordings—in the car, in the open air (often while jogging), and indoors. Churches regularly announce and distribute tickets for the appearances of CCM stars in the community. Newspapers announce those concerts in the entertainment section, not on the church page. Seniors take tours to Branson, Missouri, to attend concerts of country or country-gospel music. In addition, many churches offer concerts to the community, sometimes all sacred and sometimes in a variety of styles—classical, swing, jazz, or country.[14] In December "singing Christmas trees" appear in many churches, offering several nights of carol singing and other music.

Christian radio also helps to make music an idol in the culture. Fifty years ago, when I began my ministry at WMBI in Chicago, religious broadcasting was eclectic in style and partly educational in purpose. We sang gospel music, but also anthems and traditional hymns and psalms. Art music was given ample time, especially in recorded form. But we also presented live performances of historic and contemporary violin and piano sonatas, string trios, organ music, and art songs. I remember preparing "music appreciation" broadcasts (in small imitation of Walter Damrosch in the 1920s and Karl Haas on today's NPR), and even teaching piano improvisation on hymn tunes via radio.

Today, many radio stations broadcast contemporary Christian music twenty-four hours a day. Others specialize in country gospel music or in some other pop form, tacitly suggesting that their fans are unable or unwilling to respond to other music styles and thereby encouraging them to demand those identical sounds in church on Sunday. As a result, certain megachurches today offer worship choices on consecutive weekends: praise-and-worship style, CCM style, country style, and jazz style. In fact, *style* has become today's chief musical concern—not the text or its theology.

The Gospel Rock Phenomenon

With all the historical evidence that no music is intrinsically sacred or secular, and that many ordinary forms have become holy because of their words and their use in Christian ministry, why does the modern church have so much difficulty accepting today's prevailing popular music in Christian worship? After thirty-five years of exposure in our culture, why does Christian rock and its derivative form, contemporary Christian music (and even praise-and-worship singing with its high-decibel, driving accompaniment), still sound a bit secular to many churchgoers? I have suggested some answers in my previous chronicle of the use of music in revivalism and in sacred concerts, both of which tend to be a confusing mixture of entertainment and worship.

To be fair, it must be acknowledged that a number of contemporary Christian artists are committed to worship and ministry, not entertainment. Also, the phrase "contemporary Christian music" includes a wide variety of musical styles, some of which are quite appropriate for holy use. These should be gleaned carefully from the glut of music that's available, and used thoughtfully. Some singers and instrumentalists possess brilliant, creative gifts in both words and music, though all of them—like all of us—would profit from the refining fire of additional training and continuous self-criticism.

The following analysis refers directly to *secular rock music*. I then show how it applies to today's religious pop forms as well, because of their similarities and derivation.

Rock music's character.
The New Harvard Dictionary of Music gives this technical description of rock music:

Rock is electrical, in its use of amplification, distortion, and eventual production of sound. The electric guitar is the most important melodic instrument and is played with a sustained and florid style made possible by electronic technology. The lyrics are usually intensely personal or political and are often obscure in poetical style. Formally, rock was the first popular genre to develop extended and often complex structures, made possible by its origins in live performance and its later dissemination on long-playing records. . . .

Gradually, however, the term [rock] came to be understood again as appropriate for a single dialect of the pluralistic media-disseminated popular music of the 1970s and 80s, characterized by a basic instrumentation of electric guitars, bass, keyboard, and drums (increasingly augmented or replaced by synthesized sounds); a fast, driving rhythm punctuated by prominent and often dominant drums and bass.[15]

The dictionary names a number of related musical dialects, including jazz rock, art rock, folk rock, country rock, punk rock, New Wave rock, and heavy metal. Many of these subgenres have parallel representatives and expressions in contemporary music with Christian words.

I believe rock music is the *most primitive* popular music form to appear in modern Western culture. It possesses little significant melody and shows no harmonic development, both of which are vital in creating "integrated" music of any style. Rock is not sophisticated even in its rhythmic design. What it does have is a driving *beat* and a painful level of volume that no doubt has damaged the hearing of many listeners.

Some critics insist that damage to the auditory nerve may not be rock's greatest hurt to humanity. Charles Reich says, "The new music rocks the whole body, and penetrates the soul."[16] As a culture watcher for evangelicals, Kenneth A. Myers identifies rock music and television as the symbols of today's pop culture, whose two characteristics are a quest for novelty and a desire for instant gratification. He joins many authorities in warning that, in this and in other ways, the evangelical church largely has been taken over by that culture. Perhaps many parents have welcomed "Christian rock" as a preferred alternative to secular versions with their obscene, antisocial words.

Myers talks about the *rock myth*—a primitivist-pantheist concept that is a radical departure from historic Western ideas about thinking and being. He is convinced that the rock idiom itself is more destructive to the human spirit than dirty lyrics. Myers observes, "The essence of that myth was that rock would offer a form of spiritual deliverance by providing a superior form of knowledge, a form that was immediate rather than reflective, physical rather than mental, and emotional rather than volitional."[17]

From both a theological and a musicological viewpoint, we should be slow to condemn any style of music created by God's creatures as intrinsically evil. A study of the world's folk musics reveals many sounds which sound strange, even weird, to those outside of the culture. Yet missionaries have often used indigenous music to express Christian worship.

The one element of rock music we *must* condemn, however, is the dynamics level that destroys God's good gift of hearing. We also need to ask whether rock music is the best popular form for young people to use to express the beauty and truth of the gospel of Jesus Christ. Moreover, it is apparent that if the negative opinions of rock music are held by people in a local church, this musical genre cannot become the common form of that congregation.

Rock music's associations.

The *Harvard Dictionary* rarely includes discussion of general culture in connection with the appearance of musical forms. However, contributor Patrick Will apparently believes that rock's music style is related to the societal attitudes and actions of its creators and its listeners:

Socially, rock was aligned from the beginning with a

mostly white and young constituency claiming to be at odds with traditional American attitudes toward drug use, sex, and the work ethic. . . . [the] provocative dress and behavior by performers and audience, [dramatize] rock's continuing alliance with attitudes at variance with those of mainstream Anglo-American culture.[18]

Most observers agree that rock is an expression of *rebellion*— against parents, against society in general or political authority figures in particular, against overpowering and uncontrollable circumstances, or against God. Allen Bloom, a professor at the University of Chicago, insists that rock has one message—that of *eros,* sexual desire, and that it is a strong contributor to "the closing of the American mind."[19] The *New Harvard Dictionary* declares that heavy metal music, "a subgenre of rock music characterized by sluggish rhythms and high amplification applied to blues-derived musical forms . . . was generally associated with drug-taking, working-class audiences."[20] Other critics suggest that the music is its own kind of opiate, which may be confirmed by somebody's casual remark that their music "is more important to them than sex."

I need not discuss whether this music is the cause or simply the accompaniment of self-destructive, culture-perverting behavior. Its association with these things alone says that the phrase "Christian rock" should be an oxymoron. Of course, I am *not* suggesting that all persons who enjoy rock music commit acts of immorality or rebellion. It might be expected that in the thirty-five-year history of the rock culture, many of its early devotees have matured and cleaned up their act. Yet rock lives on, and the culture that spawned it has not improved, either in its use of drugs or in its preoccupation with virtually uncontrolled sex.

In light of the size and power of the contemporary Christian music industry, I may be simply "spitting into the wind" in expressing this concern. However, I believe such concerns must be considered in order to understand the argument that some types of contemporary worship music are secularizing the church, rendering its witness impotent. I ask again: Cannot the

Christian recording industry promote better forms to express our young people's love of, and submission to the servant-King Jesus Christ?

Rock music's commercial identity.

The admitted size and power of today's Christian music industry testifies to its commercial success. Just as in the secular music world, big money feeds it—money paid by the concert-goers and record buyers and received by the stars, promoters, and publishers. Of all the contemporary evidence of evil in the general (and the Christian) culture, the Bible warns us specifically about *materialism.* Money—a simple medium of exchange by which we purchase our needs for survival—was a temptation to believers even in the first century. "For the love of money is a root of all kinds of evil, and in their eagerness to be rich some have wandered away from the faith and pierced themselves with many pains" (1 Tim. 6:10).

"All kinds of evil" includes the manipulative character of musical icons borrowed from commercial culture. It is wise to remember that most media advertising exists to *create a need* that can be met at a cost. In such a milieu of falsehood, it is hard for the voice of truth to be heard, or, if it is heard, to be perceived as truth.[21]

Money is not a spiritual problem to us until we always want *more* and unless we use it selfishly. Many folks have criticized Christian artists who join secular record companies for multi-album deals with seven-figure bonuses. Other artists have been censured by some Christians because they have "crossed over" from the Christian market to mainline secular pop music, presumably sacrificing their Christian witness in order to make more money. These allegations may or may not be true, yet the temptations of big money are certainly there.

Rock music's identity as entertainment.

Here we arrive at the heart of today's dilemma of Christian music in worship. Thirty years ago eager young musicians justified singing religious words to blatantly secular music as "evangelism"—a means of reaching unchurched young people who were addicted to those musical sounds. Later, others rationalized it as "ministry"—perhaps a communication of God's truth or an experience of fellowship. Finally, some Christian musicians and their promoters billed their concerts as an opportunity for "worship." Admittedly, some folks still believe those are the objectives.

But more and more, contemporary Christian music is acknowledged to be an *alternative form of entertainment,* and entertainment that is preferable for Christians because words of evangelism, ministry, and worship are substituted for expressions of rebellion and addiction. But if the objectives are no longer *spiritual* ones, are those holy words not being prostituted for unholy purposes? On that basis, I applaud Christian artists who have "crossed over"! If a Christian is going to sing for purposes of entertainment, the texts should not be holy words. At the same time, if more money is involved, we can hope that these artists are practicing Christian stewardship.

A Personal Experience with Contemporary Christian Music

I have tried always to be open to all musical sounds, sacred *and* secular, from Josquin des Prés to William Bolcom, and from gospel to country to jazz to rap. Recently I attended a program featuring two contemporary Christian singers in order to evaluate how and why I respond as I do to that musical medium. The artists were believers I know well and respect highly for their faith commitment and their lives of humble, faithful witness and Christian service.

The voices wouldn't be called "beautiful" perhaps, but they had remarkable ranges, great flexibility, good intonation, and durability. My first response was positive, even enthusiastic. What energy! What power! What excitement! The music had some variety: a hard, driving song that split the eardrums was followed by one that began more quietly but ended just as big. I couldn't identify all of the words, but enough phrases were repeated so that I recognized them as true (even if incomplete) gospel. The singing included some remarkable, mesmerizing vocal gymnastics, with glides and hiccups in falsetto voice.

But after about ten minutes of pleasure, my most compelling sense was that the concert was *too much*—too much sound, too much emotion, too much repetition of words, for too long. It seemed that each selection would never end, and I tended to hope that it wouldn't and pray that it would all at the same time. And when it was over, it didn't seem to be finished. It just stopped or trailed off, and I kept hoping that the next song would bring a sense of completeness, of real satisfaction. So I stayed on, hoping and hurting.

Is this what they mean when they say that rock is a "musical fix"? Many in the audience seemed to feel the same as I. Some didn't applaud at all; others did so listlessly as if they too were a little numb—and never with the roar that follows an operatic climax of the "three tenors." I left at the intermission in order to relieve the pain in my ears and stop the roller-coaster ride of my emotions, feeling both seduced and manipulated. That music didn't provide "immediate gratification" to me—only agonizing teasing.

Every generation identifies with the music with which it has grown up. I understand that contemporary pop music is not necessarily the communicator of evil; it may even say something to some persons about God. But for all the reasons I have stated, and others, I am convinced it is a dead-end street for church music.

Definitions of Entertainment and Worship

Can a star singer shift from witness/ministry/worship to entertainment simply by announcing the fact? Is there no real difference between worship and entertainment? I believe there is a world of difference, even though I have some inkling as to why today's culture has confused the two; I have tried to explain that in this chapter.

Entertainment typically results from the *work of others* for my interest, pleasure, recreation, amusement, or diversion. Good entertainment edifies me when, through phenomena of

179

God's creation, it provides renewal for body, mind, and emotions. In the experience of entertainment, as a Christian believer I may momentarily thank God for such a gift. But, even though the setting (as in a symphony concert) may have many similarities to a church service, the experience is not holy worship, even for me personally, and certainly not for the gathered group.

Worship, on the other hand, is the *work of the worshiper* for the glory and pleasure of God. I am edified (helped, blessed, made more holy, ministered to) by worshiping God, because my attention and energy are directed toward comprehending, experiencing, and responding to who God is and what God has done. Of course, my worship, my work for God, has elements that provide pleasure, such as my recognition of friends and cobelievers; the ambiance of familiar sights, sounds, and actions; or my response to humor in the sermon or to beauty in the music. But this pleasure has "worship meaning" only as it makes me aware of God's presence or contributes to my "work for God"—*my pleasure in God himself.* It is for this reason St. Augustine felt that anything in worship that distracted him from centering on God—even if that thing was intended to help him experience God—was sinful. He said, "So oft as it befalls me to be more moved with the voice than with the ditty [song], I confess to have grievously offended: at which time I wish rather not to have heard the music."[22]

On Mixing Worship and Entertainment

It would seem, then, that all of us have difficulty preventing holy worship from degenerating into ordinary entertainment. The church sponsors (or participates in) many activities that combine worship and entertainment, so they seem to coalesce into one. A "sacred concert" is perhaps the best example.

Anyone attending a performance by Steven Curtis Chapman, Twila Paris, Dean Wilder, David Ford, George Beverly Shea or the Bowker brothers, or even Don Hustad probably will come away commenting on the artist's physical appearance, personality, vocal or instrumental skills and quality, stage presence, or the ability to communicate emotion and ideas. It is difficult to make such an occasion one in which God alone is the revered center of attention—not musical art or the performer. I would guess that, for most people, the experience is primarily one of pleasure in the performance. Listeners who are believers may recognize truthful words or a hymn tune and give a cognitive/affective "amen" that is momentary worship.

Other religious events perhaps are not so closely associated with entertainment, yet music's function in them may still be ambiguous. I have occasionally awakened my drowsy students by saying that the traditional revival or evangelistic crusade is "show business": Its singers and speakers often use God's gifts of personality and talent in purposely sensational ways, to draw attention to a communication of the gospel.[23] In the weekend seeker events at Willow Creek Community Church, performers use sacred music by soloists and instruments. Apparently, the church intends that music to be entertainment for nonworshiping seekers, though it could be true worship for believers who are present.

Billy Graham crusades often use music in the same way. One of their televised services featured the Brooklyn Tabernacle Gospel Choir. It seems to me that, when we European-American believers respond enthusiastically to African-American gospel music, we may be reacting to the titillation of unusual, more exotic sounds than our own mundane, "less colorful" music offers. Unless we translate that pleasure into something more—and this can be done, but not easily—the experience is more entertainment than worship. Even more, according to Erik Routley, when that happens, we could be trivializing the culture and spiritual situation from which it comes.[24]

The parachurch group Promise Keepers has attracted large groups of men to weekend conferences that offer unusual opportunities for high emotion in worship and sober commitment in spiritual renewal. Participants have returned home saying, "We must worship like that in our church," forgetting that part of the novel experience was due to the "men only" setting. Much of the rest can be credited to the Promise Keepers' atmosphere, which combines Super Sunday football and a county fair with a Billy Graham crusade. Even if that spirit could be duplicated in a typical Sunday service, it could not be repeated week after week.

Many churches could replicate one aspect of those meetings with great benefit to their congregations. Promise Keepers musicians sing contemporary Christian music and lead the congregation in praise-and-worship choruses. Yet at least half of their music consists of solid, traditional hymn forms, like "Holy, Holy, Holy," "Crown Him with Many Crowns," "Rejoice, the Lord Is King," "O Worship the King," "All Hail the Power of Jesus' Name," "Joyful, Joyful, We Adore Thee," "Christ the Lord Is Risen Today," and "Great Is Thy Faithfulness." In their sessions for ministers, the music leaders explain that they choose songs from both the new and the old *because they want to attract men of all ages.* Sad to say, I have never heard of a church that changed its music repertoire to a better balance on the basis of Promise Keepers' good example!

Paraworship activities in the local church contribute to the confusion as well. Evangelicals multiply church gatherings for educational, inspirational, and even recreational purposes. Music is usually part of the action—in Sunday school and other teaching sessions, prayer meetings, fellowship gatherings, missionary groups, and retreats. None of these has the concentration on serious, cognitive/emotive worship that we should expect Sunday morning; yet music is used in them all. When we sing sacred words and melodies for purely social or recreational purposes, we tend to jeopardize their holiness in worship.

Solutions—Some Radical—to the Entertainment Problem

Evangelicals cannot easily make up for their long-term worship deficiencies, even if the current infatuation with secular cultural forms passes. But we must make a beginning by doing some or all of the following things.

Safeguard the church's experiences of full worship.
Church leaders must identify the nature of each activity planned and choose the music accordingly. They should work to make all music with religious texts as meaningful as possible, whether the objective is worship, evangelism, education, ministry, fellowship, or some combination of those activities. Further, they should develop the central worship service as "most holy" in church life, choosing holy materials for its purposes and treating them as holy.

Break the controlling tie between church music and secular pop styles.
Some readers will call this suggestion impossible, even preposterous. Though church music forms have often been nourished by ordinary popular music, I believe this is not possible in today's culture. In the long history from Francis of Assisi to the gospel song era (as recounted earlier in this chapter), holy words sanctified the secular music styles with which they were associated.

Further, the music itself was altered enough to assume a new "sacred" identity. For instance, whereas the gospel song was virtually identical to its secular models in 1860, gospel music became an important sacred style that developed independently for at least a hundred years. By contrast, since 1960, contemporary Christian music has trailed along in the wake of *all* the emerging secular pop forms—pop, rock, alternative, heavy metal, reggae, and rap—none of which was well suited to express the gospel. Nevertheless, arrangers and composers imitated each new form as soon as it appeared.

I contend that church music cannot tolerate that degree of slavish attachment to secular pop styles. Those styles change too frequently to be useful in expressing the historic and continuing identity of the church. Because each generation is loyal to the secular pop style it learns as teenagers, imitating those ephemeral forms in church will cause continuing generational wars and congregational fragmentation. Finally, when secular pop styles become idols for their devotees, they cannot express unqualified allegiance to God.

So how can we break pop music's control over church music? First, acknowledge the validity of such a goal and resolve to pursue it. We do this for the long-range good of the church's worship life and the character formation of each member of the community.

Second, in addition to traditional and folk music styles, choose the very best examples of popular forms for young singers in the church—those songs with sound lyrics and good music. As in all commercial culture, the most popular forms may not be the best. Not all pop music exhibits the primitivism and aesthetic sterility of Christian rock and the poorest contemporary Christian music. Young people will enjoy the better written pop music, particularly if it is rhythmically "alive." More importantly they will learn more, musically and spiritually, by singing it.

Third, encourage church members to support those Christian musicians who sing the strongest music and who validate their performances (whether pop sacred music as genuine ministry or pop secular for good entertainment) with their own Christian witness and lifestyle.

Consider the different ways we listen to music.
I believe that we also must reexamine our responses to different music styles. Everybody listens to and understands more than one kind of music. We listen more to our favorite styles (whether rock, country, classical, or whatever). But most people can listen differently to another style, say, the national anthem, and appreciate it as a patriotic symbol of our love of country. Similarly, many folks are brought together by singing summer camp music and school fight songs but they probably do not listen to any of that music at great length.

Nicholas Wolterstorff proposes that there are three kinds of music in culture: art music, pop music, and tribal music.[25] The first two styles could encompass the favorite entertainment music of everyone. But *tribal music* is that which brings all the different members of the culture together—both classical fans and pop devotees—like the music that expresses patriotism, or school loyalty, *or worship.*

In times past, such a divergence in entertainment and unity in worship services was normal. For Wolterstorff, who worships in a Christian Reformed Church, the accepted tribal music includes Dutch versions of metrical psalms, as well as hymns, gospel songs, organ music, and anthems. Today the church in general has difficulty "coming together" in worship because many folks expect their entertainment music and their worship music to be identical. I believe the only solution is to find a new tribal music for worship upon which we can all agree, always remembering that *our music for worship should not be the music we worship!*

This means that, eventually, all Christians must enlarge their musical and textual tastes, sometimes because their preferred style (whether art or pop) has become an idol, and *always* because we must mature in our expressions of worship. In so doing, we should be able to worship with others in our human family—both our parents and our children!

Rejoice when you can.
Occasionally, we see light in the darkness—a glimmer of hope that high-quality music and hymnody will eventually prevail. The November 1994 issue of *CCM Magazine,* which promotes contemporary Christian music stars such as Petra, Carman, Sandi Patti, and Amy Grant, carried an article by former Christian artist John Fischer. He reflects:

> I've been spending a little time with some of the grand old hymns of the faith lately. Some of them make food for thought on the strength of their titles alone. Take "And Can It Be That I Should Gain" or "I Cannot Tell Why He Whom Angels Worship," for instance, as statements of grace. Or how about "Majestic Sweetness Sits Enthroned" or "O Could I Speak The Matchless Worth" as statements of worship and awe.
>
> After a steady diet of more popular contemporary worship music, walking into one of these great hymns is a little like boarding the Queen Mary and setting out to sea after rowing around the harbor for some time in a one-man

kayak. You hardly even feel like you're in a boat, and there are endless rooms to discover. A verse, a line, even a phrase, can lead to unexplored levels of reflection and insight.

This is not to fault contemporary worship music as much as it is to fault the culture out of which much of it is written. Which is why there may be something to be learned from these expressions of songwriters from across the distant waters of a hundred years or more. What doctrines were evident to them that elude us now? Are there themes that show up in hymns that don't show up in more contemporary forms of worship music? If so, it might indicate a deficiency in our spiritual understanding or, most likely, in our culture as a whole.[26]

To Mr. Fischer I say, "Welcome to the reality of unchanging paradigms, both theological and aesthetic." All of us musicians should be as honest when we realize that we have short-changed the Christian public—in church or in concert—and should show our repentance in different literature and perhaps even new music styles.

"But I Became a Believer through Christian Rock Music"

I have heard this kind of testimony all my life, with credit given to many different music styles—from gospel song to country gospel to Christian folk to whatever! We can easily understand that each style might seem to become holy to the one who was attracted to the gospel message through its use.

The truth is, each of us becomes a believer *only* through God's work of grace in which we are "born anew"—baptized by the Holy Spirit into the body of Christ. God's Spirit uses just one agent of communication: the *Word of God,* spoken or sung. The music style itself may be the "bait" used by those whom Jesus called "people fishers" (Matt. 4:19) to carry the message. I have performed many kinds of music in evangelistic crusades, and once participated in "art music" evangelism in

France in concerts sponsored by the Greater Europe Mission. Many other entertaining media—athletic events, puppet shows, clowning, or magic—have been so used, without inferring that they should become the *norm* for worship of new believers.

Closing Thoughts

Holiness is not only a matter of musical style. It also is determined by the manner of presentation, and especially by the *intent* of the artist. A musician may present a thoroughly traditional "sacred" work—an anthem, an organ piece, or a solo—in such an exhibitionistic way that the result is not worship, but entertainment.

Further, music does not deserve all the blame for secularizing contemporary worship. Early in this chapter, I mentioned speech styles that are borrowed from contemporary Christian music concerts and religious television talk shows. A recent news article identified an addition to a megachurch staff as the new "comic" preacher. (In appendix II, I discuss the obsession with stylized minidramas that "sell" the sermon.) In every instance we must ask, "Does this form or technique finally draw attention and give honor to God, or to itself and its performers?"

Very early in my ministry, I struggled with the awareness that evangelicals seemed to have a penchant for entertainment in religious contexts, like Youth for Christ rallies, evangelistic crusades, and certain Sunday evening services. At that time I reasoned that it satisfied a need created by our pietistic abstinence from "worldly" things, like theater and dance. I decided then that it would be preferable to create a Christian entertainment industry that would supply wholesome entertainers and musicians who would use ordinary, healthy styles and texts, not holy materials.

Today, we do have available Christian entertainers—drama groups, illusionists, and humorists—even though, thanks to the media, worldly entertainment forms also are enjoyed by most believers. Perhaps only in music do we still desecrate holy things—make them ordinary—by singing worship words for entertainment purposes. While we should welcome every tasteful, healthy opportunity for pleasure and recreation in our gloomy, war-torn, emotionally frayed world, we cannot be surprised if someone suggests that we evangelicals, along with the rest of our culture, are "amusing ourselves to death"[27] and thus demonstrating our unrepentant secularism.

In the next chapter, I discuss what it means to worship God in artistic truth in a culture of aesthetic relativism. Even though worship must not be viewed as entertainment or primarily as an artistic experience, it must be aesthetically "good" because we have been created and redeemed by the Supreme Creator.

7

Worshiping God
in Artistic Truth

In a Strange Land
of Aesthetic Relativism

God is good, God is truth, God is beauty, praise him!
—Percy Dearmer

Once upon a time a man, who seemed to have most of the material things needed for a good life, determined to find Truth. So he traveled to big cities and small villages. He traveled to the seacoast and to the desert. He traveled at last to the highest mountains. At the highest peak of the highest mountain, living far back in a cave he found an old hag of a woman. Her eyes were red and watery. Her hands were gnarled and twisted. Her hair was matted and tangled, her back bent with age. . . . But her voice! When she spoke, it was like a chorus of angels. And, somehow, the man knew that he had found Truth.

He stayed with Truth for a year and a day and learned all that she could teach him. At the end of that time, he said that he must return to his own home. He promised to share with everyone he met the things that he had learned from Truth.

"But," he asked, "when I tell them how I learned these things, they will ask me about my teacher. What shall I tell them about you?"

And the old ugly woman, whose eyes were red and watery, whose hands were gnarled and twisted, whose hair was matted and tangled, whose back was bent with age, . . . but whose voice when she spoke was like a chorus of angels, said: "When you speak of me, say that I am young and beautiful."[1]

It is appropriate that a chapter about aesthetics in true worship should begin with a story that is itself a work of art. It sets the imagination soaring! Does it say, like the motto at the beginning of the chapter, that goodness, truth, and beauty are closely related—a "trinity" of God's gifts to us? Does it suggest that truth and beauty are timeless—simultaneously old and freshly new? Does it challenge the popular idea that truth and beauty are always "pleasant and pretty"?

In *Jubilate II,* I point out that beauty and creativity in human experience began with the primal creation.[2] The first chapter of the Bible says, "God saw everything that he had made, and indeed, it was very good"; that is, it was what God intended. Our planet is the God-given resource for all things artistic, and it provides everything essential to sustain the life of God's creatures (Gen. 1:28-31). God created humankind "in his image," so like him, we love, and think, and create, and enjoy our handiwork. Scripture reminds us also that, from the beginning, God's Spirit endowed human beings with different thinking-planning-creating gifts. Jabal "was the ancestor of those who live in tents and have livestock," and his brother Jubal "was the ancestor of all those who play the lyre and pipe" (Gen. 4:20-21). Both Jabal's and Jubal's areas of workmanship figured prominently in the ancient Hebrew worship tradition, providing the culture's best lambs and steers for the burnt offerings, and the finest instrumental music to accompany the singing of Levite vocalists during the sacrifices.

Aesthetics matter in today's functional worship as well. We bring the arts of words and speech and gesture, of music and architecture and furnishings, as *gifts* to God and as *aids* to our experiencing of worship. This chapter will declare that, in today's culture, many of us are not measuring up to our potential in achieving scriptural standards of worship beauty. This is partly because we tend to reject the judgment of our best artists, labeling it "elitist."

I call the root cause of this problem *aesthetic relativism*—the idea that criteria of judgment are relative, varying with individuals and their environments; or *aesthetic egalitarianism*—the belief that all persons are equal, even in aesthetic discernment, so one person's standard is as valid as that of any other person. In a society in which some believe that "grunge is beautiful," agreement on worship beauty will not come easily. Such an egalitarian philosophy may be a poorly masked rationalization for our culture's failure to support aesthetic education in the public schools and the church because art must give way to more popular or more practical concerns like athletics, mathematics, and computer science.

Humanities expert George Steiner believes that Western culture is now experiencing aesthetic "twilight." He states, "A deep intuition whispers to us that the high noon of the arts, music, and possibly literature lies behind us in the West. It tells us that the chances for the reappearance of an Aeschylus, a Dante, a Michelangelo, a Shakespeare, or a Mozart are very slim."[3] Steiner reasons that this is true because our society is indifferent to questions about the existence of God. He evidently believes that even secular liberal arts education must be based on some sort of theological position:

> The question we have to ask is, Can we have a liberal program in the humanities that does not at least face the question of a theological foundation? . . . Ours is a culture of "anything goes." In it, neither the affirmation of the possibility of God nor the denial of such existence is commanding. . . . Whether certain dimensions are possible in literature, in the arts, in music, if this view prevails, seems to me at least an open question.[4]

Biblical Standards of Aesthetics

I once said that when we are responding to the admonition to "worship the LORD in the beauty of holiness" (1 Chron. 16:29, KJV), we should not confuse the "beauty of holiness" with the "holiness of beauty." At that time I was convinced that the phrase spoke of *spiritual,* not physical, beauty, based on my understanding that the ancient Scriptures associate the idea of "beauty" only with the human face (Gen. 29:17).

Now it appears that "the beauty of holiness" is "holy physical beauty" after all! Modern translations use the words "holy array" and "holy splendor" to speak of the beauty of priestly worship robes (see Exod. 28:2; 1 Chron. 16:29; 2 Chron. 20:21; Ps. 96:9). This confirms the emphasis of the previous chapter in which I suggest that ordinary, beautiful vestments become holy, beautiful vestments when they are used in the worship of God.

William Hendricks, a theologian with an interest in aesthetics, believes that God intends for humans to find the divine in art because all true beauty says something to us about God. "Beauty in all of its expressions is the first of God's ways with creatures. Beauty, truth and goodness all rest in God so they're all eternal. But, as it pertains to creation and humankind, we observe beauty before we learn to talk about goodness and conceptualize truth."[5]

The Bible itself is a work of art. For instance, the authors of the Psalms—the songbook of Solomon's temple—crafted their poetry very carefully. The introduction to the book of Psalms in the *NIV Study Bible* describes their beauty:

> The Psalms are impassioned, vivid and concrete; they are rich in images, in simile and metaphor. Assonance, alliteration and wordplays abound in the Hebrew text. Effective use of repetition and the piling up of synonyms and complements to fill out the picture are characteristic. . . . Close study of the Psalms discloses that the authors often composed with an overall design in mind. . . . A sense of symmetry is pervasive. . . . The authors of the psalms crafted their compositions very carefully. They were heirs of an ancient art (in many details showing that they had inherited a poetic tradition that goes back hundreds of years), and they developed it to a state of high sophistication.[6]

In the Torah, the detailed directions for building the tabernacle and its furnishings show that even though this was a portable worship facility in a fairly primitive culture, it was to be a structure of awe and beauty, to the glory of God. In Exodus 35 Moses tells the Israelites God's commands on how they were to proceed:

> Take from among you an offering to the LORD; let whoever is of a generous heart bring the LORD's offering: gold, silver, and bronze; blue, purple, and crimson yarns, and fine linen; goats' hair, tanned rams' skins, and fine leather; acacia wood, oil for the light, spices for the anointing oil and for the fragrant incense, and onyx stones and gems to be set in the ephod and the breastpiece.
>
> All who are skillful among you shall come and make all that the LORD has commanded: the tabernacle, its tent and its covering, its clasps and its frames, its bars, its pillars, and its bases; the ark with its poles, the mercy seat, and the curtain for the screen; the table with its poles and its utensils, and the bread of the Presence; the lampstand also for the light, with its utensils and its lamps, and the oil for the light; and the altar of incense, with its poles, and the anointing oil and the fragrant incense, and the screen for the entrance, the entrance of the tabernacle; the altar of burnt offering, with its grating of bronze, its poles and all its utensils, the basin with its stand; the hangings of the court, its pillars and its bases, and the screen for the gate of the court; the pegs of the tabernacle and the pegs of the court, and their cords; the finely worked vestments for ministering in the holy place, the holy vestments for the priest Aaron, and the vestments of his sons, for their service as priests. (Exod. 35:5-19)

Though all who were generous were invited to contribute financially, God did not sanction aesthetic egalitarianism. Only those who were "skillful" in the arts—cutters, carvers, artisans, weavers, and those working with gold, silver and bronze—were asked to participate. Later in the same chapter, Moses made it clear that (1) artistic talents are given by the Holy Spirit; (2) they are improved with training and experience; and (3) mature artists are expected to teach younger persons similarly endowed (see Exod. 35:30-35).

Christian theologians have acknowledged that all creativity is the gift of God the Spirit. Just as "all truth is God's truth," so "all beauty is God's beauty." C. S. Lewis declared:

> There is . . . a sense in which all natural agents, even inanimate ones, glorify God continually by revealing the powers he has given them. And in that sense we, as natural agents, do the same. . . . An excellently performed piece of music, as a natural operation which reveals in a very high degree the peculiar powers given to man, will thus always glorify God whatever the intention of the performers may be.[7]

The ancient Hebrew law required that everything offered in tabernacle worship was to be the *best* available—the best ox in the herd, the healthiest lamb with best conformation, the cleanest grain without mold, and the clearest, nonrancid oil. We must believe that the same standard applied to the words and music and dance that were performed in connection with the sacrifices; they were to be the best the culture could produce. In the appointment of musicians, "Chenaniah, leader of the Levites in music, was to direct the music, for he understood it" (1 Chron. 15:22). The challenge to excellence was included even in the songs of Hebrew worship, "Sing to [the LORD] a new song; play skillfully on the strings, with loud shouts" (Ps. 33:3).

Although the New Testament does not contain the same emphasis on aesthetics in human workmanship, it does express the idea that God should receive our best worship arts. In Hebrews 13:15-16, the author says that since the old covenant sacrifices are no longer needed, "through [Jesus], then, let us continually offer a *sacrifice of praise* to God, that is, the fruit of lips that confess his name. Do not neglect to do good and to share what you have, for such sacrifices are pleasing to God" (italics added).

Gifts to God under the New Covenant—gifts of fashioned words, of music, and of all other worship arts—certainly should be as complete, as perfect, as functional, and as beautiful as those under the Old Covenant. But our best gifts in worship services must be matched with our best in Christian stewardship—sharing what we have with others.

Worship Aesthetics Today

What is an acceptable standard of aesthetics for Christian worship in our day? Nicholas Wolterstorff, professor of philosophy at Yale University, believes that church music must be "generally good and satisfying to use." It must possess "aesthetic merit," which includes the requirement that it be suited to each liturgical text/action in its theological/aesthetic culture and that it contribute to a sense of "fittingness" between all parts of the worship text and action. All of this means, says Wolterstorff, that *music must serve the liturgy* "without undue awkwardness and difficulty . . . [and] without tending to distract attention from the actions." Such a standard of beauty plus functionality parallels God's creative acts and should be extended to include all worship arts. Wolterstorff says it is doubtful wisdom to use *high* art music for worship because it requires "aesthetic contemplation," which distracts us from the contemplation of God.[8]

In *Jubilate II*, I have already outlined the Christian's responsibility to live aesthetically.[9] In answer to the question "What is good church music?" I listed there four types of worship music in common use. These are:

1. High art church music (often called "classical").

Few churches possess the resources in talent necessary to produce music such as Bach's *St. Matthew Passion* or Handel's *Messiah* on a regular basis. Yet, culture watcher Kenneth Myers says that "high culture" has a greater potential for establishing a sensibility that is beneficial and constructive to Western society than more popular forms.[10] This is like saying that Leonard Bernstein has contributed more significantly to American culture than Madonna, even though he is "less popular." Until recently, most churches have felt that God was honored and the congregation edified when a single piece of art music, like Handel's "Hallelujah" chorus or Mozart's "Gloria" (from his Twelfth Mass)[11] could be learned and presented acceptably. Today, some pastors have forbidden the use of such music in church! Evidently they believe that modern audiences will not accept it or would not benefit from it.

Some Christians who are lovers of art music will object to Wolterstorff's caution stated above about using art music in church because they see a concert hall experience as one of profound worship. Certain philosophers have reminded us that the *artistic* experience is very much akin to the *religious*, and I believe one can be mistaken for the other. I remember an occasion when I was one of twenty-five hundred listeners who sat in Chicago's Symphony Hall experiencing the transcendent music of Mahler's Fifth Symphony conducted by Daniel Barenboim. Though it was midwinter, the audience sat transfixed in "cough-less" silence through each of the three long movements. Perhaps some Christians there were worshiping God for his gifts of music and musicians. For others though, I am convinced, the object of worship was the composer, the performers, or the music experience. Scripture reminds us that idolatry is worshiping "the creature rather than the Creator" (Rom. 1:25). Nevertheless, for reasons that I will give later, I believe that our culture's art music still is relevant to today's evangelical church.

2. Traditional church music (also called "liturgical" or "classical" by its detractors).

This category includes simpler, more accessible works in the forms and styles of high art music such as anthems, cantatas, and chorale/hymn preludes. These are written by "functional" composers from John Stainer in the nineteenth century to John Rutter, today's most accomplished choral writer, with a great variety of style and worth in between. This category also includes music written for strictly liturgical purposes: hymn and psalm tunes and chants of all kinds.

This material has been the core of skilled church music for the past two hundred years. It serves the church well in that it has some of the strength of the art music it imitates, yet it is available to a larger number of people. At the same time, in today's culture, traditional church music tends to be "tarred with the same brush" as high art music and often dismissed.

3. Folk music adapted for worship.

This is "historic music in the oral tradition, often in relatively simple style, . . . characteristic of a nation, society, or ethnic group."[12] It includes early American folk tunes like the setting to "Amazing Grace," African-American spirituals, and Oriental folk songs. Such music preserves the high-quality folk art of an entire culture, winnowed by passing time, and serves the church exceedingly well. The better contemporary American hymnals include such folk music (including Latino and native American hymns) in good supply.

4. Popular church music.

This includes all the forms which have been mass-produced and disseminated commercially, beginning with nineteenth-century Sunday school music and gospel songs, and also includes to-day's "country gospel," "gospel rock," contemporary Christian music, praise-and-worship music, and other related forms.

All these musics are important to our discussion because everyone is aware of them and has strong opinions about them. However, they are not always helpful to the church because their popularity allows them to crowd out stronger forms. In the previous chapter, I pointed out that some contemporary pop forms are questionable because of their musical style, their tendency to divide congregations, their extreme transience, and their status as cultural idols. Popular artists with unusual talent and discipline have produced a few gems in words and music, for which we should all give thanks. If they last in society's memory, they will become the new "folk art" of our generation.

A Strange Land of Aesthetic Relativism

What I call *aesthetic relativism* includes the idea that there are no absolutes in aesthetic quality. It implies that any person's judgment about "good church music" (what best glorifies God and edifies people in a certain congregation) is as valid as any other opinion. In other words, "beauty (in church music) is in the ear of the listener." I contend that such a concept is at odds with what we learn from Scripture and from church history; for this reason I maintain that today's relativistic culture is a "strange land" to the church and is unfriendly to its best interests.

The present situation exists because of the following developments in recent culture.

1. The triumph of commercial popular music over art music. While concerts of pop stars (in all music genres) and sales of their recordings are booming, symphony orchestra programs and other concerts in all except the major cities are in deep financial trouble because of dwindling attendance. Admittedly, high art has lost some credibility in our day because of its own "primitivism," as exhibited in the sounds (and silences) of John Cage and the visual improbabilities of Andy Warhol, among others. Yet many modern composers still write believable and accessible art music for the church, and the historic treasures are always available to us. There also is no shortage of good compositions in traditional and folk music styles.

As mentioned earlier, the problem is not measured by the number of churches that have ceased using art music or traditional music. Rather, the tragedy is that *church music has lost its historic lodestar.* Many younger listeners today do not just prefer pop music; they *dislike* art music intensely, scorn it as "elitist," and insist that pop styles are the pinnacle of achievement for this day and age.

The *New York Times* News Service recently predicted a "grim arts future" because only "graying America" is supporting the high culture performing arts. Judith Miller states, "For reasons that social scientists are trying to sort out, only art museums, jazz and . . . ballet are attracting roughly as high a percentage of people among the younger generations as among the older ones. These categories leave aside, of course, the thriving popular culture: rock music, movies and television."[13] And the situation gets worse with every succeeding generation, says Richard Peterson of Vanderbilt University: "We're talking about a massive shift in taste and tradition: from a generation of 'war baby' cultural highbrows to future generations of cultural 'omnivores,' younger Americans who think Patsy Cline, reggae, B. B. King and hip-hop are as important as the New York Philharmonic."[14]

2. The triumph of untrained talent over artistic discipline and preparation. In the 1960s and 1970s, an army of young believers picked up guitars, learned a few chords, and began to write and sing songs about their faith experiences. Of course, many hoped to graduate to professional status, so they could cash in on fame and fortune while ministering to the faithful or evangelizing the lost. We should always welcome amateur art activity by Christians because it demonstrates that we all are "created to be creative"—in the image of the Creator God; it also provides healthy diversion and refreshment for the human spirit.

But "amateurism" serves the church badly when it glorifies poor performance of poor poetry and poor music above that which requires the discipline of tedious but fruitful study and rehearsal. When amateurs are encouraged to be satisfied with what they can write and play and sing *immediately,* they have little vision and incentive for progress and development in their techniques and styles. Further, those guitar-playing beginners, who grew just a little in practicing their craft in the 1970s and 1980s, often are convinced that their achievements—and certainly, the accomplishments of contemporary Christian artists—should set the standards for the church today and in the future. I believe Scripture teaches (especially in the parable of the talents, Matt. 25:14-30) that we practice *true stewardship* when we risk "investing" God's artistic gifts in order to give them back to him in acts of worship—refined, developed, and matured.

3. The triumph of aesthetic spectatorism over aesthetic participation. Of course, only a few of the untrained performers mentioned above ever became moneymakers. The others, along with those who don't try, become the larger group of "pew potatoes" who prefer to be sung to in church rather than sing for themselves. The techniques developed in solo amateurism didn't prepare them to participate in choral singing. Congregational praise-and-worship singing can't really be counted, since full participation isn't required: one can hum, or shuffle, or clap, or even sing, but this really doesn't affect the result.

Aesthetics in Musical Worship: A Casualty List for Our Day

Definition: Excellence in the aesthetics of musical worship to the glory of God is achieved through a skilled performance of theologically true and poetically sound words set to well-crafted music that is meaningfully placed in the liturgy.

In the last half of the twentieth century, evangelicals have experienced both the birth and the death of a lofty dream of church music education. Southern Baptists, for instance, developed strong church music schools or departments in all their six seminaries; some of those divisions had been in existence since early in this century. All those school faculties were dedicated to high but practical musical standards for theological purposes—the glory of God and the blessing of the church, both locally and denomination-wide. Development of graded choir programs for all ages was seen as a sound approach to evangelism and Christian formation, both for those who participated musically and those who did not. Today, those schools or divisions are struggling, most of them just to survive. In some, arguments with critics over church music styles have done the damage. In others, changes in administration due to theological shifts have frightened away potential students who are concerned about accreditation. Admittedly, new church music programs are being developed in a number of Baptist colleges and universities, but as yet they have not demonstrated their viability.

Other evangelical churches have preferred to hire less trained musicians because they are considered to be "less idealistic and more pragmatic." Parents who became addicts of pop music in the 1970s and 1980s do not support music education as did *their* parents, and, even more, their grandparents. Where music training is maintained, the emphasis often has shifted to show-business-style activity rather than to serious development of musical technique, literature, and worship preparation. I believe that the original Southern Baptist dream was a gift from God. Churches who still cherish it should continue their dedication to the significance of music training in the life of every person. This will be the central emphasis of chapter 9.

Following is a list of areas in which church music has suffered casualties because of the pervasive influence of aesthetic relativism in our culture.

Congregational singing.
Earlier in this book I discussed the possibility that traditional hymns and hymnals are things of the past because of the prominence of praise-and-worship music sung from overhead screens in today's churches. Though this has already occurred in some congregations, I believe that it will not happen to the whole church because many mainline and liturgical churches will retain traditional hymn and psalm forms. As during the gospel song era, the great, historic songs of the church may well be preserved for us by churches whom we do not consider to be truly "evangelical."

At the same time, we should applaud the fact that styles of words and tunes of "serious" hymns are changing nowadays. Much of the older literature of English-language hymnody is being replaced by contemporary words and more varied, "folkish" music. During the last twenty years the "hymn explosion" has left us a huge corpus of fresh material by British, American, and Australasian writers,[15] much of which is strong theologically, easy to understand, and pleasant to sing. Tragically, in their obsession with praise-and-worship choruses and contemporary Christian music, typical evangelicals have totally ignored this wealth of material, including the unique songs of the Iona Community in Scotland and the Taizé Community in France.

Though individual praise choruses may function excellently in specific "response" situations, I am convinced that the typical, prolonged, charismatic praise-and-worship "experience" (like the old-fashioned revival song service) is an emotional musical "binge" that is inappropriate for mature, cognitive worship. The traditional approach that allows a congregation to sing multiple stanzas of well-written texts that express praise, thanksgiving, penitence, dedication, and petition at appropriate places throughout the service is much better. If that practice succumbs to contemporary musical emotionalism today, the church will beg for its return tomorrow!

Much has been said about the advantages of the overhead projector and screen—the centering of everyone's attention, the lifting of the head for better vocal technique, the freeing of the hands (for clapping), and so on. Without a doubt, the practice brings instant "success," if not instant gratification. The trained, rehearsed, and electronically amplified worship band sounds fine (but too loud), whether anyone else participates or not. But that is "performance music," not true congregational singing. Further, despite its manipulative attempt to guarantee attention, it does not achieve hymn singing's goal of "uniting" the congregation. Rather it creates a non-community of "participants" who somehow manage to perform independently at the same time.

On certain songs, many close their eyes to everything else in what seems to be a completely personal "love to Christ" expression. Some sing an occasional phrase while they clap and/or shuffle around in "lazy dancing." Nobody (except those on stage) seems to "work" at singing, as our song leaders once urged us to do. When we responded to their challenge—while proudly exercising our muscles by holding in our hands a collection of the historical church's memory of Christian poems and music—we had a right to feel that we had done our "work for God."

We also have lost some important artistic elements, thanks

to electronic projection of "words only." When everyone in the congregation had hymnbooks, even untrained musicians could follow the up-and-down of the notes, thereby learning the basics of music reading. In those days, most congregations had folks who sang alto, tenor, and bass, as well as melody—to God's glory; their unitedness was often experienced in delightful *a cappella* singing. It may be that only the Churches of Christ and certain Mennonites will preserve that experience, since they have no instruments to compensate for the congregation's lack of participation.

Choral music and performances.
For almost sixty years I have enjoyed and participated in the church's art of choral singing. In chapter 3 I suggested that choir music can offer a listening but still participating congregation an unusual and significant experience of the presence of our transcendent-immanent God. At the same, choral music may have more potential to be a *cognitive* worship experience than congregational singing. It is not easy to sing a hymn, especially a new one, and immediately comprehend the text. It is usually easier to understand words in a performed piece, especially if they may be read simultaneously in the bulletin.

Today it seems that this historic and meaningful aesthetic worship experience is in jeopardy. Baby Boomer adults often say that they enjoy choirs least of all the music offered in church. Charismatic groups tend to reject choir music as being "priestly," elitist, and noncongregational. Even when there is no objection to the sound or the "philosophy" of choir performance, a good singing group is difficult to recruit nowadays because of the lack of training and of interest in the age-group that normally would be expected to respond. Some churches have eliminated choirs completely, and others struggle along with a small roster of less-talented singers. Some develop choir music for only a few Sundays a year, or perhaps for the Protestant "high holidays" of Christmas and Easter.

We must also question the response of many music publishers to this dilemma. First of all, instead of giving us less difficult (unison or two-part) settings of worthy words and tunes, they have released a barrage of questionable works. Some of the most common forms are the bloated choral arrangements of hymns, the medleys of familiar hymn stanzas, and—would you believe it?—the "choralized praise chorus." Evidently they are produced in response to the current generation's stated standard of *noncreativity:* "The only music I like is something I've heard before." To which we must reply: "How then will you ever learn anything new?" Second, we must wonder why publishers cannot provide new and different poetic-musical experiences for the choir to offer, and leave the hymns to the congregation. Finally, creating medleys of a long list of only single stanzas from hymns is an indictment of the thinking capacity of the worshiper and a disservice to the hardworking hymn writer. This practice seems to be a little like eating a meal of appetizers only or reading the first chapter of several books without finishing any of them.

Having said all this, at this point I must add another development that has helped to create a "strange land of aesthetic relativism" in our day: *the triumph of the arranger over the composer.* I do so with a large dose of self-consciousness because my own limited composing gifts are better suited to arranging music than to original composing. I can remember when the smallest church choirs performed annual Christmas and Easter cantatas, with *original* texts and music. Whatever our judgment about the quality of those original works, I believe the current practice of singing mostly arrangements says something negative about today's church music aesthetics.

Of course choral *performances* are also suffering, both from poor publishing and poor training. In a day when forte-fortissimo is the normal dynamic range of church music, when did you last hear an anthem that began and ended quietly because that musical treatment was essential to the message of an important text (for instance, words like "O Rest in the Lord," from Mendelssohn's *Elijah,* based on Psalm 37)? When did you last hear a church choir demonstrate uniform vowel color, flawless diction, and musical phrasing in singing a simple piece? Or, when did you last hear a selection that achieved unity, variety, and climax without modulating to a higher key perhaps several times?

Solo music.

Many folk who reject group singing by choirs prefer the performance of pop music in various solo styles. Too many soloists today, with the help of electronics, seem to try to match the volume and emotional impact of a full choir. Sometimes the result is so grotesque that it destroys the continuity of worship. Recently I heard a soloist sing the spiritual "Were You There When They Crucified My Lord?" as an offertory solo following a sermon. She sang it excellently with powerful emotion that was increased exponentially *because* there was no accompaniment. The sound system magnified the experience even more, so that the solo became the most impressive element of the service. When the minister rose to speak afterward, all he could say was, "Wow!" In our day of emotionally overblown music expression, we need to remember that "modest" music may bring more glory to God (not praise to the singer because of an ear and mind-blowing performance).

Perhaps this is a good place to acknowledge that in every art form there are poor, good, better, and best examples. I am not an authority on contemporary genres, but I understand that the best, most creative country and rock literature is also *elitist* music: It is chosen by a relatively small number of devotees who have somehow developed the required perceptive judgment. Yet, I must confess that in typical contemporary Christian music I find little aesthetic creativity in the use of the basic elements. Too often, careless or misleading amateur theology is expressed with clichés in lines that almost rhyme. And, why must all the pieces be in duple meter (4/4 time)? Do Christian rock singers not know that in the Middle Ages, triple meter was called "perfect"—possibly because it was a reminder of the Holy Trinity?[16] And why must we always have a heavy drum accent on beats 2 and 4?

Hearing mostly pop forms in church encourages the notion that their distorted vocal techniques constitute the only expressive and/or spiritual way to sing. Granted, some pop vocal styles are pleasant to the ear and do communicate effectively. But classical styles based on healthy, disciplined development of God-given vocal cords are also beautiful, including the one which we call *bel canto* ("beautiful singing"). Further, these latter techniques are the ones on which choral singing has always been based.

Instrumental music.
Contemporary life has brought many changes in the use of instrumental music in church. Some new instruments (orchestral and electronic) are being added, while others, like the organ, are being discarded. We may call some of the results aesthetic progress and some aesthetic regress.

Many churches have created a new hallmark of evangelical worship by adding an "instrumental ensemble" as a regular feature. If the church has (or can employ) the necessary resources in talent—as does the televised Crystal Cathedral from Garden Grove, California—that semiprofessional orchestra can provide glorious accompaniment to the choir and other music. However, few churches can produce that level of playing, and *more sound is not always better!* Of course, one of the purposes of church music is to provide training and service opportunity for believers. Yet, it is doubtful wisdom to ask people to assist in this way until they can maintain proper intonation and rhythmic control; otherwise, the new accompaniment detracts from both congregational singing and performance music.

Our church features a "churchestra" that performs about once a month.[17] Since they rehearse every week, they can reach a high level of proficiency for those times of worship leadership. Such planning makes those monthly appearances special. Even then, the instruments do not play on all stanzas of the hymns, do not always accompany other music, and do not always play preludes or offertories. Sometimes one flutist playing an obbligato with a solo voice is more exciting than the entire ensemble would be. Good aesthetics always implies *variety,* and this approach insures that.

It is hard to explain the present-day antipathy to organ sounds, and as a professional organist I try not to resent the necessity to do so. I can only guess that, in the contemporary effort to attract delinquent Boomers who have rejected the church, this is another of the church's holy symbols which some people have decided "must go." Also, if late twentieth-century ears suddenly find organ sounds to be ugly, I am challenged to make my playing beautiful and to select literature that is appropriate and engaging.

Columnist Chuck Kraft of the magazine *Worship Leader* revealed something of an anti-aesthetic bias when he said that one's choice in church music instruments reveals one's view of God. If you are an organ lover, he said, you think of God as transcendent and remote, but if you envision God as immanent, friendly, and loving, you will prefer the guitar! "Can you imagine Jesus playing the organ?" he said. "How about the guitar?"[18] Kraft clearly implied that Jesus wouldn't have touched the organ, yet he might very well have played a guitar. (Would he also say that Jesus played folk style, not "classical" guitar?) But isn't our transcendent, immanent, loving God the author of *all* creation and creativity?

Considering that Jesus was an itinerant teacher and healer who mostly walked from one ministry opportunity to the next, Kraft is probably right. A first-century version of a stringed instrument would have served him well in accompanying any singing his disciples wanted to do. But I must guess that Jesus found meaning in the bolder instrumental sounds that he heard in the temple at the time of the morning and evening sacrifices. I'm quite sure that for the past one thousand years he has smiled because of the music produced expressly for his glory on all the church organs of the Western world. So I have a biased question of my own: Can you imagine Jesus playing an electric guitar in the style of Elvis Presley or some of today's contemporary Christian musicians?

I am not really worried that the instrument which has served the church for so long will disappear with the beginning of the third millennium. *Christianity Today* reported that between 1993 and 1996 organ use in American churches remained virtually unchanged.[19] No doubt the organ will continue to be an ideal instrument for the church because (1) it takes only one person to make enough sound to fill a large room; (2) with an entire orchestra of sounds available from one console, it can whisper as well as roar, and thus express both the transcendence and the immanence of God; and (3) when played masterfully, it provides the best means for leading a congregation in artistic, meaningful hymn singing.

The United States boasts more organ builders today than ever before in our history, many of them small entrepreneurs with distinctive, aesthetic concepts of tonal construction. After sixty years at the console, I still work with churches in designing organs on which I play dedication recitals. Recently the Broadway Baptist Church of Fort Worth, Texas, dedicated the largest organ in the southwestern United States and the largest organ in any Baptist church in the world. Of course, for some churches, a $50,000 electronic organ will be as much of an "alabaster-box" offering to God as the $2,000,000 pipe organ in Fort Worth. In recent years, certain companies have produced instruments that give a better than reasonable facsimile of true organ tone. Further, because of cost, more and more churches combine pipes and electronics in their organs.

We must also be thankful for the brand-new electronic sounds that have become available to us in synthesizers and in organ MIDI systems. They give new voices to speak God's praise. Electronics become a threat to aesthetic truth in worship only when they replace natural, "acoustic" sound. Some churches use too many "canned" sound tracks and so distort the sound of their own performers' voices and instruments with high-powered amplifiers that many young people have come to believe that electronic sound is the God-given norm!

Quality Performance and Our Motivation in Pursuing It

Thus far in this chapter, I have discussed mostly the materials of worship, especially musical styles, forms, and sounds of both instruments and voices. However, we must strive for excellence in the performances of worship as well. It is no aesthetic achievement and ascribes little glory to God to sing Handel's

Messiah in church if the choir cannot master its challenges to a reasonable degree.

The same is true in all the arts used in church. The sermon should be well constructed and delivered convincingly, with good speech techniques. The liturgy should be rehearsed regularly (especially the materials that change weekly), and spoken dramatically, as if it were being heard for the first time. Scripture reading especially should be prepared in advance, with coaching for both ministers and laypersons who would profit from such help. Prayers should be carefully planned and, if they are read, should sound as if they are being improvised.

In *Jubilate II,* I suggest that the worship service should be experienced as a drama in which the actors include everyone present; as such, the function of the drama's director (basically, the service planner/leader team) is important in achieving a successful worship experience. Those persons will "consider each element carefully (both in planning and in reviewing the performance) to insure that it fits into the script, and that there is a balance of faster and slower pacing, of loudness and softness, of seriousness and humor, of ecstasy and reflection, of God-centeredness and self-consciousness."[20]

Many church leaders believe that if Baby Boomers are to be attracted to church, the service performance must be "smooth flowing" with no jarring amateurism, stalling, manipulation, or confrontation. This concern no doubt reflects the routine carelessness of much traditional worship. Perhaps if, during the last forty years, worship week by week had been planned and presented as carefully as I have outlined, we would not be experiencing the present angry reaction to "meaningless" rituals and dull services. But the motivation for such excellence is not to please and provide relaxed entertainment for any group in the congregation. Like all aesthetic achievements, the purpose is the glory and pleasure of God, to whom we offer our best sacrifice of praise. Any worshiper-centered motivation should stem from a desire to proclaim the Word of God both attractively and convincingly, without distraction, so the congregation will be challenged by God the Spirit to respond, sometimes to the point of confrontation.

Developing an Aesthetically Growing Church

How does a church prepare to worship in artistic truth, in our culture's strange land of artistic relativism? Only artistically aware people will be at home in God-honoring worship through the arts; for this reason, *the arts must be part of community consciousness.* In our church, the services are planned by the pastor and a musician who is called the "Minister of Music and Worship Arts." That person works with a worship committee and supervises regular activity by teenagers in arts training: Scripture reading, drama, expressive movement (dance), puppet theater, and music (vocal, orchestra, hand-bells, and Orff instruments). We do not do everything we could, but our church sponsors concerts, both traditional and popular, presented by gifted members and by visiting artists. Our place of worship is a work of art which functions well visually (though not so well acoustically). It contains magnificent, contemporary stained glass windows that are regularly used as teaching tools by our pastor. In addition, we add decoration (including banners) according to the season of the year.

It is common practice in many churches to promote outside music activities as part of the "fellowship and recreation" program. Teenagers attend a local contemporary Christian music concert and retirees make a trip to Branson, Missouri, to hear country singers. I believe that equal, if not greater, emphasis should be given to the *art music presentations in the community.* Churches could promote local university recitals, choral union concerts, the city's orchestra performance, and such. On such occasions, the music minister could even offer a "music appreciation" presentation in advance to help in the understanding of the music.

Finally, a number of churches conduct a religious arts festival each year. Such activity may include programs of drama, poetry reading, dramatized choral works, and solo recitals, together with displays of visual art—including sculpture, photography, and painting, or other arts—prepared by members of the congregation and the community.

Sacrifices of Praise, Aesthetics, and Footwashing

In concluding this chapter, I will say something about the ways our artistic offerings are given in services of worship and the ways they are received—first by God and then by other believers. Worship artists (in every style, including both high and pop art, trained and untrained) must always be aware that they may appear to be proud—even arrogant—in the use of their talents.

In chapter 7 of his gospel, Luke tells the story of a woman (tradition says she was Mary Magdalene) who performed an outrageously extravagant and selfless act, simply because she loved Jesus so much. Like Jewish women of that time, she carried a little alabaster vial that contained very expensive perfume. Approaching Jesus, she sensed that he loved her and that he could redeem her from her shameful life. Overcome with gratitude and love for him, she began to anoint his feet with the costly liquid mingled with her tears, shamelessly kissing them and wiping them with her long hair.

All our gifts in worship should be offered to Christ in the same way. The music should be the best we have—the product of our best musicianship, our costly preparation, and our careful performance. Our motivation is the same: We are performing, not for the plaudits of the crowd, not simply to fill a slot in a worship service, but because of our great love of the one who first loved us and gave himself a sacrifice for our salvation.

Like Mary, we should be aware that such an offering has worth. There will be bystanders in our day, as in Mary's, who will view the sacrifice of praise as some kind of mistake. But Christ's response will always be the same: He will welcome the offering and receive it as magnanimously as it is given. For him, who owns "the cattle on a thousand hills," the gift of rare perfume will not be an enriching of possessions. For him, who in heaven enjoys the song of angels, our greatest music (even that of J. S. Bach) may not be the ultimate aesthetic experience. But our Lord, who endured the cross because he loved us so much, will treasure every wholehearted, loving, even extravagant response.

Of course, because in worship our love is directed to God *and* to our neighbors, our gifts of worship music are also gifts to other worshipers. They are given with the hope that the congregation may join, cognitively and emotionally, in offering the sacrifice of praise, whether the anthem of the choir, the song of the soloist, or the hymn of the whole congregation—and that, in doing so, they will experience blessing.

In this relationship to our sisters and brothers in Christ, it seems to me that we are, in a sense, "washing their feet," as Jesus did for his disciples in the Upper Room (John 13:1-15). Now we are not concerned with what a rare gift we are offering; rather, it is a simple service of hospitality, like washing the feet of friends who had been walking through hot, dusty trails in ancient Palestine. For, as the philosopher Auerbach once said, "Music washes away from the soul the dust of everyday life."

Jesus said that our attitude toward one another should be that of humble servants. If someone expresses appreciation for the music we have offered, we will respond as do our Spanish friends, *"de nada*—it's nothing." Of course, as in Jesus' foot-washing ministry, there will be those who reject the gift. They will object that the water is too hot or too cold—that the music is not "good enough" for them or that it is "too arty, too elitist." We may be tempted to retort that that's what happens when one "casts pearls before swine," but that's not the Christian response. We must not be angry, just disappointed, because we have failed to offer an acceptable vehicle of worship for our brothers and sisters in Christ and thus apparently failed to meet their needs. We must ponder whether we missed the mark in choosing the selection, or in the way it was prepared and presented, and we will return to our calling, praying that in next Sunday's services we will be more successful or that they will be more "open" to receiving what is offered.

At the same time, we will know that our Lord always accepts the offering and responds with an affirmation of his pleasure and his own unending, infinite love. Whether our gift be great or small, by human aesthetic standards, *God accepts whatever our best may be.* There is a poignant reminder of this in the story of Mary's sacrifice for her purification after she gave birth to Jesus (Luke 2:22-24). According to Hebrew law, for such an occasion a well-to-do family would bring a lamb; but a poor household (like the one in which Jesus grew up) was allowed to offer two pigeons. Of course, it must still be the best offering the family could afford—the best pigeons in the dovecote, but they would be good enough.

A Closing Prayer

Most of the issues involved in artistic activity in the church are mentioned in a remarkable prayer written by a hymnwriter-pastor who has been exemplary in developing creative "contemporary traditional" worship.

Prayer for Those Who Make Music

Our Father, in you we live and move and have our
     being.
For you are the source of all that is good.
You are the beginning of every created thing.
Therefore we praise you for every gift in our possession,
    because each gift presumes a giver,
     and each ability finds its origin in your creativity.
Without your gift of joy,
    we would have no song worth singing.
Without your making it possible,
    we would not know the art of making music
    or the delight of using word and sound to your glory.
Lord, you are our theme; you and your achievements.
    We can never exhaust so vast a subject.
For by your Spirit we find new meaning in old songs,
    and new songs are born out of the constant
     freshness of your Word.

Thank you, Father, for the rich heritage of music:
    for the poets whose words sing twice over
     when they are set to great melodies;

for the composers of today who are adding
    to the rich legacy we already possess;
for variety, innovation, and the mix of
        taste and talent that keeps our church music
        from stagnation and familiarity;
for those whose gift is to perform,
who by the use of the human voice or an instrument
    create the atmosphere of worship;
for those who taught us our expertise;
    for those who urged us to study;
        for those who financed our training;
for those who still encourage us to improve our skills.

Forgive us, Father, if we make music into a god
    to be worshiped for its own sake,
    for careless performance and for singing music
        unfit for your praise,
    for drawing attention to ourselves
        instead of pointing to you,
    for musical snobbery,
        for sentimentality,
        for neglect of the meaning of a song,
and for singing without personal commitment to you.

Help us, Father, from this moment on
    to so surrender our powers to you,
        as the one who granted them to us,
    that in cooperation with one another,
        we may be your servants, leading your people
        in the solemnity and exuberance of true worship.

To you be all the praise.

Bryan Jeffery Leech

8

Worshiping God
in Liturgical Truth

In a Strange Land of
Destructive Iconoclasm

Every church has either a ritual or a rutual.
—B. B. McKinney

Six of us were sitting in a circle, having met to plan a traditional worship service for an international conference on worship. Staring at a blank sheet of paper, with pencil poised, the leader asked, "What do we want in this service?" The questions and suggestions began:

"Can we use the choir from Russia?"

"There's a fine tenor singer coming from Korea."

"Does the church have a pipe organ?"

"We're hoping to have a member of the Billy Graham team as speaker."

"Can we expect to recruit instrumental players from the local churches?"

Suddenly someone remembered that we had met to plan a *worship* service, not a concert or an evangelistic meeting. As Kierkegaard made clear, the central "actors" in worship should be the people in the pews, not those on the platform. We started again with discussion and questions:

"Should the Call to Worship be spoken by the service leader or responsively with the congregation?"

"We must be sure to choose hymns that will be known by

all the delegates—those from Asia as well as those from eastern Europe."

"What form for the Confession of Sin and Assurance of Forgiveness would be most comfortable for the delegates?"

"Let's place the Collection after the sermon to demonstrate that our offering of money is a 'yes' response to the Word of God."

But wait a minute! I stated in chapter 1 that true worship does not ultimately depend on the details of worship activity—its location or its order and content. Persons may participate in what they consider to be an ideal service and yet not worship as Jesus commanded, with their whole person—heart, soul, mind, and strength. Or, an individual may be present in a service that few would justify in its planning and performance, yet be worshiping God fully in spirit and truth.

That progression of thought probably brings satisfaction to nonliturgical Christians, who have tended to distrust formal worship that is "just going through the motions." It also probably pleases those who advocate a shopping mall approach to worship planning: "We offer A and B (and possibly even more) services; take your pick." The idea may be welcomed also by modern "creativists," who seem to believe that worth in worship is synonymous with novelty.

I have also stated that worship content and performance *do matter* and should be consistent with our call to worship God in spirit and truth and also enable believers to worship as whole persons. Throughout this book I have discussed various aspects of worship form in the light of those standards. This chapter will deal with the subject more comprehensively.

What Is Liturgical Truth?

The dictionary's first definition of *liturgy* is "a form of public worship." So all worship is liturgical in that it has *form*—a commonly agreed upon way of doing things that is repeated week after week with small variations. What our forebears called "free" worship was only a simpler form than that of their

Roman Catholic, Orthodox, Lutheran, Episcopalian, or "high church Presbyterian" neighbors.

In more common, if less accurate and narrower usage, *liturgy* is understood to refer to the stricter, more developed forms of Orthodox, Roman Catholic, Anglican, or Lutheran churches, in which many of the same words and acts appear in each service. Other words and acts are changed according to the day and season of the church year (for instance, Advent, Christmas, Epiphany, Lent, Holy Week, Easter, or Pentecost).

If liturgical churches have a "ritual," free evangelical churches have a "rutual." Today, what may seem to be spontaneous, creative worship (including the succession of praise choruses and the number of repetitions of each) actually has been worked out in great detail. Its sponsors simply are *substituting a new ritual for the old.* They are hiding its identity as a form of liturgy by offering no worship bulletin, thus giving the impression that it is spontaneous.

When I say that both historic free church services and contemporary, creative worship have ritual that is liturgical, I mean to say that the same *actions* (preaching, singing, praying, body movement, drama, receiving an offering, or sharing the Lord's Supper) are used regularly to express certain *experiences* (gathering, praise, confession, hearing God's Word and responding to it, thanksgiving and supplication, dedication, or dismissal). The order of experiences may or may not change week by week, and the specific words and actions may be completely improvised.

The worship of the ancient Jews in the tabernacle, temple, and synagogue was strictly liturgical, with specific readings from the Law and the Prophets and prayers prescribed for each day of the year. After the Christian Pentecost, the first Jewish believers continued to gather in the synagogue and the temple for prayer and preaching.[1] They also met by themselves on the first day of the week to "remember the Lord's death" in the supper Jesus instituted.

After Christians were no longer welcome in the Jewish sabbath meetings, *some* freer worship emerged that was less developed than that of the synagogue. As Paul encouraged, "What should be done then, my friends? When you come together, each one has a hymn, a lesson, a revelation, a tongue, or an interpretation. Let all things be done for building up" (1 Cor. 14:26). From this tradition many modern "free," or nonliturgical, churches argue for their simple, unfettered orders.

However, by the second century prescribed Christian forms appeared and those forms increased in complexity through the years. Eastern Orthodoxy's highly symbolic and aesthetic worship has not changed greatly since the eleventh century. In the West, the official liturgies continued to develop; Roman Catholic rites were standardized at the Council of Trent in 1562, and radically reformed (partly by adopting congregational participation in vernacular languages) at the Second Vatican Council in 1962.

With the sixteenth-century Reformation, the Anglican and Lutheran communions simplified their worship drastically, yet they remain quite strictly liturgical to this day. Calvin also left a worship order for his followers, and many Reformed churches around the world still follow its modern adaptation quite faithfully.[2]

What we know today as free—or nonliturgical—worship began with Anabaptists in sixteenth-century Europe and with Baptists, Quakers, and Congregationalists in England in the early seventeenth century. All of this is to say that Christian worship has been liturgical throughout most of its history, and for most people who bear the name "Christian" it remains so today.[3]

Early Christian leaders found that liturgical consistency was important in order to assure that "true" words were spoken in worship. In that dynamic missionary period, churches were formed faster than new converts could be trained to be pastors and bishops; following a "worship book" and reading a sermon prepared by an older, experienced pastor ensured that worship would be doctrinally pure. Today, those who follow the Scripture lectionary of the church year argue that such a practice ensures that a broader range of Scriptures will be read and all doctrines of our faith will be preached. They also confess that they do not have the talent or the time to prepare prayers on a regular basis without at least borrowing ideas from biblical prayers or from others developed by highly skilled writers.

Those committed to traditional liturgies insist also that repetition of the same actions (including some of the same words) Sunday after Sunday can make them more meaningful. First, worshipers know in advance what the experience will be, so they prepare their hearts and minds for it. Second, when the same words and actions are repeated over and over again, they become part of the deep memory of an individual, returning to the consciousness in times of stress and tragedy. One Baptist-turned-Episcopalian minister told me that the difference between his former and his present approach to spirituality is the difference between a glaze (you spread it on) and a marinade (you soak in it)!

Since the time of the Reformation, disputes about the form of worship have caused much conflict in the church, even as it does today. I have become convinced that the traditional nonliturgical position is not tenable. To most people, freedom in worship implies that form and content really do not matter. Such an attitude encourages a church either to let its ritual become a meaningless "rutual," or to sample every worship novelty that comes along.

I believe strongly that *most churches today need change in their worship,* not only because congregations are calling for change but also because our recent past practices have been inadequate. However, I am convinced that many contemporary approaches to change have been superficial at best and destructive at worst. It seems to me that we will find liturgical truth when:

- we agree that the form and content of worship do matter;
- we discover what Scripture teaches about (and models in) worship practice; and
- we update or adequately replace the ways in which the historical church has confirmed that biblical authority.

I hope this discussion will contribute to that discovery and will challenge readers to appropriate renewal that reclaims the wonder and majesty of true worship.

What Is Iconoclasm?

I define *iconoclasm* as a "radical housecleaning of worship elements," sometimes to the point of throwing out essentials of worship along with nonessential elements. The *Random House Dictionary* describes an *iconoclast* as "one who attacks cherished beliefs, traditional institutions, etc., as being based on error or superstition." Iconoclasts can be God's agents of cleansing and renewal when they oppose worship actions that truly *are* based on error and superstition.

Martin Luther was such a *constructive* iconoclast when he substituted German for Latin in the worship of his sixteenth-century church, opening the way to cognitive, participatory worship for every person. However, some Lutherans believe that he indulged in *destructive* iconoclasm when he reduced the Eucharistic prayer of his German mass (1526) to the Words of Institution. Insofar as Luther eliminated good, orthodox words that add to the meaning of the Lord's Supper experience (which have since been returned to Lutheran worship), I agree.[4]

A Strange Land of Destructive Iconoclasm

It is interesting to note that today's "creative" worship reform movement is known best for what it has subtracted from worship. The cover story of the August 1996 issue of the *Atlantic Monthly* begins with this description of contemporary destructive worship iconoclasm:

> No spires. No crosses. No robes. No clerical collars.
> No hard pews. No kneelers. No biblical gobbledygook.
> No prayerly rote. No fire, no brimstone. No pipe organs.
> No dreary eighteenth-century hymns. No forced solemnity.
> No Sunday finery. No collection plates.[5]

To be sure, there are substitutes for some, but not all, of these items in newer forms of worship. Yet I believe that many of today's worship reformers have been destructively iconoclastic. In their zeal to eliminate what they judge to be in error—because "folks don't understand it or find it relevant"—they have thrown out much that is commanded or modeled in Scripture, without replacing it with anything better.

Many churches today have little corporate prayer and almost no reading of Scripture. Calls to Worship and Benedictions are considered to be timeworn and irrelevant—even those whose words come directly from the Bible. The loss of a sense of the holy—both in the absence of significant worship symbols and the resulting lack of a sense of reverence—may be as important as any change, especially at this time when the visible and the emotive are culture's strongest communicators.

In this chapter, I will list briefly Scripture's worship rubrics—commands and examples—in both Old and New Testaments. Second, I will describe one contemporary example of the more destructive iconoclastic church services I have witnessed in modern worship. Finally, I will outline the actions of a historic yet modern liturgy—the Geneva Order of the Reformed Church—that I find to be God-honoring and people-blessing.

Worship Instruction in the New Testament

The New Testament records the beginnings of Christian worship and our study will begin there.

Specific rubrics given.
Earlier in chapters 1 and 2, I discussed Jesus' words on which this book is based: "God is spirit, and those who worship him must worship in spirit and truth" (John 4:24). Our Lord also gave a specific directive for Christian worship celebration, when at the last supper in the Upper Room he said: "Do this in remembrance of me" (Luke 22:19). Because these words of Jesus were confirmed by Paul (1 Cor. 11:24) as a command for the whole church, we call the *Lord's Supper* an ordinance ("a rule"). Many groups also call it a sacrament, meaning "a visible sign to signify or confer grace."

A second specific ordinance or sacrament is that of *Christian baptism*. This was expressed in Jesus' words at the time of his ascension: "Go therefore and make disciples of all nations, *baptizing them* in the name of the Father and of the Son and of the Holy Spirit" (Matt. 28:19, italics added).

Apostolic examples in the early church.

The church has always considered that the directions given and examples set by first-century believers constitute additional rubrics for worship. In fact, some groups believe that *unless* a worship action occurred in the New Testament church, it is not authorized for use at any time in human history.[6] Many contemporary churches have ignored some of these recorded elements or have so minimized their use that they have lost their intended spiritual potential.

1. Scripture Reading

Until I arrive, give attention to the public reading of scripture. (1 Tim. 4:13)

In the apostle Paul's day, the first Christian congregations followed the synagogue practice of reading both the Law (*Torah*) and the books of the prophets (*Haftarah*). In addition, the apostle instructed them to read his letters (Col. 4:16), which suggests that he believed that his words also contained God's message for them. In some churches today, a visible Bible and visible readers are rejected symbols. Frequently, if God's Word is heard, it comes from an offstage, electronic voice. Supposedly, the novel practice adds authority and mystery, as if God's voice was actually being heard.

I believe that a *visible* Bible is significant. Seeing God's Word shows that the written revelation of God is complete in one book which we should treasure and study. The visible reader is also important, recalling Ezra's festive, seven-day-long ceremonial reading of the law after Israel returned from captivity (see Neh. 8:1-18). God's Word must be understood to be to and for *us,* along with the "cloud of witnesses" (Heb. 12:1). It is inspired (breathed to life by God) in its reading and hearing as well as in its writing (2 Tim. 3:16). Whenever we meet to worship, we should expect to read the Bible aloud and explain the reading in the sermon. In this aspect of worship all liturgical churches do better than evangelicals; in every Eucharistic service, Roman Catholics read extended portions from the Old Testament (or the Apocrypha), an Epistle, and one of the Gospels. They also sing a psalm responsively.

2. The Sermon

> On the first day of the week, when we met to break bread, Paul was holding a discussion with them . . . speaking until midnight. (Acts 20:7)

Paul evidently was a gifted and sometimes lengthy proclaimer of God's Word. The church always has acknowledged that God, Three-in-One, speaks in the sermon as well as in the Scripture readings, offering grace and calling for obedience. On occasion, other art forms have been used in the communication. During the Middle Ages, the Western church used several kinds of drama. In the eighteenth century, J. S. Bach produced solo and choral cantatas that were musical expositions of Scripture.

3. Singing

> Sing psalms, hymns, and spiritual songs. (Col. 3:16)

In writing to the churches at Colossae and Ephesus, Paul assumed that Christians would use a broad expression of congregational music, including historic *psalms* expressing every type of prayer, fresh *hymns* to teach the new theology of the emerging church, and *spiritual songs* that were at least more emotional than rational, and probably improvised and/or glossalalic.

Obviously, this musical triad is a much more complete worship expression than a diet of praise-and-worship choruses, even when contemporary Christian music is added. It is also better than singing only gospel songs or only dated hymns. (This matter was discussed at length in chapters 3 and 4.)

4. Prayers

Therefore confess your sins to one another, and pray for one another, so that you may be healed. The prayer of the righteous is powerful and effective. (James 5:16)

I urge that supplications, prayers, intercessions, and thanksgivings be made for everyone, for kings and all who are in high positions, so that we may lead a quiet and peaceable life in all godliness and dignity. (1 Tim. 2:1-2)

In the first Scripture quotation, the apostle James refers no doubt to the act of being reconciled with those we have wronged or who have wronged us. Beyond this, I believe he calls us to confess our sins to God in each other's presence, that is, in corporate worship.

Writing to Timothy, Paul gives standards for both spoken and musical prayer that call for *variety, specificity,* and *discipline.* In contrast, the typical, casual judgment about public prayer for modern evangelicals seems to be that a prayer is a prayer is a prayer, and it should be improvised without careful planning. At best, a single prayer often tries to combine all the modes mentioned by Paul—and perhaps more. Adult Christians should not continue to pray the typical "around the world," "bless everybody" prayers of a five-year-old. They should mature in prayer life—in theology, in vocabulary, and in structure. Worship scholars traditionally have thought it wise to separate prayer types, expressing at one point in the service thanksgiving, and at another, supplication, and so on.

When did you last hear a corporate prayer that made you sit bolt upright with goosebumps, because it made you aware that the eternal, holy God was actually present, listening and answering? Is typical ho-hum praying the reason why so many evangelicals don't take Paul's instructions seriously?

5. The Congregational "Amen"

How can anyone in the position of an outsider say the "Amen" to your thanksgiving, since the outsider does not know what you are saying? (1 Cor. 14:16)

In historical worship practice, many prayers are spoken by the whole congregation in unison. Others, voiced by a single individual, conclude with a spoken congregational "Amen," affirming that it was offered on behalf of the whole church.

By contrast, typical evangelicals suggest by their silence and, I fear, often assume that a "pastoral" prayer is strictly a solo performance. Teaching worshipers to "join minds and hearts" in all prayers—and to show this by a united-and-uniting "Amen"—may be the most significant change we could initiate in our services.

6. Confession of Faith

> Take hold of the eternal life, to which you were called and for which you made the good confession in the presence of many witnesses. (1 Tim. 6:12)

Certain noncreedal churches object to the reciting of a creed or a confession of faith. Yet they require baptismal candidates to declare their faith in Jesus Christ as "Lord," which may have been the circumstance of Timothy's confession mentioned in the verse above. All Christians should be grateful that, since the third or fourth centuries, the Apostles' Creed and the Nicene Creed have remained unchanged as verbal bulwarks of our faith that have withstood many attacks. When I speak such a confession in public worship, I affirm and rejoice in the essentials of my faith.

7. Collection

> Now concerning the collection for the saints . . . On the first day of every week, each of you is to put aside and save whatever extra you earn, so that collections need not be taken when I come. (1 Cor. 16:1-2)

From this statement, one might think that Paul was embarrassed to have a "love offering" received when he was present! Though the apostle speaks of money collections in almost utilitarian terms, we must believe that, from his Jewish "tithes and offerings" heritage, he understood that this is one of the most joyous and most demanding expressions of our ministry to God in worship.

8. Physical Actions

I want everyone everywhere to lift innocent hands toward heaven and pray. (1 Tim. 2:8, CEV)

Greet one another with a holy kiss. (1 Cor. 16:20)

These passages vindicate the use of bodily action in worship, thus rejecting the Neoplatonism that has occasionally plagued the church.[7] I believe that it opens the door to all sorts of "embodied prayer," including even dance. Recently I noticed that certain non-charismatic Roman Catholics held their hands palms-upward, but not over their heads, during prayer.

The church has always considered the kiss of peace ("holy kiss," 1 Thess. 5:26) to be a divine rubric, but some congregations still believe it makes visitors uncomfortable.

9. Greetings and Benedictions

Grace to you and peace from God our Father and the Lord Jesus Christ. (1 Cor. 1:3)

The grace of the Lord Jesus Christ, the love of God, and the communion of the Holy Spirit be with all of you. (2 Cor. 13:13)

More than anything I want these gifts—grace, peace, love, and communion—from God, and I am glad to hear them promised to me at the beginning and the end of public worship. One Bible commentator says that the order of these blessings is significant: "The *grace of Christ* expresses and leads one toward the *love of God,* and the love of God when actualized through the *Spirit,* produces *communion* with God and with one another."[8]

General rubrics from the apostle Paul.

To complete our study of worship instruction in the New Testament, we must consider two more statements of Paul.

In his first letter to Christians in the Greek city of Corinth, he includes a long discussion of speaking in tongues, which ends with the directive: "All things should be done decently and in order" (1 Cor. 14:40). This admonition obviously places limitations on individual freedom in worship, and the entire chapter of 1 Corinthians 14 implies that such discipline both edifies believers and glorifies God. "Let all things be done for building up" ("for edifying," KJV) says Paul in verse 26. Earlier in chapter 1, I characterized worship as ministry to God; however, building up or edifying others undoubtedly refers to the ministry of worship *to the congregation of believers.*

Such a concept may seem to cast doubt on the idea that corporate worship is essentially purposeless except that it exists for the glory of God. Australian scholar David Peterson reminds us that Paul frequently wrote about the importance of worship for the edification of the church as a community of the people of God. We should ponder these words carefully in our day when much so-called "creativity" seems to be tearing the church apart! Peterson goes on to reaffirm that the central focus of worship is *not* the serendipities of evangelism, Christian education, or pastoral ministry.

> This does not mean that prayer or praise is a means to an end, namely edification. We worship God because of who he is and because of his grace toward us. However, participating in the edification of the church is an important expression of our devotion and service to God. God is glorified by the growth of the church towards the goals he has set for us.[9]

I believe Paul is saying that when in worship God is glorified in a way that calls forth the best from worshipers—both in worship participation and in changed lives, the service edifies those worshipers and witnesses to nonbelievers.

Using the above actions and perhaps others, I hope to answer the question: What worship order and content in our day best glorifies God, builds up Christians, and calls the unchurched to faith?

An Old Testament Model for Worship

The vision recorded in Isaiah 6 is the account of the prophet Isaiah's encounter with God in full worship. It also suggests standards and even a good order of worship events for God's gathered people. Since, from New Testament passages I listed actions of worship (for instance, preaching and singing), I will note *spiritual experiences* in this Old Testament passage.

Spiritual Experiences	Isaiah 6:1-13
An Encounter with God	[1]In the year that King Uzziah died, I saw the LORD sitting on a throne, high and lofty; and the hem of his robe filled the temple. [2]Seraphs were in attendance above him; each had six wings: with two they covered their faces, and with two they covered their feet, and with two they flew. [3]And one called to another and said:
God Is Praised	"Holy, holy, holy is the LORD of hosts; the whole earth is full of his glory."
Confession of Sin	[4]The pivots on the thresholds shook at the voices of those who called, and the house filled with smoke. [5]And I said: "Woe is me! I am lost, for I am a man of unclean lips, and I live among a people of unclean lips; yet my eyes have seen the King, the LORD of hosts!"
Forgiveness/ Cleansing	[6]Then one of the seraphs flew to me, holding a live coal that had been taken from the altar with a pair of tongs. [7]The seraph touched my mouth with it and said: "Now that this has touched your lips, your guilt has departed and your sin is blotted out." [8]Then I
God Speaks/ We Respond	heard the voice of the Lord saying, "Whom shall I send, and who will go for us?" And I said, "Here am I; send me!" [9]And he said, "Go and say to this people: 'Keep listening, but do not comprehend; keep looking, but do not understand.' [10]Make the mind of this people dull,

and stop their ears,
and shut their eyes,
so that they may not look with their eyes,
and listen with their ears,
and comprehend with their minds,
and turn and be healed."

We Pray
for Help

[11]Then I said, "How long, O Lord?" And he said:
"Until cities lie waste
without inhabitant,
and houses without people,
and the land is utterly desolate;
[12]until the Lord sends everyone far away,
and vast is the emptiness in the midst of the land.
[13]Even if a tenth part remain in it,
it will be burned again,
like a terebinth or an oak
whose stump remains standing
when it is felled."
The holy seed is its stump.

From this awesome passage we can extrapolate certain characteristics that I believe are the *sine qua non*—the essentials—of full worship.

1. "I saw the Lord" (v. 1): *a full, general self-revealing (including self-giving) of God,* as shown in God's attributes of holiness, omnipotence, mystery, and in God's loving actions, such as redemption (v. 7) and providence.

2. "I said: 'Woe is me!' " (v. 5): *the continual interacting of God's glory with human "woe,"* that is, human weakness, sin, and suffering.

3. "Your sin is blotted out" (v. 7): *God's saving acts* are the central motivation for our worship celebration. Though we contend correctly that worship's central focus is not evangelism, in repeated acts of forgiveness/cleansing/reconciliation, and through our continual sanctification, God "saves" us in the actions of corporate worship.

4. "I heard the voice of the Lord" (v. 8): *God's specific*

revelation to his redeemed people during a particular service, normally presented through Scripture and homily.

5. "I said, 'Here am I, send me!'" (v. 8): *a full human response,* including verbal witness and complete submission of all we are and have to God's purposes.

6. "I said . . . and he said": *a full conversation with God,* with several types of prayer represented, including adoration (v. 3), confession (v. 5), dedication (v. 8), and petition with a suggestion of lament (v. 11).

Interestingly, Isaiah's God-crafted worship was full of audible, visible, and palpable right-brain images, as well as left-brain logic. Of course, a counterpart to the Lord's Supper is not included here, and Isaiah's experience does not include mention of remembrance and thanksgiving. Also, this is an account of a solo worship encounter, and typical Sunday worship must be corporate, with the congregation uniting to be one body—a part of the body of Christ.

Otherwise, I dare to suggest that Isaiah's worship scenes suggest all the essentials of a typical Service of the Word worship (without Communion). With this in mind, let us examine a leading example of contemporary worship today to see how it compares.

An Example of Contemporary Iconoclastic Worship

The acknowledged paradigm among churches committed to "church growth" is Willow Creek Community Church in South Barrington, Illinois, of which Bill Hybels is founder-pastor. On weekends the church presents four "seeker events" that they insist are *not* worship. (However, many other churches in the process of change have mistakenly imitated Willow Creek's style and content by implementing what is called "seeker-sensitive" or "seeker-friendly" *worship.*)

Hybels' sincerity and success in seeking to bridge the chasm between church and culture to reach the uncommitted are evident. I hesitate to criticize any soul-winning method, even the most strange and wonderful, and will not examine the seeker events here.

Once Willow Creek seekers become believers, they are encouraged to be baptized and to become integrated into the full life of the church; this includes participation in small groups for learning, fellowship, and ministry. Requirements for membership at Willow Creek are demanding, but the church welcomes eight thousand or more people on Wednesday and Thursday evenings for their "New Community" services, which are intended to be bona fide worship services.

I believe Bill Hybels seeks to lead Willow Creek's converts into mature Christian living. The one thing I question about Willow Creek is the worship presented on weeknights for its believers (former "seekers") who compose the New Community. The following order was printed in the worship bulletin for a service I visited in February 1992:

"I Love You, Lord"	Vonda Dyer and New Community Chorus
Exaltation	Don Cousins and Congregation
"So Much More"	Barb Olita and New Community Chorus
Family Concerns	
Message:	
"How to Be a Wife"	Jill Briscoe

The service, held in Willow Creek's five-thousand-seat theatre-style auditorium, was essentially one-half musical worship and one-half Bible teaching, with no connection between the two segments. It began with the curtain opening on a stage filled with the choir and praise band. An opening music selection by solo and chorus featured a montage of swing styles.

The best worship action of the evening followed: a well-planned presentation based on Scripture, in which seven readers alternately stated some spiritual blessing of believers, followed with supporting Scriptures paraphrased, and ending with an ascription—"Our God is a wise God . . . a gracious God . . . a giving God . . . a great God." For me, this was the high worship moment of the evening.

Next came a long period of singing called "Exaltation" in the printed bulletin, all of it in the short, repeated forms of praise-and-worship music. The texts were divided between typical pure praise (for instance, "I will bless the Lord and give him glory") and words of devotion and dedication (for example, "Everything I am I bring to you"). Singing began quietly, seemingly in an order improvised by the worship leader and supported by his six-voice worship team, and gradually increased in fervor and volume.

A brief interruption occurred when an offering was received "to support the ministries of the church"—with no mention that this was an action of worship. Next was a call to prayer—silent, personal prayer. "What are the one, two, three blessings God has given you? Give thanks. What do you want from God? Tell him." All of this was accompanied by piano "background music."

Exaltation singing then resumed. Everybody stood and each increasingly more emotional song was accompanied by clapping and body movement and followed with applause, whistles, and yelling. When the planned and prepared choruses and overhead transparencies were exhausted, three additional choruses were sung from memory with even more excitement and pleasure. The music concluded with another solo with choir in contemporary Christian style. The program listing of "Family Concerns"—which I expected to be "Prayers of the People"—turned out to be announcements of activities for the New Community.

The leader introduced the evening speaker and prayed briefly for her speaking. The message, which was a quiet, reasoned exegesis of Ephesians 5:22-23, with bits of humor, read in lecture style from a script, lasted fifty minutes. The speaker, a pastor's wife, explained that the Scripture calls for mutual submission of husband and wife, with the husband being "first among equals." At the end, she prayed briefly, the audience applauded, and we all got up and left.

Evaluation of Iconoclastic Worship

Structurally, the Willow Creek service resembled a typical evangelistic meeting, which features a lengthy song service—with both congregational and "performance" music—followed by a full sermon. It also had much in common with Sunday morning revivalist prayer-preaching-and-song worship, which omits many New Testament essentials. Using the nine New Testament rubrics for worship laid out earlier in this chapter, let's evaluate the New Community service I attended.

1. Scripture Reading
Scriptures were quoted (though not identified as such) in the opening litany, "Our God is a . . . [great] God," and the Ephesians passage formed the basis for the teaching ministry, but there was no recognizable public *reading* of Scripture.

2. The Sermon
The message was instruction about a central issue in today's culture; but it was not true preaching in that there was no call from God for decision and action and no opportunity to respond.

3. Singing of Various Types
The total singing did not add up to the standard of "psalms, hymns, and spiritual songs."

4/5. Prayers and Congregational Amen
Nobody knows what forms of prayer were present, since the "prayers of the people" were silent and personal. In true corporate worship, the church prays as Christ's undivided body, so there can be a united-and-uniting "Amen."

6. Confession of Faith
The absence of voicing a Creed was not startling, since few typical evangelical churches use a confession of faith.

7. Collection
A collection was received, though it was not identified as an "offering" to God.

8/9. Physical Actions and Greetings and Benedictions
There was body action such as hands lifted or clapping during singing, whistling, and yelling. But there was no "kiss of peace"

or other greeting in the name of Christ, not even a handshake or hello.

Evaluating it against the Old Testament model of Isaiah 6, this service featured iconoclasm in other details, some of which are suggested in Isaiah's vision.

Little of the symbolism of traditional worship is left. The room is the same auditorium used for seeker events; we see no cross, no Bible, no hymnals, no pulpit or baptismal font. There is no sense of awe, nobody singing "holy, holy, holy," no shaking of the house (except by ear-splitting sound), no mystery-filled cloud. True, it was dark in the room much of the time, but that theatricality only increased our sense of aloneness, our lack of "togetherness." We came in alone, without corporately greeting God or our neighbors; we left alone without saying goodbye ("God be with you") or "Vaya con Dios" (as in a benediction). As in all the megachurches I have visited, it seemed to be expected that any worship would be *personal,* not corporate.

To be sure, as always, there was symbolism present, and this is what is said to us: "This is a *new, fresh* way of expressing worship to God. What is significant is your personal, immediate feeling of worship. You have no stake in the two-thousand-year history of your Christian forebears. That's why we do not tell the story of God's mighty, loving deeds on behalf of his people, do not cherish any of the historic symbols of our faith, and do not sing any traditional church music. Further, don't let this 'theater' symbolism confuse you. This is vaudeville, not drama. There really is not a logical sequence of events in worship. At least, don't hesitate to discard the order in that tired church you normally attend."

Admittedly, this was just one example of a service that, as one of Willow Creek's staff has said, is "different every time."

> Worship needs to start somewhere, go somewhere. People come to worship from the battlefield of the expressway, after wolfing down a hurried supper. They have many different needs, and the worship planners seek to meet

them by varying the tone of the services. Sometimes people need to be comforted, sometimes they need to be challenged to submit to God. Sometimes they come to a great sense of celebration, and other times to a service that is tender and quiet.[10]

But how do worship planners determine what a congregation needs on any specific night? Doesn't a typical congregation need *all* these messages and perhaps *all* these emotional moods in *every* service? What I hear in this rationale is an apologetic for "surprise worship"—an experience based on titillation of the emotions. This is a typical statement of today's "creativist" worship changers that needs to be challenged.

In 1997 I again visited a worship service of the New Community. That service was more like a midweek prayer meeeeting in my church: half musical "worship" (both congregational and solo "performance") and half "inspirational" speaking (in this instance, Hybels' annual review of the young church's history and goals, with a challenge to meet the latter). There was less opportunity for true worship than on my previous visit.

It is difficult to evaluate a church's worship on the basis of two visits, one of them six years ago. A friend who attends Willow Creek regularly tells me that nowadays a choir is rare, greeting one another is a regular feature, the collection is recognized as an act of worship, and most of the speaking is excellent Bible teaching by the ministering staff. Otherwise, the basic pattern is unchanged. Willow Creek is still young and the church has come a long way toward worthy objectives. Perhaps they will yet develop maturity in the area of Christian worship.

The Geneva Order of Worship, Updated

Finally, I will present a contemporary traditional order of worship in order to compare its potential with that of Willow Creek's New Community and other iconoclastic worship styles. The Geneva Order is based on the outline devised by John

Calvin in the sixteenth century for Reformed services in Geneva. It is similar to the other Western liturgies.[11]

This order contains all the worship actions listed in the New Testament (except baptism), includes all the spiritual experiences of Isaiah 6:1-13, and incorporates a Communion service of "thanksgiving and remembrance." (See outline on next page.)

Here is a description of the parts of worship included in the Geneva Order. The first part of the service, the Gathering, includes the most radical departure from tradition. It suggests beginning with informal fellowship and moving toward a conscious encounter with God in worship.

The Gathering.
The opening acts of worship may be considered partly preparatory. The objective is to help people center their minds and hearts on becoming a community of faith and love, an assembly called together by God. "Preworship" activities may include informal singing (perhaps of experience songs or choruses), "faith witness" (personal testimony), rehearsal of worship materials, announcements, greeting one another, and personal prayer and meditation (possibly with music played).

Full worship begins with a Greeting and/or Call to Worship and a Hymn of Praise, perhaps related to the day or season of the church year. These acts, more than all others in the service, *identify the God we worship.* God's presence is acknowledged by a Prayer of Praise or an Invocation (with petitions concerning the worship service).

The second-century document known as the *Didaché* stated that believers came together on the Lord's Day to break bread and give thanks "after first *confessing their sins.*" This act helps free us to renew our relationship with God. It should always be followed with the assurance that God forgives us (1 John 1:7, 9). A joyful hymn or psalm, or a Trinitarian "Gloria," would appropriately close this section.

All of the materials in this part of the service should be brief, fresh, and challenging, yet easily recognizable and understood. In the Gathering, worshipers are just beginning to focus on the reality of worship, and they are not ready for the more

The Geneva Order of Worship

GATHERING

Preparation (some of the following):
Informal singing, possibly with testimonies or prayers/
rehearsal of music or worship acts/announcements/
kiss of peace/meditation or personal prayer (with music)
Greeting (or Call to Worship) and Hymn of Praise
Opening Prayers: Invocation/prayer of the day/prayer of
praise/Scripture greeting
Prayer of Confession; Assurance of Forgiveness or Litany with response
Act of Praise: Psalm/Hymn/Doxology/Gloria Patri/Gloria in excelsis

PROCLAMATION AND RESPONSE
(Service of the Word)

Prayer for Illumination
Scripture Readings, with responses
Sermon
Response:
Hymn of Corporate Response
Declaration of faith
The Offering (with music)
Prayers of the Congregation (Thanksgiving and Petition)

(If Communion is not observed at this point, continue with Dismissal)

REMEMBRANCE AND THANKSGIVING
(Service of the Table)

Confession and Assurance (if not included earlier)
Invitation to the Lord's Table
Salutation and *Sursum Corda* ("Lift up your hearts")
Prayer of Thanksgiving:
Preface (Salvation history) and *Sanctus* ("Holy, holy, holy")
Remembrance of God's acts through Jesus Christ
Words of Institution
Memorial Acclamation
Prayer to the Holy Spirit (that God's people may be united in
communion with him and with each other)
Doxology and Great Amen
The Lord's Prayer
Communion (with music)
Prayer after Communion

DISMISSAL

Hymn/Charge/Benediction/Silent Prayer/Music

intensive cognitive activity required by the sermon and later prayers.

Proclamation.
Once the church has gathered, has reminded itself who God is, has praised God for his person and his work, and has confessed its sin and been forgiven, cleansed, and reconciled, it is ready to worship God more completely. It does so by *listening carefully to God speak through his revealed Word* and then responding fully. When the Scriptures are read and explained in the church, God himself speaks to his people, for "through the Holy Spirit, Christ is present in the sermon offering grace and calling for obedience."[12] Often a "Prayer for Illumination" is used to ask the Holy Spirit to help us understand God's Word in both Scriptures and Sermon.

Many churches read three portions of Scripture in worship— Old Testament, Epistle, and Gospel—demonstrating the unity as well as the importance of Scripture. As St. Augustine succinctly said, "In the Old Testament the New is hidden; in the New Testament the Old appears." Increasingly, the Psalms are being used as they were intended: as musical responses to God's Word, usually following the Old Testament reading.

In this worship order, the joining of the Scriptures read with God's Word explained (without prayers and offering or other acts between) is purposeful; it ensures that we will identify the relationship of the sermon to the readings. However, music may follow the Old Testament reading or the Epistle without any sense of interruption: it could be congregational, choral, or solo, and should relate to the theme of the day, or express general praise and thanksgiving.

Response.
By this time, the logic of the Geneva Order should have become apparent. In the Gathering, we prepare to worship, centering our minds and hearts on the true God, giving him praise and adoration, confessing that we fall short of his glory, and claiming once again his assurance of forgiveness and acceptance through Christ. Then we listen carefully to what God says

to us, through a full range of Scriptures and through the explanation and application of Scripture in the sermon.

Now we are ready to *respond to God,* both in our hearts and in specific actions. At this point, most churches use a hymn that speaks specifically to the sermon's challenge, perhaps with an opportunity for personal dedication (as in accepting Christ as Savior, or in joining the worship, work, and fellowship of the local church). Many congregations use a Declaration of Faith (or Creed) as well; it affirms that we believe the historical doctrines of our faith and accept God's message of the day as well. Finally, the offering is the worshipers' "amen" to God, whether it is a shout or a whisper. It is our practical, monetary "here am I, send me" response, which also sanctifies our daily work that provides us with money to give.

A few evangelical churches, whose services are televised, place the offering after the sermon, so that the entire message will be heard; but very few offer the "Prayers of the Congregation" (once called the Pastoral Prayer) at this point. Yet this is their placement in Calvin's Geneva Order as well as in all historic Western liturgies. I would affirm this for two reasons: First, God called the meeting in order to reveal himself, his actions, and his will; it is simply good etiquette to "hear God out" and to offer a full affirmative response, before breaking in on the conversation to remind God of our needs and those of others. Second, it is a moving and uniting experience for believers to pray together—to express their humanness and their dependence on God—as the closing act of a community at worship.

At this time the church prays for those who are hurting in the gathered congregation, and also remembers those who are absent for any reason. Because worshipers are part of Christ's body, they pray also for the whole church around the world. Petitionary prayers also include remembrance of government leaders, and of all people everywhere, especially those in distress of any kind. At this point, the prayer is a Christian response to the contents of the week's newspapers and news telecasts! Jesus prayed for the world; his people should do no less. Finally, gratitude is one of the most attractive Christian graces, and it is proper for our petitions to be preceded by *prayers of thanksgiving* for the answers God has already given to our cries for help.

Remembrance and Thanksgiving.
Throughout this book I have spoken of the Lord's Supper in almost sacramental terms, partly because I believe its meaning has been diminished by many evangelicals, especially in my own Baptist fellowship. Timothy George, one of our "historical" theologians, has said:

> We must also guard against a minimalist understanding of the Lord's Supper which reduces this vital ordinance to an empty ritual detached from the spiritual life of believers. . . . We need not fall prey to the lure of sacramentalism or the false doctrine of transubstantiation to reclaim the historic Baptist understanding of the Lord's Supper, which has nowhere been better described than in the *Second London Confession* (of Baptists) of 1689:
>> "Worthy receivers, outwardly partaking of the visible elements in this ordinance, do then also inwardly by faith, really and indeed, yet not carnally and corporally, but spiritually receive, and feed upon Christ crucified and all the benefits of His death: the Body and Blood of Christ, being then not corporally, or carnally, but spiritually present to the faith of believers, in that ordinance, as the elements themselves are to the outward senses."[13]

All worship centers in Christ's victory over sin and death for our salvation, and the Service of the Table is an opportunity to tell that story frequently and effectively. This segment of worship is *most important for seekers* who may be present because it can present the core of the gospel in less than five minutes. Many of our experiences of the Lord's Supper are not as meaningful as they should be, not because we do not dramatize them or because we do not sing the correct music, but because we do not tell the *whole story* and do not offer a complete experience. Follow the outline of this suggested Service of the Table (see page 237).

All Christian believers are invited to the Lord's Table after confessing their sins and being assured of God's forgiveness, cleansing, and reconciliation (unless that has been done earlier in the service).

The *Salutation* ("The Lord be with you; and also with you") and the *Sursum Corda* ("Lift up your hearts . . . Let us give thanks to the Lord . . . ") are biblical phrases that have been used in this connection at least since the third century.

The *Preface* in the Prayer of Thanksgiving begins to tell the story of God's revealing to his people, beginning with creation. It ends with the *Sanctus,* the "three holies" of Isaiah 6:3, in which earth's people join the inhabitants of heaven in singing praise to God.

Remembrance of salvation history (God's story) continues with a reciting of God's revealing through Jesus' incarnation, life, death, resurrection, ascension, and continuing ministry.

The *Words of Institution* (1 Cor. 11:23-26) tie the experience to the supper of Jesus and his disciples in the Upper Room and present our authorization for this experience of worship.

The *Memorial Acclamation* is a concise congregational statement of the basis for our remembrance and thanksgiving: "Christ has died, Christ is risen, Christ will come again."

The *Prayer to the Holy Spirit* is important because it acknowledges the third person of the Trinity; it is only through the Holy Spirit that the Supper or any act of worship will have any meaning to us, either as ordinance or sacrament. It should not be necessary to argue the significance of the *Lord's Prayer,* which should be spoken regularly in worship, either here or as a conclusion of the earlier Prayers of the Congregation.

The prayer closes with a *Doxology* of praise to the Trinity and a united *Amen.*

During *Communion,* the receiving of the bread and cup, music for contemplation or celebration may be sung.

The Service of the Table closes with a *Prayer of Thanks* for God's gift of the Holy Supper for our reminding and our spiritual food.

Dismissal.

When all the central actions of worship have been completed, there is nothing more to do but to send the congregation out into the world of everyday life, where they continue their worship and service to God. Dismissal actions may include some of the following: a hymn, psalm, song, or doxology; a charge (challenge/commission); a benediction, assuring us that we go with God's presence and blessing; and a time of silent prayer, in which we contemplate and confirm the experience just completed. The closing music, usually instrumental, traditionally conveys the ideas of summary or transition to worship and service in everyday life.

The Role of Music

Much of today's argument about worship centers in the music used. Throughout this book I have argued that if God's people are to be the undivided body of Christ, worship planners need to use *both* historic and contemporary music in carefully selected art and traditional styles, folk idioms, and popular forms. I will not be dogmatic about a "balance" of styles, but "tokenism" should be shunned; it will always be recognized as a lack of commitment to one form or another.

I believe that the contemporary concept of a "song service led by a worship leader and team" (including the praise-and-worship format described in chapter 4) is not helpful in worship, for two reasons. First, it suggests that God's presence is apprehended only in a long progression of emotional-musical experiences. I fear that it also encourages the idea that if the singing produces the expected *emotions,* we have certainly met God and "worshiped." Music could be an effective part of *each* of the spiritual experiences outlined above. I recommend especially that if worship choruses are meaningful to the congregation, they can be used for the "preservice" gathering and as congregational responses to prayers. Those and other repetitive forms (like Taizé prayer chants) may serve well also during the Communion service.

Worship Is an Active Verb

Worship scholars have heralded Robert Webber's book *Worship Is a Verb* because it says that worship is *something we do,* not something that service leaders—like preachers and choirs—do for us. Perhaps most people believe the motto infers that congregational hymns are better vehicles of worship than choir anthems, and the best prayers are those we speak with our own lips, lungs, and vocal cords. When today's prophets call us to active participation, they usually remind us that we should not be "couch potatoes" in church.

However, I have observed that many folk watching a football game at home are very active, emotionally and cognitively involved couch potatoes. On the other hand, I fear that many singing, speaking worshipers in church are still quite thoroughly passive and uninvolved, mouthing words without either cognitive or emotional participation!

I noticed recently in a Russian Orthodox service that while the congregation is not required to say or sing anything, they were very much involved in everything that took place. All except the aged and infirm stood throughout the long service, with their eyes riveted on the action of the leaders. I could not prove that they heard every word that was spoken, but they seemed to be thoroughly caught up with biblical and theological phrases they had heard over and over again since childhood. They relaxed their "at attention" position only when they responded by making physical motions of their own, sometimes bowing to touch the floor with their hands or even kneeling to touch it with their foreheads.

I believe that both our singing/speaking and our watching/listening as evangelicals should be thoroughly and intensively active, not passive. In this regard, the choir at my church sets an example for the congregation whenever we have a baptism. Because the baptistry is located above and behind the choir seats, our singers stand and turn around to face the baptismal action. You may be sure that the congregation is more attentive to that worship act than it would be otherwise!

Making Worship Changes in the Church

When we remember the suddenness with which worship iconoclasm descended on us, we might presume that we could reverse the process quickly and proceed to a full, mature worship that incorporates the biblical rubrics we have discussed. I believe this is a propitious time to discuss the topic of change, since the subject is at the forefront of all church life today. However, since most "changing" congregations either have moved or are moving in the direction of destructive iconoclasm, a constructive, reactionary response for worship change needs to be carefully prepared, clearly explained, and well executed.

Church leaders who believe that the worship life advocated in this book is both our privilege and our duty—integral to mature discipleship—have no other choice. But they will first assess their own ability to "lead" a church at this time in history, and the likelihood that their congregation will respond positively. If they believe they are adequately committed and prepared, and the church is sufficiently "open," then worship should be placed at the top of the church agenda, ahead of education, ministry, and proclamation.

I believe that the chosen nature of worship and its underlying rationale should also be described in the church's promotional material. A strong evangelical church in Memphis, Tennessee, has produced an excellent brochure entitled "Worship—Our Gift to God," which states:

> Worship is a response to God for who he is and for what he has done for us in Jesus Christ. The focus of Christian worship should not be on what we get (good feelings, peace, fellowship—though indeed these may be perfectly legitimate by-products), but rather on what we give. We are called to adore and pay homage to God Almighty, and are privileged to be invited to do so: worship is thus an end in itself—indeed the highest of all ends. God seeks, and delights in, the praises of his people.
>
> Worship also serves to reorient us (after the relentless

onslaught of the world and its perspective) to the center of our existence and his will for our lives.[14]

The pamphlet also lists and describes five foundational principles undergirding the "practice of corporate worship" at the church: Blended Worship, Thematic Worship, Participatory Worship, Theocentric Worship, and Dignified Worship.

In most situations, leaders will find it necessary to move slowly, making the "easier" changes first and others as rapidly as the congregation can be prepared for them. The theological integrity and aesthetic quality of each *present* worship action (singing, praying, preaching) may be most important and easiest to achieve; I have dealt with those subjects in other chapters of this book. Especially in our day, corporate services should also incorporate the arts which contribute largely to our emotive, sensory, "wonder and majesty" worship expression.

I believe also that all the worship experiences from Isaiah 6 listed in this chapter are essential and that all the actions recorded in the New Testament epistles are normative for the church. However, if service leaders prepare adequately, a full service can be spoken spontaneously, without any evident "reading."

Also, certain accommodations may be made in the education process. If a church has never used a full Prayer of Confession, that idea may be introduced by combining confession with the Invocation; then later, a full Confession Prayer with Assurance of Pardon could be used. Again, in the Prayers of Thanksgiving and Petition, one Sunday's service could emphasize more thanksgiving, and another, petition. Because "free worship" people are skeptical about repeating the same words week after week (for instance, the Lord's Prayer, the "Glory to God," or the Salutation and *Sursum Corda* of the Communion service), it may be wise to use such elements only occasionally at first.

Finally, though the Geneva service is a logical *order* of worship, other patterns are possible. Offering *full* worship is more important than the order in which the actions occur.

Full Praise of God and Full Ministry to People

Christian worship is our affirming, life-changing response to God's self-revealing and self-giving, through Jesus Christ, as enabled by the Holy Spirit. Full worship, then, requires a *full revelation* of God, Three-in-One, and a *full response* by God's people.

In a culture obsessed with novelty and destructive iconoclasm, a service in the Geneva tradition may sound complicated, rigid, and long. However, if the words (read or improvised) and the music and other arts are well chosen and well used, in the power of the Holy Spirit, this service outline offers the opportunity for more complete worship of God and more blessing for the congregation than iconoclastic substitutes. The following chart shows how God is praised and the church edified in the six experiences of full liturgical worship:

The Experience	God is praised	We are edified
We praise God.	for his transcendent, all-holy Being and his mighty works.	by being assured that our trust is in the only true and living God.
We confess our sins and are forgiven.	as our Judge and Redeemer.	by being forgiven, cleansed, reconciled.
We hear God's Word read and preached.	as the Author and Source of all we need to know for spiritual life.	by the truth of God's Word, which teaches, guides, and molds us.
We respond —"yes"—to God.	as our Lord and Sovereign.	by obeying God, and thus being conformed to his image.
We pray for God's help.	as our Help, our Refuge, our Healer.	by "casting our care" on God.
We give thanks and remember in the Lord's Supper.	as our Savior and our Sustainer.	by "feeding on Christ" in our hearts by faith.

In the next and final chapter of this book, I will encourage church leaders to take the lead in supporting arts education in connection with worship. I also will suggest additional ways to teach the significance of true worship in the life of the church.

9

Worshiping God
in Educational Truth

In a Strange Land of
Intellectual Ambivalence

Education has really only one . . . *sine qua non:*
one must want it.—George E. Woodberry

*A*s children, many of us learned firsthand the meaning of
a biblical motto (along with "I'm doing this for your own
good") often quoted to us with parental discipline:
"Train children in the right way, and when old, they will not
stray" (Prov. 22:6). This educational truth—which also works
in school and in a church music program—has been demonstrated recently in both negative and positive ways.

Thirty years ago we saw the largest youth choirs in church
history, all eager to perform the new musicals and other contemporary music that were appearing. Ministers of music allowed them to sing the new compositions without requiring
them to learn other styles—whether high art, folk song, or
traditional church music. Today those young people have
grown up to be Baby Boomers, and they're back in church
insisting on singing and hearing only their own musical choices
just as they did before. Their musical taste is a case of arrested
development because they were not nurtured by a balanced
diet. Further, they seem to have little interest in well-rounded
music education for their own children or grandchildren.

Education still works in positive ways as well. In University

Baptist Church of Fort Worth, Texas, the youth choir numbers fifty members. It has a waiting list of young singers eager to join, to rehearse two nights a week, and to sing a wide variety of music from memory in the early morning service *every* Sunday. Many other congregations enthusiastically participate in worthy, if less spectacular, ventures. If a church, its ministers, and parents support a strong training program, then a gifted, loving, and patient musician can still minister effectively through church music education, to the glory of God. That's educational truth and another unchanging paradigm!

Reviewing Where We've Been

Before developing this idea of educational truth, let's review our thought pilgrimage. This book is a treatise on Jesus' words about worship: "God is spirit, and those who worship him must worship in spirit and truth" (John 4:24). It has endeavored to explain what those words might mean in these closing years of the twentieth century, in a Western culture that may be less friendly to Christian worship than at any time since A.D. 313, when Constantine decreed that Christianity would be a lawful religion throughout the Roman empire. Because the emphasis has been placed on the arts of worship, especially music, I have referred to our inhospitable culture in the words of Psalm 137:4: "How shall we sing the LORD's song *in a strange land?*" (KJV, italics added) The question voices our frustration, but also asks for positive, helpful answers, which I have tried to give. Here is a summary of my discussion thus far.

Chapter 1 pointed out that much of today's church is preoccupied with forms and styles. God's concern is for worship by the whole person—heart, soul, mind, and strength—"in spirit and truth"—specifically, in Trinitarian truth. When we worship, we must consciously encounter and acknowledge the revelation of God the Father, God the Eternal Son, and God the Holy Spirit, and respond to that revealing.

The second chapter emphasized the primacy of intelligible words in communicating divine truth. Today's culture often seems to be more interested in the affective expressions of symbolic things, such as musical styles, and the novelties of dance or drama. Worship leaders should balance the cognitive and emotive, choosing the best texts available and making sure they are identified. Understanding is often helped when words are both heard with the ear and seen by the eye.

In chapter 3—worshiping God in theological truth—we said that contemporary services have been influenced too much by the charismatic renewal movement, whose theology and practice of worship are very different from those of historical evangelicalism. In our desire to extend evangelical fellowship to include folk of different doctrinal persuasions, we should be careful to "sing up to our own theology" in worship.

The fourth chapter's discussion of biblical truth reminded us that the Bible sets standards for our worship, sometimes by specific commands and sometimes by principles and examples. In continuing the emphasis of chapter 3, this section said that we should examine carefully the biblical interpretations of others, while "rightly explaining the word of truth" ourselves (2 Tim. 2:15). Further, we should demonstrate our biblical understanding in our worship.

Chapter 5 examined worshiping as a community in ecclesiological truth in the light of the growing practice of dividing congregations according to worship style. This chapter urged worship leaders to keep Christ's body—the church—undivided by carefully choosing from a variety of musical styles in a single, inclusively designed service that might be called "contemporary traditional."

The sixth chapter dealt with our culture's effect on worship and raised some of the same questions H. Richard Niebuhr posed in his book *Christ and Culture:* Do we preach a "Christ of culture" or a "Christ against culture"?[1] Many modern observers believe that evangelicalism is attempting to sanctify the unsanctifiable by combining entertainment with worship, especially in its use of some of the more extreme musical styles of secular pop culture. My answer is the same as Niebuhr's: We should preach and exemplify a "Christ who *transforms* culture."

We suggested in chapter 7 that today's conflicts about what

constitutes beauty in worship art stem partly from "aesthetic anarchy"—a failure to acknowledge any authority other than personal preference. It reminded us that God is the source of all beauty, as well as of all truth, and that Christians should be aesthetically creative, bringing to God their best artistic expressions, in worship as in all of life.

Chapter 8 argued that form and content of public worship *do* matter in a day when many churches seem to be cleaning out traditional forms and, in the process, "throwing out the baby with the bath water." It espouses *complete worship*—a full self-revealing of God and a full response by God's adoring, obedient children.

Which brings us to this final chapter on what it means to worship in educational truth in today's strange land of intellectual ambivalence. This topic is a logical conclusion for this study because it calls for Christian education to meet the challenges of our day. Here we face yet another cultural antagonist, perhaps two: our society's disinterest in arts education and evangelical failure to study and to teach worship—almost to the point of anti-intellectualism.

Many observers believe that the church is experiencing the contemporary wilderness of conflict, frustration, and failure, because of our past failure to understand, to live by, and to *teach the truth* involved. If we are to reclaim God's full blessing, it will come through repentance, returning to that truth, and teaching and demonstrating it to our children.

Theological Education in the Scriptures

To begin, I will discuss a biblical approach to education in general and then give the history of music education in particular. Ancient Israel learned from the Torah that God was the first teacher and that they were required to communicate *all of God's truth* to subsequent generations. Moses reminded the Israelites of what God had said on Mount Horeb:

> So now, Israel, give heed to the statutes and ordinances that I am teaching you to observe, so that you may live to

enter and occupy the land that the LORD, the God of your ancestors, is giving you. . . . Take care and watch yourselves closely, so as neither to forget the things that your eyes have seen nor to let them slip from your mind all the days of your life; make them known to your children and your children's children. (Deut. 4:1, 9)

Later we read these instructions about pedagogy in faith, together with parallel symbolic actions that are practiced to this day by Orthodox Jews:

Keep these words that I am commanding you today in your heart. Recite them to your children and talk about them when you are at home and when you are away, when you lie down and when you rise. Bind them as a sign on your hand, fix them as an emblem on your forehead, and write them on the doorposts of your house and on your gates. (Deut. 6:6-9)

Deuteronomy 32 contains Moses' great hymn of witness and challenge to Israel, delivered before his death and burial on Mount Nebo. The accompanying instructions say something significant about the importance of solid, historical, congregational music:

Now therefore write this song, and teach it to the Israelites; put it in their mouths, in order that this song may be a witness for me. . . . *And when many terrible troubles come upon them, this song will confront them as a witness,* because it will not be lost from the mouths of their descendants. (Deut. 31:19, 21, italics added)

The New Testament also reveals that faith is communicated by teaching. During Jesus' ministry on earth he was known as *Rabbi* ("teacher"). His final teaching to his disciples included the challenge that they should continue the same ministry in his stead: "Go therefore and make disciples of all nations, baptizing them in the name of the Father and of the Son and of the Holy Spirit, and *teaching them to obey everything that I have commanded you"* (Matt. 28:19-20, italics added). So we have in Scripture a directive to teach others spiritual truths we have learned.

Worship Arts Training in the Old Testament

Teaching our Christian faith certainly should include instruction in how to worship God, the Three-in-One. Such training should begin with general biblical-theological principles and proceed to such practical matters as the use of words, music, and other arts that express God's self-revealing to us and our life-transforming response to God.

In chapter 7, I noted God's instructions for the artwork of the ancient Hebrew tabernacle. The same passage says that artistic talents are a gift from God which should be passed on to others.

> Then Moses said to the Israelites: See, the LORD has called by name Bezalel son of Uri son of Hur, of the tribe of Judah; *he has filled him with divine spirit, with skill, intelligence, and knowledge in every kind of craft*, to devise artistic designs, to work in gold, silver, and bronze, in cutting stones for setting, and in carving wood, in every kind of craft. *And he has inspired him to teach,* both him and Oholiab son of Ahisamach, of the tribe of Dan. (Exod. 35:30-34, italics added)

The choral singing of the tabernacle and temple was also under the tutelage and direction of experts, as recorded in detail in such lengthy passages as 1 Chronicles 6:31-48 and 15:16-22. The latter reading ends with this statement of required proficiency for all would-be art teachers: "Chenaniah, leader of the Levites in music, was to direct the music, *for he understood it"* (italics added). In these long lists of musical worship artists, the names "Asaph, Heman, and Jeduthun" stand out and are repeated in several subsequent Scriptures. Asaph in particular seems to have established something of a guild or school of worship music, whose members are identified as "sons of Asaph" (1 Chron. 25:1-2; 26:1; 2 Chron. 5:12; 20:14; 29:13; 35:15; Ezra 2:41; 3:10; Neh. 7:44; 11:17,22; 12:35; and in superscriptions of some psalms).

Education through Music in the New Testament

The apostle Paul passed along Christ's commission to teach to the believers at Colossae, and thus to the whole church, in Colossians 3:16, "teach and admonish one another." David Pass argues that this charge should be linked directly to the phrase "psalms, hymns, and spiritual songs" as it is in the King James Version: "teaching and admonishing one another *in* psalms and hymns and spiritual songs" (italics added). Pass calls this charge the "Magna Carta of church music."[2] Most modern translations do not follow the King James pattern, but group the ideas like the *New Revised Standard Version:* "Let the word of Christ dwell in you richly; teach and admonish one another in all wisdom; and with gratitude in your hearts sing psalms, hymns, and spiritual songs to God."

It is not necessary to restructure this verse to find warrant for Christian education in the music experiences provided in our churches. Without doubt, in these words, teaching "the word of Christ" is linked to our singing, however closely. In this case, Scripture gives us direction *by example,* if not by direct rubric. In Old Testament times, music was the bearer and teacher of God's good news—in the Song of Moses before his death, in many other canticles, and primarily in the book of Psalms. In the early church, *music was God's pedagogue* through the psalms, hymns, and spiritual songs mentioned by Paul (Eph. 5:19), and perhaps uniquely in the "Jesus hymns" found throughout the New Testament. One example is 1 Timothy 3:16:

> He was revealed in flesh,
> vindicated in spirit,
> seen by angels,

proclaimed among Gentiles,
 believed in throughout the world,
 taken up in glory.

The Place of Music Education in Western History

Of course, all artistic activity in the church will be affected pro or con by education in the home and in the general culture. Formal training in the arts has had a checkered history since before the Christian era and seems to be seriously threatened in our day. Throughout this long period, public education has taught music more than any other art.

No society has given larger place to music training than that of ancient Greece, where free men (though not women) studied Homer, mathematics, music, and gymnastics. In the ancient church, sophisticated or "serious" music activity was limited to the clergy; Gregory the Great (ca. 540–604) is said to have established the *Schola cantorum* in Rome to standardize and teach the official chant of the church. As Christianity spread throughout the Western world, cathedrals, monasteries, abbeys, and collegiate churches established choir schools where boys received their general education and were trained in music for the church's worship.

The first American music education for groups of people occurred in early eighteenth-century "singing schools," organized to "combat what the clergy perceived as a serious decline in the musical skills of parishioners."[3] Public education became common early in the nineteenth century, and by 1838 Lowell Mason (1792–1872) had introduced music into the curriculum of Boston schools. By the end of the nineteenth century, most American children received training in sight-singing.

In the twentieth century, music education was broadened to include an introduction to the tradition of Western art music. Middle schools and high schools formed and trained bands, orchestras, and choruses, and offered elective classes in music appreciation, theory, and history. "General music" (including singing, music appreciation, and increasing use of the techniques of Kodály, Orff, Suzuki, and Dalcroze) continued to be required for the elementary grades.

Of course, churches profited from public music education and built on its foundation in their own training activities. Early in the twentieth century, John Finley Williamson developed the "graded choir" concept and taught it at Westminster Choir College. Many urban churches soon adopted this pattern as the norm for their music education programs. Today, many churches offer music training for preschoolers to senior adults and performance opportunities for all except the youngest children.

Beginning in the 1950s, the costs associated with new emphases on science and technology forced public schools to reevaluate their curricula. In the 1970s and 1980s, pressures to limit or drop arts education increased as school populations and tax revenues decreased. At the moment the future of public school music is at best iffy.

Music Education's Contribution to Society

Why should we worry if typical children in the early grades are not taught to sing? Many people believe that for all except professional artists, education in the arts has little to do with earning a living or functioning well in society.

Ancient Greece was convinced that individuals could be good citizens only if music was a large part of their *general* education. More than two thousand years later, one would think that, with the emergence of "right-brain/left-brain" thinking, modern society would agree that the emotive (aesthetic) brain needs the discipline and nurture of formal training just as much as the cognitive (rational) brain. Many educators still believe that is true.

In *Foundations and Principles of Music Education,* Charles Leonhard and Robert House list fifteen tenets of their philosophy of music education, of which I will name only three:

■ Aesthetic experience grows out of and is related to ordinary experience. "Aesthetic quality is the source of man's highest satisfaction in living, and while all experience that is carried on intelligently has aesthetic quality, *man's most valued experience is in connection with art objects consciously and feeling-fully conceived and contemplated"* (italics added).

■ All human experience is accompanied by feeling. Music bears a close similarity to the forms of human feeling and is the tonal analogue of the emotive life.

■ Every person has the need to transform experience symbolically and has the capacity for symbolic experience with music.[4]

Partly for these reasons, many community leaders believe that schools must maintain arts education. Campaigns to preserve music programs have been supported by recent research which shows that aesthetic training makes many contributions to culture that are not generally recognized.

Wendell Harrison has asked the question, "Does playing a musical instrument make a child smarter?" His answer:

Studies have been done for some time now on basic intelligence as it relates to playing a musical instrument. While once it was said that smart kids are in the band or orchestra, for sometime now neurologists have been finding that the kids are smart *because* they are in the band or orchestra [italics added].[5]

A 1992 study developed by the Center for Music Research at Florida State University provided evidence that participation in the arts is a powerful tool for motivating at-risk students to stay in school.[6] Another report demonstrated that first-graders who received Kodály training (which uses folk songs and emphasizes melodic and rhythmic elements) exhibited significantly better reading scores than other students.[7] In yet another case, when singing lessons were combined with keyboard instruction, children showed remarkable improvement in space perception.[8]

The future of music education in the United States is still in doubt, since the culture at large does not support it. Perhaps too few folks know about this research or have confidence in the conclusions reached. Perhaps in our materialistic culture, not enough people really care.

A Parable from Contemporary Culture

A remarkable picture of today's "strange land of intellectual ambivalence" in music education is presented in the 1996 movie *Mr. Holland's Opus.* Glenn Holland is a musician who has dreams of being a successful composer, but completes a music education degree "just in case." After ten years of bare subsistence in traveling show business, he reluctantly takes a job teaching music in a high school during the 1960s.

In his first years of teaching, Glenn spends every unscheduled moment working on his first "symphony." However, he soon discovers that if he is to meet the needs of his students, his free time must be given to special rehearsals and coaching his "very average" students. His idealism almost disappears in his first classes and rehearsals because his students are neither talented nor very interested in music. Gradually he learns how to teach music appreciation by beginning with the music most students prefer—rock 'n' roll.

As Glenn follows the advice of his wise principal to "give students a compass" to guide them in meeting life's challenges, he develops the too rare insight that characterizes a master teacher. He teaches a shy girl to play the clarinet "because she wants to be good at something, like all the rest of the family." After a long period of frustration, he finally teaches an unmusical boy to play the bass drum in order to earn an academic credit and qualify for athletic activity in which he has unusual talent.

Over the next thirty years of his career, he goes through great difficulties in balancing the demands of teaching with the emotional and financial needs of his often dysfunctional family. He frequently is embroiled in conflict with the new principal and the school board over his educational philosophy and techniques. In spite of all this, he survives and succeeds in developing a strong music and drama program, even during the tumultuous 1960s, 1970s, and 1980s. In the process of struggling to teach public school music, he has become a mature person who understands the relationship of love and responsibility. Even more, through the unique one-on-one process of music teaching, his students have developed work habits and true character, which enable them to meet their most important life challenges.

But the symphony never gets finished.

Later, Glenn is just short of retirement age when he is informed that, because of budget pressures, the entire music/art/drama education program is being dropped from the curriculum. In the movie's closing scenes, as he is leaving the school building for the last time, he hears music in the auditorium. He goes to investigate and finds the room jammed with present and former students. The shy girl he had taught clarinet was there, now a woman who has become governor. At the speaker's podium she declares that Mr. Holland's *principal opus* is his students who have gathered to honor him. "You have touched every life in this room, and, as a result, we are better persons," she says. The picture ends at a high emotional level with the school band playing his now finished symphony.

I found the motion picture amazingly true to contemporary culture, even in its somewhat disappointing conclusion. All my friends have said, "Isn't that a wonderful movie?" Of course I enjoyed it and was glad that Holland realized finally that his life's struggle had been worthwhile. But why did no one speak up at the gathering and *say* that the school and the community would be much poorer without arts education? They were losing something that could not be replaced by better reading, writing, arithmetic (and computer science), subjects the principal decided were "more important than Mozart." Surely his ex-student-now-governor remembered what music had contributed uniquely to her development. If she ever considered it important to find money for art study or even to urge citizens to vote to increase their taxes for that purpose, it unfortunately wasn't mentioned on that final day. The best way they could have honored Mr. Holland would have been to preserve that character-building education for their children and grandchildren!

It's still hard to say whether or not aesthetic training will survive in our public schools, despite the recent passage of the Goals 2000: Educate America Act. Here the arts are listed as an equal partner with other school subjects. One of the eight stated national education goals is as follows:

> All students will leave grades 4, 8, and 12 having demonstrated competency in challenging subject matter, including English, mathematics, science, foreign languages, civics and government, economics, *arts,* history, and geography, and every school in America will ensure that all students learn to use their minds well so that they may be prepared for responsible citizenship, further learning, and productive employment in our nation's modern economy [italics added].[9]

I believe that, in the light of biblical teaching and the research reported above, Christian parents should support this standard for both public and private schools.

Music Education's Contribution in the Church

Many church leaders and members believe that if music education does not survive in the general culture, it is pointless to try to maintain it in the church. Others insist that, if necessary, the church should take the lead in developing the artistic gifts of its members as it has done in the past.

Music training in church offers an important opportunity for the physical, intellectual, aesthetic, and spiritual formation of individuals in the church—as persons, as musicians, and as Christians. That formation includes all the positive effects mentioned in connection with public music education. Uniquely in the church, choir members are taught also that by developing God-given talent they are practicing stewardship in offering to God their best "sacrifice of praise," for God's glory and the blessing of all worshipers. This too is an unchanging paradigm.

Music education in the church, then, *is inseparable from Christian education.* Roger L. Shinn defines Christian education as "the effort to introduce persons into the life and mission of the community of Christian faith." To demonstrate how this is linked to music, I will relate music education to Shinn's three components of Christian education, the first one being:

> 1. The educational ministry of the church invites and incorporates persons into the life of the Christian community. It engages them in the characteristic acts by which this community responds to God.
>
> This community finds modes of expression that communicate and evoke faith: . . . (1) worship, (2) Christian thought, and (3) ethos (spirit of the community) and ethic (ethos in action).

Music is a primary mode of expression in *worship* and in proclaiming *Christian thought* (in the words of hymns and other music). It also expresses the *spirit* of the community, both in small-group music activity, like rehearsals, and in the whole congregation, when it worships together. Finally, music expresses the community's *ethic:* We rehearse and perform together in mutual esteem, cooperation, and love, offering our musical gifts to God.

> 2. The educational ministry of the church is the appropriation of a heritage. It involves individuals in a past that significantly constitutes their present. . . . Christian education requires the internalizing of a meaningful history.

A comprehensive music ministry appropriates the heritage of God's acts in history with and through human beings. This heritage is conveyed in words that relate God's mighty deeds in history and in the verbal and musical art forms that have come down to us through the centuries. We dare not cripple either Christian education or music education by catering to our culture's obsession with "modernity."

3. The educational ministry of the church is training in mission. It requires learning by service and for service of God in his world.[10]

The music program is a means of service and of mission. This concept is incarnated by choir members and instrumentalists in their regular ministry to a congregation and community and perhaps in mission tours by musical groups. It may even include a challenge to some individuals for lifetime service in music ministry, either at home or in overseas missions.

The Ministry of Music: Music Education Plus Christian Education

I have always believed that music activity in the church (especially for younger ages) is more important for what it offers to the participants in complete spiritual-intellectual-emotive-physical formation, than for what the participants offer to the congregation in performances. Ministers of music educate "Christianly" through music activity, so they must be aware of musical and spiritual capabilities at every age level. The following paragraphs give an example of their challenge.[11]

Some church musicians believe that the older elementary group of children (ages nine to eleven) is the most exciting age to work with. The child's voice is beautiful at this age and can cover a wide range of pitches with a lot of tonal contrast, so long as the dynamic level is not forced. These children can develop sound singing techniques and maintain them with a sense of perfection in actual worship performance, as the boys in English cathedral choirs demonstrate. They are able to experience personal worship of God and are therefore qualified to lead the congregation in worship. They can and should become aware of music's functions in worship, as well as of the meaning of other liturgical actions.

Unfortunately, in recent years children's music activity in

some churches has suffered from the attempt to match pop performances in the entertainment world. In one church I know, parents rejected the ministry of a superb children's music specialist "because she emphasized learning more than fun." The children weren't bored, only the parents! Another church boasted recently that it supported "worship in the *real world*," attracting teenagers by playing contemporary Christian music with accompanying music videos. (Perhaps it *would* be better to "worship in God's world"!) Certain music publishers have met the "dumbing down" expectations of modern culture by supplying children's musicals with the razzle-dazzle and glitz we expect from the half-time extravaganzas on TV's athletic broadcasts. But such negative examples are neither good Christian education nor good music pedagogy.

Despite the examples cited at the beginning of this chapter, many folks still believe that in order to keep teenagers in the church we must give them *Christian versions* of the secular pop music preferred by their age group. A study by music educator Barbara Resch indicates that that is not true.

In classrooms in public and private high schools, Resch played a tape of forty excerpts of music heard in American churches today, including (1) traditional organ and choral music (from Gregorian chant to twentieth-century anthems); (2) religious easy listening (contemporary Christian music, gospel, jazz, and folk); (3) improvisatory vocal genres (African-American gospel, jazz, and rock); (4) traditional instrumental music; (5) solo performances with instrumental backup group (vocal jazz, classic aria, country gospel); and (6) rock and twentieth-century instrumental music (with high volume, fast tempos, and percussiveness). Students were not asked whether they *liked* the music or not, but whether they considered it *appropriate* for use in church.

Resch reports that "the responses of unchurched teenagers—those who lacked a context from which to judge appropriateness—lined up with typical teenage music preferences, with the highest ratings going to soloistic styles and rock music." However, the overall response of all students gave the highest ratings of appropriateness to traditional choral music and the lowest to Christian rock music. Students who attended church showed that there is a close tie between their perception of appropriateness and how often they hear a particular type of music in church. Resch concludes:

> Therefore, it is clear that the music young people consider appropriate for worship is likely the music they already hear in the context of the church service. Rather than bringing an external set of standards from the world of leisure listening to the church situation—which is what we have assumed teenagers are doing—the church situation itself seems to determine what teenagers feel is right for that setting.[12]

These examples should suggest the musical and spiritual training possibilities for every group in the church: preschool, elementary, middle school, high school, adults, senior adults, and "exceptional" (handicapped) people.

Teaching Worship in the Church

In conclusion, I must say something about education in the totality of worship, adding to the suggestions already given at the ends of chapters 2 and 8. Church members need to be prepared for their roles as members of the faith community. Most congregations provide regular instruction for Sunday school teachers (and, of course, pupils). They also help church members learn how to witness to their faith and how to carry out social ministries. Very few offer training in what Paul Richardson has called our "common and essential vocation"—the worship of God![13]

If, during recent years, pastors had understood the significance of true, full worship actions and words and had practiced and taught the same to their congregations, we might not now be experiencing such a turbulent revolution. If we are to move on from this wilderness experience into God's Promised Land of true worship, we must *again and forever study and teach* the essentials of worship philosophy and procedures.

Resistance may be expected in the "strange land" of congregational intellectual ambivalence—perhaps in the often expressed opinion that believers "automatically" worship correctly and that worship education (like prepared prayers) is somehow a threat to sincerity and reality. Evangelicals can hope to develop sound concepts and patterns of worship only through long-term education in the local church. Here are four ways we can teach believers about how to worship in spirit and truth.

In preparing for church membership.
Historically, Christian believers in liturgical churches have prepared for full participation in the body of Christ in catechism classes, which teach the doctrines of the particular tradition and lay foundations for worship participation. To a lesser degree, certain evangelical churches have conducted "new members' classes." Such classes should be required. They can provide answers to such questions as:

- Why and how should we worship as a group on Sunday morning, as families at home during the week, and as individual believers in every experience of life?
- In corporate worship, what is the meaning of a Call to Worship or a Benediction?
- Why do we celebrate the Lord's Supper as we do?
- Why do we sing particular styles of music? How do congregational hymns, choral anthems, and contemporary Christian music contribute to full worship?
- How should laypersons lead in public prayer?
- When does handclapping glorify God and benefit other worshipers, and when does it not?

In preparing for services.
Many churches that publish a weekly newsletter list the principal materials of worship for each Sunday: sermon title, Scriptures, hymns and anthems, and so on. This is a reminder that all these elements are important to the service; it can encour-

age members to read the Scriptures in advance and to look forward to the musical items.

Such a newsletter could also include articles about worship and worship orders, and even analyses of hymn texts.[14] For instance, the inclusion of worship materials like this sixteenth-century prayer poem of John Donne would help many worshipers understand the significance of the Prayer of Confession and Assurance of Forgiveness:

Wilt thou forgive that sin where I begun,
    which was my sin though it were done before?
Wilt thou forgive that sin through which I run,
    and do run still, though still I do deplore?
When thou hast done, thou hast not done,
    for I have more.

Wilt thou forgive that sin by which I've won
    others to sin, and made my sin their door?
Wilt thou forgive that sin which I did shun
    a year or two, but wallowed in a score?
When thou hast done, thou hast not done,
    for I have more.

I have a sin of fear, that when I've spun
    my last thread, I shall perish on the shore;
but swear by thyself that at my death thy Son
    shall shine as he shines now, and heretofore,
and having done that, thou hast done;
    I fear no more.

The opening segment of worship orders—the Gathering—is also preparatory in nature. In our church it includes a "gathering hymn," announcements about important activities, a welcome, especially to visitors, and preparation for the "invitation" that will be given at the end of the sermon. Full worship begins with a Call to Worship, sometimes following an instrumental prelude. Such a time of preparation can also include explanation, and sometimes rehearsal, of worship actions and elements, including new hymns.

Some pastors oppose such an activity, apparently because they believe it detracts from the dignity of the worship experience to follow. I fear that such reluctance is based on the idea that worship is a performance *for* the worshipers. However, if worship is the worshiper's work, practicing a new hymn makes just as much sense as the choir's short rehearsal of the anthem before the service. Even at the symphony concert, all the musicians will be "warming up" and practicing difficult passages in the scheduled music until just before the conductor enters.

In the worship bulletin.
The Order of Worship itself is worship education, and some churches call it the "worship guide." In our church it gives the service actions in bold type: **Gathering** (as described above), **Praise** (Call to Worship, Hymn of Praise, Invocation, Anthem), **Proclamation** (Scripture, Pastoral Prayer, Response Hymn, Sermon), and **Response** (Hymn of Invitation, Offering, Musical Offering, Sharing of Decisions).

Of course, it is important that there be "truth in advertising." An announced Call to Worship should not turn out to be a bit of choral praise or a spoken Invocation. A Benediction should always announce the blessing of the Trinity, rather than state a congregational "charge" based on the sermon emphasis. If possible, song texts should be specifically identified as a "Hymn of Praise" or an "Anthem of Witness" or a "Psalm of Lament." Prayers should be listed as "Invocation," "Dedication," "Confession," "Praise," or "Thanksgiving and Petition." In some church bulletins, each hymn listing is even followed with a short statement of the words' emphasis.

In the service itself.
Perhaps the best worship teaching is done in the service itself. A well-planned, well-executed service is its own best apologist. However, because any repeated ritual ("liturgical" or "charismatic") may anesthetize its participants, we should go out of

our way repeatedly to sensitize them to the Holy Spirit's wake-up call!

Pastors can repeat words of the hymns in prayers following, thus tying the service elements together. A hymn can be announced with a brief statement about its significance in that particular service. The *purpose* of each worship action should be described occasionally. In different instances the service leader could include explanations such as:

"In the Prayer of Confession, we have an opportunity to be assured that we worship God with pure hearts, free of unconfessed sin."

Or "Our offering of money gifts acknowledges that all we have is a gift from God, and says a very practical 'amen' to God's will for our lives."

Or "In the Scriptures, Jesus Christ speaks to us: listen to the Word of God!"

Similarly, special actions such as baptisms, family dedications (in presenting a child), and the Lord's Supper should be explained on a regular basis.

Education for Heaven's Worship

As mentioned in the first chapter, I believe that a sense of God's presence in our services is necessary if we are to worship with the whole person—heart, soul, mind, and strength—"in spirit and truth." We often should remind our congregations that all earthly worship is preparation and training as part of our eternal vocation: praising God forever and ever, unto ages of ages, in God's very Presence.

Whenever we sing the "three holies," we declare that the glory of God is celebrated in heaven and on earth simultaneously because our human voices and actions join those of angels around God's throne, "Holy, holy, holy is the Lord of hosts: the whole earth is full of his glory" (Isa. 6:3) and "Holy, holy, holy, the Lord God the Almighty, who was and is and is to come" (Rev. 4:8).

One day there will be but one choir—all singing "like the

sound of many waters and like . . . mighty thunderpeals, crying out":

> "Hallelujah!
> For the Lord our God the Almighty reigns.
> Let us rejoice and exult and give him the glory,
> for the marriage of the Lamb has come,
> and his bride has made herself ready;
> to her it has been granted to be clothed
> with fine line, bright and pure"—
> for the fine linen is the righteous deeds of the saints.
> (Rev. 19:6-8)

In that truth, we should be sure that our worship echoes more a vision of heaven than that of an unbelieving culture. Otherwise our earthly rehearsal might do us little good! Let us pray with Erik Routley:

> God of Glory, around whose eternal throne all the
> heavenly powers offer their ceaseless songs of praise:
> Grant that we may overhear these songs, and with our
> own lips and lives interpret them to all in whose
> presence we play or sing;
> That your church may behold the beauty of its
> King, and see with mortal eyes the land that is afar
> off, where all your promises are celebrated, and
> where all your love in every sight and sound is the
> theme of eternal rejoicing; through Jesus Christ our
> Lord. Amen.[15]

A Final Word of Hope

If some of this book has sounded like a jeremiad, I must close with a statement of hope and challenge.

I believe that some groups in the larger church are becoming aware that they have been "on spiritual detour" recently in their consuming preoccupation with novel worship forms and styles. They are almost ready to head down the "straight and narrow," if the correct road can be identified in the current maze of opinions and possibilities. Certain parachurch groups, such as Promise Keepers, have learned that they need historic hymns as well as contemporary choruses to attract men of all ages and to help them express their identity in more mature worship. Some churches are retreating from their decision to be segregated into "contemporary" and "traditional" ghettos, and are choosing more inclusive, contemporary traditional worship. When that happens, the *new is joined with the old,* which should always have been the paradigm. Nobody doubts that the church is in serious trouble, particularly in its relationship to modern culture. But more and more thinking leaders are convinced that the solution to its problems will not be found in thoughtless tinkering with its worship forms and arts.

The Christian commitment necessary for such a renewal in worship is expressed well in a "Postmodern Confession of Faith" by Leonard Sweet, partially quoted here:

> I am a member of the Church of the Out of Control. I am an out of control disciple. I've given up my control to God. I trust and obey the Spirit. I've jumped off the fence, stepped over the line. I've pulled out all the stops. There's no turning back, looking around, slowing down, backing away, letting up or shutting up. It's a life against the odds, outside the box, over the wall, the game of life played without goal lines other than "Thy will be done." . . .
>
> I am not here to please the dominant culture or to serve any all-show, no-go bureaucracy; I live to please my Lord and Savior. My spiritual taste buds have graduated from fizz and froth to fire and ice. Sometimes I'm called to sharpen the cutting edge and sometimes to blunt the cutting edge. . . .
>
> I won't be seduced by popularity, traduced by criticism, travested by hypocrisy, or trivialized by mediocrity. Just because the show must go on, whether in Hollywood, Washington, Nashville or Denver, doesn't mean the show is worth watching. . . .

My fundamental identity is as a disciple of *Jesus*—but even more, as a disciple of Jesus who lives *in Christ,* who doesn't trek through history simply "in His steps" but seeks to travel more deeply *in His Spirit.*[16]

As I come to the end of this writing project, I notice that, without really planning it, this book on Christian worship has taken on the character of an actual Service of the Word. The arguments I've put forth are much like a homily, which, beginning with the first words of the Prologue, has been based on Holy Scripture. Throughout there have been occasional songs and prayers. So in keeping with the Service, I must close with a Benediction that prays for the ending God desires to the present "worship wars":

Peace be to the whole community, and love with faith. (Eph. 6:23)

The grace of the Lord Jesus Christ, the love of God, and the communion of the Holy Spirit be with all of you. (2 Cor. 13:13)

Appendix I

More Definitions of Worship

Since no one definition will suffice for the activity we call worship, I offer here some of the best-known definitions of or statements about that holy calling. The added commentary is intended to clarify what it means to worship "in spirit and truth," so this appendix might also be titled "Tests of True Worship."

From the Hebrew Scriptures: The Hebrew word for "worship" is *shachah*, "bowing down" (see Exod. 34:8). In ancient times, worship was expressed with the physical action of bowing, sometimes to the point of being prostrate ("Then Abram fell on his face . . ." Gen. 17:3). We worship in spirit and truth when we bow in submission to God's will for us because we love God, Three-in-One, with our total selfhood.

From the New Testament: The Greek word for "worship" is *latreuo*, "the work of the people" for God (see Rev. 19:10). True worship requires thoughtful, disciplined effort. People who want to meet God in spirit and truth will reject so-called worship in which they are encouraged to be passive or entertained.

Martin Luther: "In worship, we assemble in order to hear and to discuss God's Word, and then to praise God, to sing, and to pray."[1] The true heart-worshiper will welcome God's full Word of truth and will seek to respond to it fully in praise and prayer, and also in a changed life.

John Calvin: "The principal work of the Spirit is faith. . . . The principal exercise of faith is prayer."[2] Jesus called the Jerusalem temple his Father's "house of prayer," and in one historic worship tradition, services are known as Morning Prayer and Evening Prayer. True worshipers do not "say" prayers or "hear" prayers. Even when they read prayers in the worship order, *they pray,* through Jesus Christ as enabled by God's Spirit. Further, mature faith will produce full, mature prayer, beginning with confession, and balancing petition with praise and thanksgiving.

Evelyn Underhill: "Christian worship is the total adoring response of man to the one Eternal God self-revealed in time."[3] My own adaptation of this statement for the purpose of this book is: "Christian worship is the affirmative, transforming response of human beings to God's self-revealing and self-giving, through Jesus Christ, in the power of the Holy Spirit." Because God always makes the first move, says the first word, worship begins with God's self-giving and self-revealing. The in-spirit-and-truth worshiper will be eager to hear all that God reveals and to receive all that God gives, and faithful to respond fully—in sincere praise and in full dedication of self and means to God's glory.

Appendix I

Ken Medema: "Worship is telling the story of God's gracious, mighty acts on behalf of his people, and finding our place in the story."[4] God's actions in history began with Creation and will close when all believers are gathered in God's eternal Presence. When we worship in spirit and truth, we will bring the story up-to-date, acknowledging our union with Christ and his church through the new birth and our present relationship with Christ as a disciple and follower.

Robert Webber: "Worship is a verb."[5] Worship is something we do, not something that is done for us (by ministers and musicians). Again, the mental and physical "doing" must be acts that express the love and commitment of our total selves. For instance, true worshipers do not give money in the offering primarily to support the work of the church. They do so as an act of worship, a token that all they are and have belongs to God, One-in-Three.

Welton Gaddy: "The people of God exist to serve God. No higher service to God is possible than the worship of God."[6] Ordinary human employment can be performed as a matter of duty or a necessary means to an end, that is, to sustain or to improve the human condition. Worship, our work for God, is wasted effort unless it originates in our total selfhood's love of God.

James White: "Called from the world, we come together, deliberately seeking to approach reality at its deepest level by encountering God in and through Jesus Christ and by responding to this awareness."[7] God says the first word; by the Holy Spirit, we are "called from the world." But human beings must *deliberately* seek to "encounter God in and through Jesus Christ" and to respond.

Donald Hustad: "The worship service is a rehearsal for the everyday life of worship."[8] Someone has said that everyday life is the "true liturgy," since, for the Christian believer, all of life should be worship. If the rehearsal is true worship in spirit and truth, life itself should be worship with the whole person—heart, soul, mind, and strength.

From Choristers' Guild material (ascribed to Martin Luther): "They who sing pray twice," that is, they pray with the mind (through the words) and with the emotions (through the music). This means more than understanding the words and feeling the emotions associated with them and with all aspects of the music. Worshipers in spirit and truth are saying a spiritual "amen" to the words, sensing God's presence as reality, and joyfully "making melody to the Lord" in their hearts (Eph. 5:19). This is worshiping God in both cognitive and emotive truth.

Appendix II

Worship Drama:
Holy and Ordinary

One hundred fifty years ago, Søren Kierkegaard used the metaphor of a stage drama to remind us that worship must be active participation, not passive observation.[1] Yet modern worship "creativists" have encouraged us to "relax and sit back in our seats" in order to enjoy the latest liturgical innovation—a short dramatic skit that serves to "set up" the sermon. Is this another opportunity to substitute ordinary entertainment for holy worship? Perhaps, but not necessarily so.

Scripture presents many dramatic occasions of worship: Abraham's journey to Mt. Moriah to sacrifice his son Isaac; Moses' meeting with God at the burning bush in the desert; Israel's crossing the Red Sea followed by Miriam's song and dance of victory; the temple's magnificent pageantry of sacrifices; Isaiah's vision; the prophets' gripping modes of communication; Jesus' baptism and transfiguration; and the Upper Room supper of our Lord with his disciples. Finally, John on Patmos, in the book of Revelation, expressed his "vision" in apocalyptic language and images, and some scholars believe he was influenced by the forms of Greek drama.

There is no specific reference in the Old or New Testaments to actors on a secular stage, performing with or without music. However, Michael Perry shows us how the Psalms give evidence of a dramatic worship script, complete with staging instructions.

> We have only to look at Psalm 118 to see that it is neither a hymn nor merely a meditation. There are obvious character parts and choral parts. And there are even "stage" instructions embedded in the text. For example, verse 27—"with boughs in hand, join in the festal procession up to the horns of the altar"—which, in some traditions, we blindly *sing* as though the psalm were homogeneous. It does not take much imagination to see that what we are dealing with is the script of a drama or the libretto of an opera, set in the context of a magnificent act of worship. Here the intending (and noble?) worshiper approaches the door of the temple and asks to enter to give thanks for God's deliverance. The ministers/priests tell him righteousness is a prerequisite of an approach to God. And the drama progresses from there. Permeating the drama are the resonant choruses of the Hebrew liturgy:

Leader	Let Israel say:
All	His love endures forever.
Leader	Let the house of Aaron say:
All	His love endures forever.
Leader	Let those who fear the Lord say:
All	His love endures forever!

Finally, the worshiper is admitted ("Blessed is he who comes in the name of the Lord") and the celebration begins.[2]

Worship Dramas in History

Between the tenth and the thirteenth centuries, Roman Catholic worship used various kinds of drama to communicate the biblical message to non-literate serfs and privileged nobles alike. The first examples were brief insertions in the mass called *tropes.* In a well-known Easter trope, an angel meets the three Marys (Magdalene, Lazarus's sister, and Jesus' mother) at Jesus' tomb:

> *Angel:* Whom seek ye in the sepulchre, O followers of Christ?
> *Marys:* Jesus of Nazareth who was crucified, O celestial ones.
> *Angel:* He is not here; he is risen as he foretold; go, announce
> that he is risen from the sepulchre.

Over the centuries this Easter trope developed into a full drama, with costumes, properties, and explicit directions for staging. Performers sang the text, probably in monody (a single melody line), and mostly in Latin, with occasional vernacular phrases.[3]

Other musical dramas told the stories of the post-Resurrection Emmaus journey, the passion of Christ, Jesus' birth, the raising of Lazarus, the conversion of St. Paul, the Last Judgment, Esau and Jacob, and the life of Daniel. Scholars classify such dramas in three types: (1) *mystery plays,* based on Scripture stories; (2) *miracle plays,* based on lives of Christian saints; and (3) *morality plays,* which dealt with human vices and virtues. The plays became increasingly bawdy and secular and were banished from worship in 1250.[4]

Passions (sung by the clergy and the congregation, but without costumes and staging) continued to appear in Palm Sunday worship of the Roman Catholic church. They also became a favorite choral form for Lutheran composers from the sixteenth through the eighteenth centuries, culminating in the magnificent *St. Matthew Passion* of J. S. Bach. Bach, like many of his predecessors, also wrote many church cantatas which used opera-like conversations of biblical characters or between Christ and the believer; similar works for seasonal use have continued to be written to the present day.

Why Worry about "Holy or Ordinary"?

This brief chronicle should remind us to be especially careful in using worship elements that are not sanctioned either by Scripture or by widespread, continuous use throughout history. However, Warren Wiersbe insists that "whenever people get blind to spiritual things, God does something dramatic to get their attention." [5] Old Testament prophets used vivid, impassioned language that conjured up dramatic mental images (like Ezekiel's "vision of the dry bones," Ezek. 37:1-14).

Jesus used stories (parables) from everyday life to preach the good news of the gospel. But one "worship prompter" (to use Kierkegaard's image) is not nearly so prone to detract from the congregation's "work of worship" as a stage-full might be. Perhaps that's the reason why religious drama has more often occurred as a separate and independent expression of faith—a means of evangelism or renewal—rather than a feature of regular worship.

Today's Sermon-Related Dramas

The contemporary sermon-related, dramatic skit which seems to be getting the most attention is related to the medieval morality plays, and has been a prominent feature of the seeker events at Willow Creek Community Church. Typical examples portray a scene from modern secular life to set up the Christian faith answers in the spoken message that follows. A theater expert at Willow Creek Church describes them:

> Much of the material in these sketches may seem "secular" in that there is no specific "Christian" content in the sketch. However, when the sketch is performed in connection with a biblically based message that addresses the same question or problem, it takes on spiritual significance. *Keeping Tabs,* for example, presents a character who is possessed by the idea of paying back people for kindness shown toward her. While the theme is comically explored, the point it makes is a serious one. Many have a difficult time accepting the mystery of grace—a gift given with "no strings attached." This "secular" sketch has a strong Christian application when presented along with a message on grace.[6]

The word *secular* in the above description is significant, since such dramatic sketches appear only in Willow Creek's seeker events; the church uses no drama in its weeknight worship for believers. Yet, Willow Creek's imitators insist on presenting the same type of minidramas in worship services, with little concern that they may be more secular entertainment than sacred worship.

For many congregations, using drama in worship signifies being "modern and relevant." The question "for what purpose?" often evokes only a blank stare; evidently, using the new form matters more than any purpose it might have. Willow Creek's dramas have a purpose: to help nonbelievers diagnose their own spiritual malaise in preparation for the gospel message spoken by the preacher. As such, they make sense in a context where that message is the only reason for the gathering. In a worship service, such theatrical skits should have less significance, partly because believers should not need convincing that the sermon contains important truth which they should hear. Also, adding time to sermon communication reduces the time available for sermon response—praise, thanksgiving, petition, dedication, and other worship actions.

I am convinced that dramatic sketches of this kind are out of place as a regular feature in a worship service. Many of those I have witnessed seem to provoke such raucous hilarity that they wipe out any sense of reverent purpose. Perhaps, like the musical *Godspell,* they might achieve better results in a theater setting. But even there, most of them would fall short of the idea that good worship drama is *participation,* not just spectatorism.

What Makes a Worship Drama Acceptable?

But isn't that weakness characteristic of all stage dramas? Not necessarily. Recently Michael Linton reviewed the Crystal Cathedral's "Glory of Easter" passion play, with its cast of hundreds, live animals, thunderstorm, and earthquake, thinly veiled dancing girls, and angels that seem to fly. The performance is good, Linton says, but the theology expressed is bad; as a result, the audience really never "gets involved." He reminds us also that traditional presentations of the Passion Story, like that at Oberammergau in Germany, "have been careful to stress the immediate relationship between the presenters of the story and its hearers." As in Bach's *St. Matthew Passion,* listeners should find that they are not "mere observers of a moving story, but the cause of the tale, participants in it, and its beneficiaries." But, says Linton,

> This is not the case with the Crystal Cathedral "Glory." Here there is no congregation participating in the action, reflecting on their responsibility in the torture and death of the Savior of the world. There is only audience, thrilled, amused, and perhaps even emotionally moved by the drama—but always distanced from it.[7]

That is what makes many of today's typical worship dramas ordinary, not holy—entertainment, not worship.

Having established the standard for staged dramas that can qualify as worship, I can recommend all the biblical stories treated in medieval mystery plays and more. Most churches favor the Easter and Christmas narratives, and some celebrate Christ's Second Coming in a drama presented on the Feast of Christ the King.

Dramatic Elements in Regular Worship

Certain portions of typical Sunday services also can be treated dramatically in what may be called "readers' theater." Scripture readings can be spoken dramatically by a group of individuals; large portions of the Bible have been arranged and published for such use.[8] The same treatment can be given to other worship acts—a call to worship, a call to hymns or carols, a call to prayer, a parting challenge, or a benediction.[9] A sermon could be delivered as a dramatic monologue, complete with costuming and appropriate gestures, or even be a provocative dialogue, with one person serving as "devil's advocate."

The Indispensable Drama of Worship

However, in using any of these examples I urge caution, lest the "play within a play" detract from Kierkegaard's concern for the "drama of the total service." The full experience of worship, like its partial microcosm in Isaiah 6, is a logical, life-changing sequence of spiritual experiences in our encounter with God:

- Our gathering as God's called-out and called-together people for the holy purpose of worship.
- Recognizing God in all his holy glory, and responding appropriately with wonder and praise.
- Confessing our continuing need of God's forgiveness, cleansing, and reconciliation.
- Receiving God's grace in the accomplishment of his saving work.
- Listening to God speak in Scripture and sermon.
- Responding to God in dedication of self and resources.
- Acknowledging dependence on God, in prayers of thanksgiving and petition.
- In the Lord's Supper, remembering and giving thanks for all God's actions for us through Christ, as we "feed on him in our hearts by faith."
- Departing to continue the life of worship in the world.

In *Jubilate II*, I borrowed Kierkegaard's metaphor in speaking of worship's *cast* (the congregation, with help from the "leaders-prompters"), worship's *book* or script (the full service order), worship's *direction* (by planners and leaders, as guided—and sometimes overruled—by the Holy Spirit), and worship's *staging* (the worship space and all it contains).[10] To me, this is the only indispensable drama of worship.

Appendix III

Teaching Hymns in the Church:
A Hymn Festival

In recent years church musicians have complained that they have lost their traditional opportunities to teach hymns. Sunday schools no longer sing hymns in an "opening worship period." Evening services with their protracted song times are rarely held in churches. Only a few believers regularly attend a weeknight service where hymns might be taught. Worship with singing happens once a week for most church attenders. If a new hymn is to be learned, it must happen in the regular "struggle through" experience of Saturday night or Sunday morning, perhaps with an opening stanza introduced by the choir.

I am convinced that a *hymn festival* or a *hymn sermon* is the best way to teach hymns today. On such an occasion, hymns are the largest part of the service, so everyone is aware that worship-work is singing from the hymnal. Because of the concentration on singing, new hymns can be mixed with the old and introduced by instruments, soloists, or the choir. Because the hymns are placed in the context of a theological outline, their meaning is made clear without pedantic teaching. I have experienced that though congregations may begin such a service cautiously, before long they are caught up in the realization that something significant is happening, and the festival ends with a high level of satisfaction.

Below I've outlined just such a service which I have conducted many times in churches, frequently in the context of a hymnal dedication. I lead the singing myself from the organ, and turn toward the congregation to speak before each selection. The hymn singing is enhanced with choral and solo stanzas, and additional accompaniment by handbells and other orchestral instruments. This presentation will take the largest part of a one-hour service. A similar hymn sermon of thirty minutes (with perhaps three or four hymns included) could be the homily in a typical worship setting.

This service may be used by readers without the publishers' written permission, providing credit is given. Song selections are found in *The Worshiping Church: A Hymnal* (Carol Stream, Ill: Hope, 1990). If another hymnal is used, different hymns may be chosen, of course. Ideally the narration would be rewritten and amplified in the speaker's own words. Similar hymn festival outlines are available from The Hymn Society in the United States and Canada, Boston University School of Theology, 745 Commonwealth Ave., Boston, MA 02215-1401.

A Hymn Festival:

The Vision of Isaiah

The sixth chapter of Isaiah is a remarkable passage of Scripture which speaks of the prophet's personal, emotionally moving and transforming experience of worship. Liturgical scholars tell us that it is also a good picture of corporate worship, with all the necessary spiritual experiences in a logical order of progression. In fact, that order is followed in all the historic Western liturgies, including John Calvin's worship order introduced in Geneva in 1540.

In our worship today, we will read the verses describing each successive experience. I will make a few comments about the reading and we will sing hymns and other music which illustrate that experience. In so doing, we may learn more about the nature of true worship. We will also discover what hymn texts say. Hopefully, at the same time, we will worship God.

> In the year that King Uzziah died, I saw the LORD sitting on a throne, high and lofty; and the hem of his robe filled the temple. Seraphs were in attendance above him; each had six wings: with two they covered their faces, and with two they covered their feet, and with two they flew. And one called to another and said:
> "Holy, holy, holy is the LORD of hosts;
> the whole earth is full of his glory."
> The pivots on the thresholds shook at the voices of those who called, and the house filled with smoke. (Isa. 6:1-4)

Above all, worship is an encounter with the living God. Isaiah's dramatic experience revealed a God who is transcendent or, as Rudolf Otto said in *The Idea of the Holy,* the *mysterium tremendum et fascinans*—"the mystery, tremendous and fascinating." We identify a revealing of the attributes of God in the physical phenomena: his perfect holiness or "otherness" in the song of the "three holies"; his power, in the phrase "the pivots on the thresholds shook at the voices of those who called"; and his inscrutability, in the words, "and the house filled with smoke." Someone has suggested that the seraphs present significant images of worship as our response to God in worship: *reverence*—"with two [wings] they covered their faces," *humility*—"with two they covered their feet," and *willing service*—"with two they flew."

Our first hymn speaks of God's holiness, his perfect goodness, his freedom from any sin. The word also signifies God's otherness, his utter "differentness" from human beings whom he has created. The three repetitions of the word "holy" in Hebrew simply intensify the meaning of the word, but Christians have taken it to be a symbol of the Trinity.

True Worship

Hymn 2: "Holy, Holy, Holy, Lord God Almighty" (Heber, Dykes)

We frequently speak of the mighty power of God in references to his created world. The first two stanzas of the next hymn speak of the power of God as seen in nature; the third stanza tells of his power in salvation through Christ; and finally, stanza 4 says that we shall sing of God's greatness throughout eternity.

Hymn 21: "How Great Thou Art!" (Hine, Swedish)

Have you ever seen the sun? Don't answer too quickly! Scientists tell us that we cannot actually see the sun, which is only a moderate-size star, because of the radiance of the gases which surround it. In this hymn, Walter Chalmers Smith says that it is the glory of God which makes him invisible—finally incomprehensible—to us. God is mystery and there is much about God which as mortals we cannot understand. As 1 Timothy 6:16 says, "It is he alone who has immortality and dwells in unapproachable light, whom no one has ever seen or can see." In this case, *light obscures rather than reveals!* The hymn is based on the doxology of 1 Timothy 1:17 and emphasizes the word "invisible": "To the King of the ages, immortal, invisible, the only God, be honor and glory forever and ever. Amen."

Hymn 62: "Immortal, Invisible, God Only Wise" (Smith, Welsh)

> And I said: "Woe is me! I am lost, for I am a man of unclean lips, and I live among a people of unclean lips; yet my eyes have seen the King, the LORD of hosts!" (Isa. 6:5)

When I sit in church for worship, if I really knew all about the persons who sit around me, and compared myself—my actions, my words, my thoughts—to them, I might feel quite comfortable. But when I see God as he is—especially as revealed in the God-man Jesus Christ, I can only identify myself as a sinner, and plead for mercy. We will sing Ken Medema's setting of the invitation to cleansing from Isaiah 1:18, speak a historic prayer of confession, and then sing J. Edwin Orr's words that acknowledge that we are forgiven, cleansed, and reconciled to God.

Hymn 456: "Come, Let Us Reason Together" (Medema)

> Most holy and merciful Father: We confess in your presence the sinfulness of our nature, and our shortcomings and offenses against you. You alone know how often we have sinned, in wandering from your ways, in wasting your gifts, in forgetting your love. Have mercy, O Lord, upon us, who are ashamed and sorry for all we have done to

displease you; and forgive our sins, through Jesus Christ your Son, our Savior. Amen.

Hymn 458: "Search Me, O God," stanza 2 (Orr)

> Then one of the seraphs flew to me, holding a live coal that had been taken from the altar with a pair of tongs. The seraph touched my mouth with it and said: "Now that this has touched your lips, your guilt has departed and your sin is blotted out." (Isa. 6:6-7)

At this point, someone—perhaps all of us—should say "Hallelujah!" Friends, believe the good news of the gospel! In Jesus Christ, we are forgiven and cleansed from sin; we have become new persons because the Holy Spirit lives within us. We often sing about this truth in words of Christian experience, like those of Henry Smith's contemporary song of joy.

Hymn 496: "Give Thanks with a Grateful Heart" (Smith)

> Then I heard the voice of the Lord saying, "Whom shall I send, and who will go for us?" (Isa. 6:8)

Is it possible? The transcendent God—holy, powerful, loving, inscrutable— needs the person of unclean lips to do his work in the world. Yes, it is not only possible, but inevitable. There is no delay for maturing, no waiting for additional training. As soon as we are forgiven, cleansed, and reconciled, we are called to service in God's kingdom. Jesus Christ must be our Lord as well as our Savior.

In typical evangelical worship, this call is heard in worship acts—hearing the Word of God read and explained, learning what God wants us to be and to do. Our hymn tells us that we are called to be "God's people, God's servants, and God's prophets."

Hymn 710: "We Are Called to Be God's People" (Jackson, Haydn)

> And I said, "Here am I; send me!" (Isa. 6:8)

I often wonder how the story would have continued if at this point we had the deafening silence that sometimes occurs when we ask for a volunteer to do something in the church, like teach a Sunday school class or assist with a children's choir. But the affirmative response is inevitable. The person who has seen God in Jesus Christ, who is forgiven, healed, and reconciled, who has heard his call, cannot do otherwise. God has no other provision for accomplishing his purposes in the world. We are his ambassadors and servants.

In worship, we respond to God's call in many ways: by word and by giving money to signify that we are wholly God's. In many churches, response sometimes calls for the physical act of walking to the front of the church to speak to the pastor. We respond today in a hymn of dedication.

Hymn 566: "Take My Life, Lead Me, Lord" (Rawls)

> And he said, "Go and say to this people:
>   'Keep listening, but do not comprehend;
>   keep looking, but do not understand.'
> Make the mind of this people dull,
>   and stop their ears,
>   and shut their eyes,
>   so that they may not look with their eyes,
>   and listen with their ears,
>   and comprehend with their minds,
>   and turn and be healed."
> Then I said, "How long, O Lord?" (Isa. 6:9-11)

On this occasion I'm not going to try to tell you what these words mean. But one thing is apparent. The prophet, in responding to God's call, has run into trouble. People didn't listen, or didn't understand, or didn't respond as he had expected. So we hear his agonizing cry for help; "How long, O Lord, how long?"

These words represent our prayers in worship, especially the prayers of petition or supplication. In all the historic liturgies they come after the response to Scripture reading and the sermon. In our hymns, we ask God for help in many ways. For one thing, we need guidance and wisdom. The Welsh hymn, "Guide Me, O Thou Great Jehovah," uses imagery from the Israelites' journey through the desert to their Promised Land.

Hymn 634: "Guide Me, O Thou Great Jehovah" (Williams, Hughes)

A hymn which comes to us from Ghana in Africa prays that Christ's love may fill our hearts, so that we will love our neighbors, despite racial, social, or cultural differences.

Hymn 436: "Jesu, Jesu, Fill Us with Your Love" (Colvin, Ghana)

There are times when all of us, young and old, feel that life's problems—in health, in our relationships, in our work—are overwhelming. At such a time of utter darkness and weariness, we need a hymn like this.

Appendix III

Hymn 638: "Precious Lord, Take My Hand" (Dorsey)

"How long, O Lord?" And he said:
  "Until cities lie waste
    without inhabitant,
  and houses without people,
    and the land is utterly desolate;
  until the Lord sends everyone far away,
    and vast is the emptiness in the midst of the land."
(Isa. 6:11–12)

How long, O Lord, how long? Until the world falls down around our ears—that's how long! There is no furlough and no retirement from God's call to service and discipleship. We are not called to be successful, *only faithful.*

In the end, as in the beginning of Isaiah's vision, there will be only praise to God and to Jesus Christ, with the Holy Spirit, one God, for ever and ever! Amen.

Hymn 98: "Majesty, Worship His Majesty" (Hayford)

Notes

Foreword

1. Martin E. Marty, foreword, *The Church Musician*, rev. ed. by Paul Westermeyer (Minneapolis, Minn.: Augsburg Fortress, 1997) xiv-xv.

2. Marva Dawn, *Reaching Out without Dumbing Down: A Theology of Worship for the Turn-of-the-Century Culture* (Grand Rapids, Mich.: Eerdmans, 1995).

3. Erik Routley, *Church Music and the Christian Faith* (Carol Stream, Ill.: Agape, 1978) 134.

Prologue: Singing the Lord's Song in a Strange Land

1. Joel Arthur Barker, *Future Edge* (New York: Morrow, 1992) 140.

2. Mike Regele, *Death of the Church* (Grand Rapids, Mich.: Zondervan, 1995) 47ff.

3. Ibid., 70, 75.

4. The following representative books are recommended: George Barna, *The Frog in the Kettle: What Christians Need to Know About Life in the Year 2000* (Ventura, Calif.: Regal, 1990); Barna, *Marketing the Church: What They Never Taught You About Church Growth* (Colorado Springs: NavPress, 1988); Doug Murren, *The Baby Boomerang* (Ventura, Calif.: Regal, 1990); Lyle Schaller, *Forty-four Ways to Increase Church Attendance* (Nashville, Tenn.: Abingdon, 1988); George G. Hunter, *Church for the Unchurched* (Nashville, Tenn.: Abingdon, 1996).

5. Tom F. Driver, *The Magic of Ritual* (New York: HarperCollins, 1991) 131ff., 152ff., and 166ff.

6. See Søren Kierkegaard, *Purity of Heart Is to Will One Thing* (New York: Harper, 1938) 160-166.

7. See Marva Dawn, *Reaching Out without Dumbing Down* (Grand Rapids, Mich.: Eerdmans, 1995).

8. William E. Hull, *The Broadman Bible Commentary: John*, vol. 9, (Nashville, Tenn: Broadman, 1970) 254.

Chapter 1: Worshiping God in Spirit and Truth

1. Charles Willis, "Worship," four articles in *Western Recorder*, vol. 167, no. 35:15.

2. Robert E. Webber, "Seven Styles of Morning Worship," *The Complete Library of Christian Worship*, vol. 3, (Nashville, Tenn.: Star Song, 1994) 111-127.

3. *The Divine Liturgy of Saint John Chrysostom* (Brookline, Mass.: Holy Cross Orthodox Press, 1992) 31-32.

4. William Barclay, *The Gospel of John*, vol. I, The Daily Study Bible (Philadelphia, Pa.: Westminster, 1955) 154.

5. David Peterson, "Worship in the New Testament," in *Worship: Adoration and Action,* ed. D. A. Carson (Grand Rapids, Mich.: Baker, 1993) 63.

6. Welton Gaddy, *The Gift of Worship* (Nashville, Tenn.: Broadman, 1992) 33.

7. See Lynne and Bill Hybels' discussion of this in *Rediscovering Church* (Grand Rapids, Mich.: Zondervan, 1995) 175-177. My reference to Billy Graham is based on my years of personal acquaintance with him. In *A Biblical Standard for Evangelists* (Minneapolis, Minn.: World Wide, 1983), pages 103-113, Graham discusses the uniqueness of his calling as an evangelist, in contrast to the local church roles of pastor and teacher.

8. Don E. Saliers, *Worship As Theology* (Nashville, Tenn.: Abingdon, 1994) 108ff.

9. Ibid., 47.

10. Annie Dillard, *Teaching a Stone to Talk* (New York: Harper and Row, 1985) 40, 58.

11. Davis Duggins, "The Worship Gap," *Moody Monthly,* March–April 1996: 20.

12. The biblical Greek word for *worship* (*leitourgia,* "liturgy") means "work of the people." The word first referred to the work of civil servants but later came to mean the work (or ministry) of the people for God.

13. James B. Torrance, *Worship, Community and the Triune God of Grace* (Downers Grove, Ill.: InterVarsity, 1996) 15.

14. Carol Doran and Thomas H. Troeger, *Trouble at the Table* (Nashville, Tenn.: Abingdon, 1992) 24-25.

Chapter 2: Worshiping God in Cognitive and Affective Truth

1. Quoted in Timothy Dudley-Smith, *Authentic Christianity: From the Writings of John Stott* (Downers Grove, Ill.: InterVarsity, 1995) 94.

2. Ibid., 277.

3. A. S. Herbert, *Worship in Ancient Israel* (Richmond, Va: John Knox, 1959) 26.

4. Austin C. Lovelace and William C. Rice, *Music and Worship in the Church* (Nashville, Tenn.: Abingdon, 1960, 1976) 19-20.

5. See Donald Hustad, *Jubilate II* (Carol Stream, Ill.: Hope Publishing, 1993) 33-34. See also my analysis of the hymn in *Crusade Hymn Stories,* ed. Cliff Barrows (Carol Stream, Ill.: Hope Publishing, 1967) 48-50.

6. The congregational singer must read the words one at a time while giving attention also to vocalizing the music. This makes comprehension very difficult.

7. "Private communion" may have some connection to votive masses in the Middle Ages, but it has no place in evangelical worship. To begin, the Lord's Supper in church is for the whole body of Christ. It would have been less offensive (at least to God) to have served the wedding cake only to the bride and groom! Further, to serve the elements without any theological

explanation or prayer of thanksgiving, to say nothing of the authorization in the Words of Institution, should be unthinkable.

8. This may need a bit of explanation. Certain parts of the Roman liturgy are not consistent with evangelical theology, but the five songs listed here contain nothing that is not true to Scripture.

9. There is little need to explain the imagery of the first two windows. But in the Holy Spirit window, the artist has combined an image of our previous building with the new structure that replaced it; the fire which destroyed the first merges with fire that emanates from a dove, which represents the Holy Spirit. The rest of the window is filled with figures who represent the congregation—folks of all ages dressed and equipped for many different vocations in serving God.

10. See Thomas H. Troeger, *Borrowed Light* (New York: Oxford University Press, 1994) 26; and Brian Wren, *Piece Together Praise* (Carol Stream, Ill.: Hope Publishing, 1996.) 4, 5, 7ff.

11. Ruth C. Duck. *Finding Words for Worship* (Louisville, Ky.: Westminster John Knox, 1995) 23-24.

12. From the *Iona Community Wild Goose Songs,* by John L. Bell and Graham Maule, (c) 1987 by Wild Goose Publications. The wild goose is a Celtic symbol of the Holy Spirit, and it serves as the logo of Iona Community publications.

13. G. Robert Jacks, *Getting the Word Across: Speech Communication for Pastors and Lay Leaders* (Grand Rapids, Mich.: Eerdmans, 1995).

14. These three volumes are published by Baker Book House, Grand Rapids, Mich. *The Dramatized New Testament,* 1993; *The Dramatized Old Testament, Volume One* (Genesis to Esther), 1994; and *The Dramatized Old Testament, Volume Two* (Job to Malachi), 1996. All are based on the New International Version.

15. J. D. Crichton, "A Theology of Worship," *The Study of Liturgy,* eds. Cheslyn Jones, Geoffrey Wainwright, and Edward Yarnold. (New York: Oxford University Press, 1978) 10.

Chapter 3: Worshiping God in Theological Truth
1. See Robert G. Clouse, "Pentecostal Churches," *The New International Dictionary of the Christian Church,* gen. ed. J. D. Douglas (Grand Rapids, Mich.: Zondervan, 1978) 763-764.

2. See H. V. Synan, "Classical Pentecostalism," *Dictionary of Pentecostal and Charismatic Movements,* eds. Burgess and McGee (Grand Rapids, Mich.: Zondervan, 1988) 219-222.

3. Peter D. Hocken, "Charismatic Movement," *Dictionary of Pentecostal and Charismatic Movements,* 132.

4. *Newsweek,* July 4, 1960; *Time,* August 15, 1960.

5. For example, Gordon Fee at Wheaton College, Gordon-Conwell Theo-

logical Seminary, and Regent College; Chuck Kraft and John Wimber, at Fuller Theological Seminary.

6. Hocken, "Charismatic Movement," 155-156.

7. Harvey Cox, *Fire from Heaven: The Reshaping of Religion in the Twenty-First Century* (New York: Addison-Wesley, 1995). Cox's study is concerned more with classic Pentecostalism and especially with African-American churches. Cox does not give the modern charismatic renewal movement the credit it deserves for extending the earlier phenomenon.

8. R. P. Spittler, "Glossalalia," *Dictionary of Pentecostal and Charismatic Movements*, 336.

9. Cox, *Fire from Heaven*, 82, 83.

10. Spittler, "Glossalalia," 335.

11. Ibid., 340.

12. Gordon Fee, outstanding New Testament scholar and an ordained minister in the Assemblies of God, believes that the gift of tongues is intended to be practiced principally in private worship. See his *Paul, the Spirit, and the People of God* (Peabody, Mass.: Hendrickson, 1996).

13. Paul Hoon, *The Integrity of Worship* (Nashville, Tenn.: Abingdon, 1971) 91-94.

14. Ibid.

15. Robert Webber. "Father Worship," *Worship Leader*, vol. 5, no. 5, Sep–Oct 1996: 12.

16. Compare Saul's experience of ecstasy ("frenzy," NRSV) following his musical experience at Gibeah-elohim (1 Sam. 10:5-6).

17. This mood is sometimes called the "warm fuzzies," a term borrowed from contemporary psychologists.

18. These are captions from Terry Law, *The Power of Praise and Worship* (Tulsa, Okla.: Victory House, 1985) 143-158. The last statement from Psalm 22:3 is often quoted in this context.

Chapter 4: Worshiping God in Biblical Truth

1. For further information on this topic, see Hustad, *Jubilate II* (Carol Stream, Ill.: Hope Publishing, 1993) 129-164.

2. John Calvin, *The Necessity of Reforming the Church*, trans. W. Robert Godfrey (Dallas, Tex.: Protestant Heritage Press, 1995) 17-18.

3. See *The Piety of John Calvin*, trans. and eds. Ford Lewis Battles and Stanley Tagg (Grand Rapids, Mich.: Baker, 1978) 117-136.

4. For further discussion, see Donald Hustad, *Jubilate! Church Music in the Evangelical Tradition* (Carol Stream, Ill.: Hope Publishing, 1981) 41-44.

5. See "Jewish Church Music History" in *Key Words in Church Music*, ed. Carl Schalk (St. Louis, Mo.: Concordia, 1978) 87-91.

6. This has been called one of the sharpest satires on non-Hebraic religion in Holy Writ. "He has wandered away" is probably a euphemism for "he is relieving himself."

7. See the discussion of "sacred concerts" in chapter 6, pp. 169 ff.

8. Paul Wohlgemuth, "Praise Singing," *The Hymn,* January 1987, 19-20. The ark of the covenant had earlier been stolen by the Philistines, then returned and housed in the house of Abinadab. After David became king, he retrieved the ark and brought it, not to the official tabernacle at Gibeon, but to his own tent in Jerusalem, his political capital. The tent has been called "David's Tabernacle" and it was there that David established the music leadership of Asaph, Heman, and Jeduthun, which characterized the worship of Solomon's temple (1 Sam. 4:2-10; 2 Sam. 6:2-4 and 6:17; 1 Chron. 16:4; 25:1-31).

9. Terry Law, *The Power of Praise and Worship* (Tulsa, Okla.: Victory House, 1985) 247.

10. Ibid., 140-141.

11. See Robert E. Webber, "The Praise-and-Worship Renewal," *Twenty Centuries of Christian Worship,* vol. 2 of *The Complete Library of Christian Worship,* ed. Robert E. Webber (Nashville, Tenn.: Star Song, 1994) 131-134. See also my prior discussion of the theology of praise in chapter 3.

12. Ken Barker, *Songs for Praise and Worship,* eds. Ken Barker and Tom Fettke (Waco, Tex.: Word, 1993) 474.

13. See Donald Hustad, "Doxology: A Biblical Triad," *Ex Auditu,* vol. 8, 1992.

14. See my discussion of the daily offices in "The Services of the Hours," *Jubilate II,* 177-179.

15. Ralph P. Martin, "Hymns in the New Testament: An Evolving Pattern of Worship Responses," *Ex Auditu,* vol. 8, 1992: 34-42.

16. See Egon Wellesz, "Early Christian Music," *The New Oxford History of Music,* vol. 2 (London: Oxford University Press, 1954) 1-6.

17. Eric Werner, *The Sacred Bridge* (New York: Schocken, 1970) 168-169.

18. Taken from the editor's comments in the *NIV Study Bible* (Grand Rapids, Mich.: Zondervan, 1985) 817.

Chapter 5: Worshiping God as the Community of Faith

1. Marva Dawn, *Reaching Out without Dumbing Down* (Grand Rapids, Mich.: Eerdmans, 1995) 10. The term "principalities and powers" is found in the King James rendering of Romans 8:38; Ephesians 1:21; 6:12; and Colossians 2:10.

2. Paul King Jewett, "Church," *The New International Dictionary of the Christian Church,* ed. J. D. Douglas (Grand Rapids, Mich.: Zondervan, 1978) 226-227.

3. Ibid.

4. Ibid. Jewett adds that the Reformed tradition (since Calvin) has also practiced church discipline to ensure the integrity of Word and sacrament (ordinance) in the church fellowship.

5. William Barclay, *The Letters to the Galatians and Ephesians* (Philadelphia, Pa.: Westminster, 1956) 102.

6. Ibid., 107.

7. In fact, Southern Baptists have little glue to hold them together, since each local church congregation is autonomous in every area of authority.

8. See Hustad, *Jubilate II* (Carol Stream, Ill.: Hope Publishing, 1993) 219-220, quoting Walter Shurden and John Loftis.

9. Lynne and Bill Hybels, *Rediscovering Church* (Grand Rapids, Mich.: Zondervan, 1995) 57-58.

10. George G. Hunter, "Church for the Unchurched," *Next*, vol. 2, no. 12, August 1996: 1.

11. Ibid., 2-3.

12. Willow Creek's New Community service, however, also falls short of ideal worship. This is discussed in chapter 8.

13. Ken Barker and Tom Fettke, eds., *Songs for Praise and Worship* (Dallas, Tex.: Word Music, 1992).

14. One organization that specializes in presenting conferences for church leaders recently changed the title of its journal to *Next*. Perhaps, to maintain this particular parachurch enterprise, it is important to anticipate that there will always be another problem for which it will have the solution!

15. Paul W. Hoon, *The Integrity of Worship* (New York: Abingdon, 1971) 96-97.

16. William Barclay, *The Letters to the Corinthians* (Philadelphia, Pa.: Westminster, 1954) 112-113. The passage in quotes is credited to "a great Church historian," with no other identification.

17. *The New Oxford Annotated Bible (NRSV)* (New York: Oxford University Press, 1991) footnote on 242. See also Barclay, op. cit., p. 116: "Paul has just been rebuking those who with their divisions and their class distinctions divide the Church; so this may mean that the man eats and drinks unworthily who has never realized that the whole Church is the body of Christ and who is at variance with his brother, who looks on his brother with contempt, or who, for any reason is not one with his brethren."

18. James I. Packer, "On from Orr: The Cultural Crisis, Rational Realism, and Incarnational Ontology," *Crux*, vol. 32, no. 3, September 1996: 14-15.

19. Ibid., 15.

20. James B. Torrance, *Worship, Community and the Triune God of Grace* (Downers Grove, Ill.: InterVarsity, 1996) 41.

21. Dawn, *Reaching Out*, 135-136.

Chapter 6: Worshiping God in Cultural Truth

1. Ira Sankey, *My Life and the Story of the Gospel Hymns* (New York: Harper & Bros., 1906, 1907) 61-62.

2. See Arthur Holmes, *All Truth Is God's Truth* (Grand Rapids, Mich.: Eerdmans, 1977).

3. For persons living away from Jerusalem, services in the synagogue were important but inferior substitutes for the temple.

4. Alfred Sendrey, *Music in Ancient Israel* (New York: Philosophical Library, 1969) 169.

5. Samuel J. Mikolaski, "Neoplatonism," *The New International Dictionary of the Christian Church*, ed. J. D. Douglas, (Grand Rapids, Mich.: Zondervan, 1978). As Mikolaski explains, "[Neoplatonism] maintained an infinite qualitative distinction and distance between the material world, including the flesh, and divine goodness."

6. See my discussion of ordinary music forms becoming holy in *Jubilate II* (Carol Stream, Ill.: Hope Publishing, 1993) 135-136, 180, 189, 193-194, 225-228.

7. See Harry Eskew and Hugh T. McElrath, *Sing with Understanding* (Nashville, Tenn.: Broadman, 1980) 115-117.

8. Ibid., 180-188.

9. See *Grove's Dictionary of Music and Musicians*, 5th ed., vol. 5, 86.

10. See Stanislaw and Hustad, *Companion to the Worshiping Church: A Hymnal* (Carol Stream, Ill.: Hope Publishing, 1993) 3-4. Evangelical hymnists frequently have said that the final result was an incongruous mix of Watts's penitential devotion and revivalism's glib joy.

11. Cited in Gustave Reese, *Music in the Middle Ages* (New York: W. W. Norton, 1940) 65.

12. George Stebbins, *Reminiscences and Gospel Hymn Stories* (New York: AMS Press, 1971) 202.

13. C. E. Jones, "Jesus People," *Dictionary of Pentecostal and Charismatic Movements*, eds. Stanley M. Burgess and Gary B. McGee (Grand Rapids, Mich.: Zondervan, 1988) 491-492.

14. Coral Ridge Presbyterian Church in Ft. Lauderdale, Florida, considers such a concert program to be part of their outreach "ministry" and offers seminars on how to conduct similar efforts.

15. Patrick T. Will, "Rock," in *The New Harvard Dictionary of Music*, ed. Don Randel (Cambridge, Mass.: Belknap, Harvard University Press) 710-711.

16. Charles A. Reich, *The Greening of America* (New York: Random House, 1970) 245.

17. Kenneth A. Myers, *All God's Children and Blue Suede Shoes* (Westchester, Ill.: Crossway, 1989) 137.

18. Will, "Rock," 711.

19. Allen Bloom, *The Closing of the American Mind* (New York: Simon and Schuster, 1987) 73.

20. Patrick T. Will, "Heavy Metal," *New Harvard Dictionary of Music*, 375.

21. An insight from Paul Richardson in a personal letter of October 6, 1997.

22. Quote from *Source Readings in Music History*, ed. Oliver Strunk,

vol. I, (New York: W.W. Norton, 1965) 74. See also "pleasure meaning in music" in Hustad, *Jubilate II*, 12, 29-31.

23. See "Billy Sunday" in Hustad, *Jubilate II*, 249-250.

24. Erik Routley, *Christian Hymns Observed* (Princeton, N. J.: Prestige, 1982) 64-67.

25. Nicholas Wolterstorff, *Art in Action* (Grand Rapids, Mich.: Eerdmans, 1980) 21-23.

26. John Fischer, "Gospel Ship," *CCM Magazine*, November 1994: 94.

27. Neil Postman, *Amusing Ourselves to Death: Public Discourse in the Age of Show Business* (New York: Viking Penguin, 1985).

Chapter 7: Worshiping God in Artistic Truth

1. This story was told to me by Loralee Cooley of Pampa, Texas, a professional storyteller. It is adapted from "The Old Woman in the Cave" (c) 1986 by Jane Yolen.

2. See Donald Hustad, *Jubilate II* (Carol Stream, Ill.: Hope Publishing, 1993), especially pages 3-10 and 16-21.

3. Quoted by Martin Marty in *Context*, December 1, 1996, 4-5, originally from an article by George Steiner in *Chronicle of Higher Education*, June 21, 1996.

4. Ibid.

5. From *The Tie*, journal of Southern Baptist Seminary, vol. 62, no. 4: 24.

6. *NIV Study Bible*, ed. Kenneth Barker (Grand Rapids, Mich.: Zondervan, 1985) 783-784.

7. C. S. Lewis, "On Church Music," *Christian Reflections* (Grand Rapids, Mich.: Eerdmans, 1967) 98.

8. Nicholas Wolterstorff, *Art in Action* (Grand Rapids, Mich.: Eerdmans, 1980) 183-189.

9. Hustad, *Jubilate II*, 16-21, 43-70.

10. Kenneth A. Myers, *All God's Children and Blue Suede Shoes* (Westchester, Ill.: Crossway, 1989) 121.

11. This is the common title, though Mozart's authorship has been questioned.

12. Bruno Nettl, "Folk Music," in *The New Harvard Dictionary of Music*, ed. Don Randel (Cambridge, Mass.: Harvard University Press, 1986) 315.

13. From Judith Miller, "Older Audiences Point to Grim Arts Future" in the (Louisville, Ky.) *Courier-Journal*, Feb. 12, 1996.

14. Ibid.

15. For instance, Fred Pratt Green, Brian Wren, Margaret Clarkson, Fred Kaan, Timothy Dudley-Smith, Shirley Erena Murray, Thomas Troeger, Carl P. Daw Jr., Jane Parker Huber, Jaroslav Vajda, and Christopher Idle.

16. Admittedly, I make this comment with "tongue in cheek." But see Gustave Reese, *Music in the Middle Ages* (New York: W. W. Norton, 1940) 272ff.

17. The term "churchestra" was invented by Douglas Smith, the instrumental director at my church, who teaches at the School of Church Music and Worship at Southern Baptist Theological Seminary. It really means "any group of instruments that is available, based on four-part brass sound."

18. Charles Kraft, *Worship Leader*, April–May 1993.

19. John C. LaRue Jr., "The Changing Sound of Music," *Christianity Today*, October 6, 1997, 67.

20. Hustad, *Jubilate II*, 338-349.

Chapter 8: Worshiping God in Liturgical Truth

1. See Acts 2:42: "They devoted themselves to the apostles' teaching and fellowship, to the breaking of bread and the prayers." "*The* prayers" suggests strongly that these were the formal, liturgical prayers of the synagogue or the temple. See also Acts 2:46; 5:25, and many similar passages.

2. A brief account of this history (through the eighteenth century) may be found in Donald Hustad, *Jubilate II* (Carol Stream, Ill.: Hope Publishing, 1993) 157-211.

3. Here I am using *liturgical* in the narrow sense (Orthodox, Roman Catholic, Anglican, Lutheran, etc.). They greatly outnumber nonliturgical Christians.

4. For my discussion of Luther's changes, see *Jubilate II*, 186-188.

5. The writer is Charles Trueheart and this excerpt was quoted in *Next*, December 1996: 4.

6. For example, certain groups have banned instrumental music for this reason.

7. As noted in chapter 6, the pagan philosophy of Neoplatonism includes the idea that all physical things, including the body, are devoid of divine goodness.

8. *The New Oxford Annotated Bible (NRSV)* (New York: Oxford University Press, 1991) footnote 262 NT.

9. David Peterson, "Worship in the New Testament," *Worship: Adoration and Action*, ed. D. A. Carson (Grand Rapids, Mich.: Baker, 1993) 80.

10. From an instruction tape, "Discovering the Dimensions of Worship," (#C9220), Seeds Tape Ministry, 1992.

11. See also Hustad, *Jubilate II*, 259-262, 330-345. There I show comparative outlines of Roman Catholic, Lutheran, Anglican (Episcopalian), and Reformed (Presbyterian) worship, as well as a more complete analysis of a modern Geneva Order.

12. From the *Book of Common Worship* (Louisville, Ky.: Westminster/John Knox, 1993) 37.

13. Timothy George, "Southern Baptist Theology: Whence and Whither?" in *The Founders Journal*, Winter-Spring 1995: 30-31. English Baptists thoroughly separated themselves from Church of England theology and liturgical life. Yet the Anglican *Book of Common Prayer* (1662) says that the

minister will pronounce these words when distributing communion bread: "Take and eat this in remembrance that Christ died for you, and feed on him in your heart by faith with thanksgiving."

14. This is the First Evangelical Church of Memphis, Tennessee, where Ron Man is pastor of Worship and Music.

Chapter 9: Worshiping God in Educational Truth

1. H. Richard Niebuhr, *Christ and Culture* (New York: Harper and Row, 1951).

2. David B. Pass, *Music and the Church* (Nashville, Tenn.: Broadman, 1989) 85.

3. "Education in the United States," *The New Harvard Dictionary of Music*, ed. Don Randel. (Cambridge, Mass: Harvard University Press, 1986) 276-278. See also Hustad, *Jubilate II* (Carol Stream, Ill.: Hope Publishing, 1993) 78, 213-214, 231-232.

4. Charles Leonhard and Robert W. House, *Foundations and Principles of Music Education* (New York: McGraw-Hill, 1959) 100-101.

5. Wendell Harrison, "Does Playing a Musical Instrument Make a Child Smarter?" *Orchestra Monitor,* January 1985: 26.

6. "Arts Education Improves At-Risk Students' Overall Performance, Study Finds," in *Music Educators Journal,* November 1992: 11.

7. Norman Weinberger, ed., "Music and Cognitive Achievement in Children," *MUSICA Research Notes,* vol. 1, no. 2, Fall 1994. Other sources quoted in the article: Hurwitz, Wolff, Bortnick, and Kokas, "Nonmusical Effects of the Kodály Music Curriculum in Primary Grade Children," *Journal of Learning Disabilities,* (1975) vol. 8: 45-51; Mohanty and Hejmadi, "Effects of Intervention Training on Some Cognitive Abilities of Preschool Children," *Psychological Studies,* (1992) vol. 37: 31-37; Rauscher, Shaw, Levine, Ky, and Wright, paper presented at the annual meeting of the *American Psychological Society,* Los Angeles, Calif., August 13, 1994.

8. Ibid.

9. From a pamphlet of the National Coalition for Music Education, n.d.

10. Roger L. Shinn, *An Introduction to Christian Education* (Nashville, Tenn.: Abingdon, 1966) 12-18.

11. Hustad, *Jubilate II,* 427-438.

12. Barbara J. Resch, "Teens and Church Music," *Reformed Worship,* vol. 44: 4-6.

13. Paul Richardson wrote this phrase on the margin of my manuscript for this book. He first suggested it in "Hymnology: A Crucial Intersection," *Review and Expositor,* vol. 91, no. 3: 433.

14. Materials are available from The Hymn Society in the United States and Canada, Boston University School of Theology, 745 Commonwealth Ave., Boston, MA 02215-1401, and in such books as Kenneth W. Osbeck, *Amazing Grace* (Grand Rapids, Mich.: Kregel, 1990); William J. Reynolds,

Songs of Glory (Grand Rapids, Mich.: Zondervan, 1990); and Austin Lovelace, *Hymn Notes for Church Bulletins* (Chicago: GIA Publications, 1987).
15. Quoted in *The Worshiping Church*, ed. Donald Hustad (Carol Stream, Ill.: Hope Publishing, 1990) 795.
16. Leonard Sweet, *Worship Leader,* vol. 5, no. 2, Mar-Apr 1996: 39.

Appendix I: More Definitions of Worship
1. Martin Luther, *Larger Catechism,* vol. III, 84.
2. Quoted in "The Principal Practice of Faith," by Raymond K. Anderson, *Christian History,* vol. 5, no. 4: 21.
3. Evelyn Underhill, *Worship,* rev. ed. (Guildford, U.K.: Inter Publishing Service Ltd., 1991) 48.
4. I heard Ken Medema say this at a workshop in which we both participated. He may have been referring to Jean-Jacques von Allmen's statement: "Christian worship is a recapitulation of what God has already done (culminating in our salvation through Christ by the operation of the Holy Spirit), and the anticipation of what is yet to be." In *Worship: Its Theology and Practice* (New York: Oxford University Press, 1965) 33.
5. Robert Webber, *Worship Is a Verb* (Waco, Tex.: Word, 1985).
6. Welton Gaddy, *The Gift of Worship* (Nashville, Tenn.: Broadman, 1992) xv.
7. James F. White, *Introduction to Christian Worship* (Nashville, Tenn.: Abingdon, 1980) 21.
8. See Donald Hustad, *Jubilate II* (Carol Stream, Ill.: Hope Publishing, 1993) 124.

Appendix II: Worship Drama
1. See Søren Kierkegaard, *Purity of Heart Is to Will One Thing* (New York: Harpers, 1938) 160-166. The Danish philosopher-theologian said that in Christian worship, the actors are not the people who seem to be on stage. The actors are the congregation; God is the audience; the preacher, liturgist, and other artists are "prompters" who remind us what God has said and done and what we should do and say. See also Hustad, *Jubilate II,* 106-107.
2. *The Dramatized New Testament*, ed. Michael Perry (Grand Rapids, Mich.: Baker, 1993) 10.
3. W. L. Smoldon, "Liturgical Drama," *The New Oxford History of Music,* vol. 2 (London: Oxford University Press, 1954) 175-219.
4. Robert Webber, "A Brief History of Drama in Worship," *Music and the Arts in Christian Worship*, Book Two, vol. 4 of *The Complete Library of Christian Worship,* ed. Robert E. Webber (Nashville, Tenn.: Star Song, 1994) 657-659.
5. In a personal letter of April 6, 1998, Wiersbe wrote about the "action sermons" of the prophets: "Isaiah walked around for three years dressed

like a prisoner of war. Jeremiah broke jars, buried sashes and wore a yoke. Ezekiel played war, got a haircut and did strange things with the hair, and wasn't allowed to weep when his wife died. The people we preach to today are blind and deaf, so there's a desperate need to get their attention. There's a place for the dramatic."

6. Steve Pederson, "Drama in the Seekers' Service," in Webber, "A Brief History of Drama in Worship," 672-674, 686-688.

7. Michael R. Linton, "Smoke and Mirrors at the Crystal Cathedral," *First Things*, June–July 1997: 12-13.

8. See *The Dramatized Old Testament* (2 vols., 1994 and 1996) and *The Dramatized New Testament* (1993), ed. Michael Perry (Grand Rapids, Mich.: Baker).

9. Examples of such materials and instructions for their use may be found in *Dramatized Scripture* by Mozelle Clark Sherman. Contact Dr. Sherman at 3601 Coronado Drive, Louisville, KY 40241.

10. Donald Hustad, *Jubilate II* (Carol Stream, Ill.: Hope Publishing, 1993) 313-349.

Selected Bibliography

Allen, Ronald and Gordon Borror. *Worship: Rediscovering the Missing Jewel.* Portland, Ore.: Multnomah, 1982.

Ashton, Joseph N. *Music in Worship.* Boston: Pilgrim, 1943.

Barclay, William. *The Daily Study Bible.* 17 vols. Philadelphia, Pa.: Westminster, 1955.

Battles, Ford Lewis and Stanley Tagg, trans. and eds. *The Piety of John Calvin.* Grand Rapids, Mich.: Baker, 1978.

Benz, Ernst. *The Eastern Orthodox Church: Its Thought and Life.* Garden City, N.Y.: Doubleday, 1963.

Best, Harold M. *Music through the Eyes of Faith.* San Francisco: HarperCollins, 1993.

Blackwood, Andrew W. *The Fine Art of Public Worship.* Nashville, Tenn.: Abingdon, 1939.

Book of Common Worship. Louisville, Ky.: Westminster/John Knox, 1993.

Bruggink, Donald J. and Carl H. Droppers. *Christ and Architecture.* Grand Rapids, Mich.: Eerdmans, 1965.

Brunner, Peter. *Worship in the Name of Jesus.* Trans. by M. H. Bertram. St. Louis, Mo.: Concordia, 1968.

Burgess, Stanley M. and Gary B. McGee, eds. *Dictionary of Pentecostal and Charismatic Movements.* Grand Rapids, Mich.: Zondervan, 1988.

Burkhart, John E. *Worship.* Philadelphia, Pa.: Westminster, 1982.

Calvin, John. *The Necessity of Reforming the Church.* Trans. by W. Robert Godfrey. Dallas, Tex.: Protestant Heritage Press, 1995.

Carson, D. A., ed. *Worship: Adoration and Action.* Grand Rapids, Mich.: Baker, 1993.

Carson, Tim and Kathy Carson. *So You're Thinking About Contemporary Worship.* St. Louis, Mo.: Chalice Press, 1997.

Clapp, Rodney. *A Peculiar People: The Church as Culture in a Post-Christian Society.* Downers Grove, Ill.: InterVarsity, 1996.

Cornwall, Judson. *Let Us Worship.* South Plainfield, N.J.: Bridge Publishing, 1983.

Cox, Harvey. *Fire from Heaven: The Reshaping of Religion in the Twenty-First Century.* New York: Addison-Wesley, 1995.

_____. *The Seduction of the Spirit.* New York: Simon and Schuster, 1973.

Dawn, Marva. *Reaching Out without Dumbing Down: A Theology of Worship for the Turn-of-the-Century Culture.* Grand Rapids, Mich.: Eerdmans, 1995.

Dillard, Annie. *Teaching a Stone to Talk.* New York: Harper and Row, 1985.

Doran, Carol and Thomas H. Troeger. *Trouble at the Table.* Nashville, Tenn.: Abingdon, 1992.

Douglas, J. D., ed. *The New International Dictionary of the Christian Church.* Grand Rapids, Mich.: Zondervan, 1974, 1978.

Driver, Tom F. *The Magic of Ritual.* New York: HarperCollins, 1991.

Duck, Ruth C. *Finding Words for Worship.* Louisville, Ky.: Westminster/John Knox, 1995.

Edersheim, Alfred. *The Temple: Its Ministry and Services.* Grand Rapids, Mich.: Eerdmans, 1958.

Egge, Mandus A., ed. *Worship: Good News in Action.* Minneapolis, Minn.: Augsburg, 1973.

Erickson, Craig Douglas. *Participating in Worship.* Louisville, Ky.: Westminster/John Knox, 1989.

Ferguson, George. *Signs and Symbols in Christian Art.* New York: Oxford, 1954, 1961.

Frame, John M. *Worship in Spirit and Truth.* Phillipsburg, N.J.: Presbyterian and Reformed, 1996.

Furr, Gary A. and Milburn Price. *The Dialogue of Worship: Creating Space for Revelation and Response.* Macon, Ga.: Smyth & Helwys, 1998.

Gaddy, C. Welton. *The Gift of Worship.* Nashville, Tenn.: Broadman, 1992.

Gaddy, C. Welton and Don W. Nixon. *Worship Resources for Christian Congregations: A Symphony for the Senses.* Macon, Ga.: Smyth & Helwys, 1995.

Gagne, Ronald, Thomas Kane, and Robert VerEecke. *Introducing Dance in Christian Worship.* Washington, D. C.: Pastoral Press, 1984.

Grove's Dictionary of Music and Musicians, 5th ed. New York: St. Martin's, 1954.

Halter, Carl and Carl Schalk, eds. *A Handbook of Church Music.* St. Louis, Mo.: Concordia, 1978.

Hardy, Daniel W. and David F. Ford. *Praising and Knowing God.* Philadelphia: Westminster, 1985.

Hayford, Jack W. *Worship His Majesty.* Dallas, Tex.: Word, 1987.

Herbert, A. S. *Worship in Ancient Israel.* Richmond, Va.: John Knox, 1959.

Hoon, Paul W. *The Integrity of Worship.* Nashville, Tenn.: Abingdon, 1971.

Horn, Henry E. *Worship in Crisis.* Philadelphia, Pa.: Fortress, 1972.

Hunter, George G. *Church for the Unchurched.* Nashville, Tenn.: Abingdon, 1996.

Hustad, Donald P. "Baptist Worship Forms: Uniting the Charleston and Sandy Creek Traditions." *Review and Expositor.* Winter 1988.

_____. "Doxology: A Biblical Triad." *Ex Auditu.* Vol. 8, 1992.

_____. "Fellow Artists in Celebration," *Review and Expositor.* Vol. 71, no. 1, Winter 1974.

Hustad, Donald P. *Jubilate! Church Music in the Evangelical Tradition.* Carol Stream, Ill.: Hope, 1981.

_____. *Jubilate II: Church Music in Worship and Renewal.* Carol Stream, Ill.: Hope, 1993.

_____. "Music and the Church's Outreach." *Review and Expositor.* Vol. 69, no. 2, Spring 1972.

Hustad, Donald P., ed. *The Worshiping Church: A Hymnal, Worship Leaders' Edition.* Carol Stream, Ill.: Hope, 1991.

Jacks, Robert. *Getting the Word Across: Speech Communication for Pastors and Lay Leaders.* Grand Rapids, Mich.: Eerdmans, 1995.

Johansson, Calvin M. *Discipling Music Ministry.* Peabody, Mass.: Hendrickson, 1992.

_____. *Music and Ministry: A Biblical Counterpoint.* Peabody, Mass.: Hendrickson, 1992.

Jones, Cheslyn, Geoffrey Wainwright, and Edward Yarnold, eds. *The Study of Liturgy.* London: Oxford, 1978.

Kendrick, Graham. *Learning to Worship as a Way of Life.* Minneapolis, Minn.: Bethany House, 1984.

Kierkegaard, Søren. *Purity of Heart Is to Will One Thing.* New York: Harper, 1938.

Killinger, John. *Leave It to the Spirit.* New York: Harper and Row, 1971.

Klauser, Theodor. *A Short History of the Western Liturgy.* New York: Oxford, 1969.

Lathrop, Gordon W. *Holy Things: A Liturgical Theology.* Minneapolis, Minn.: Augsburg Fortress, 1993.

Law, Terry. *The Power of Praise and Worship.* Tulsa, Okla.: Victory House, 1985.

Liesch, Barry. *People in the Presence of God.* Grand Rapids, Mich.: Zondervan, 1988.

_____. *The New Worship.* Grand Rapids, Mich.: Baker, 1996.

Lovelace, Austin C. and William E. Rice. *Music and Worship in the Church.* Rev. ed. Nashville, Tenn.: Abingdon, 1976.

Luther, Martin. *Liturgy and Hymns.* Vol. 53 of *Luther's Works.* Edited by Ulrich S. Leupold. Philadelphia, Pa.: Fortress, 1965.

Maldonado, Luis and David Power. *Symbol and Art in Worship.* New York: Seabury, 1980.

Martin, Ralph P. *The Worship of God.* Grand Rapids, Mich.: Eerdmans, 1982.

_____. *Worship in the Early Church.* London: Marshall, Morgan and Scott, 1964.

Morganthaler, Sally. *Worship Evangelism.* Grand Rapids, Mich.: Zondervan, 1995.

Moule, C. F. D. *Worship in the New Testament.* Richmond, Va.: John Knox, 1961.

Myers, Kenneth A. *All God's Children and Blue Suede Shoes.* Westchester, Ill.: Crossway, 1989.

Nichols, James Hastings. *Corporate Worship in the Reformed Tradition.* Philadelphia, Pa.: Westminster, 1968.

Niebuhr, H. Richard. *Christ and Culture.* New York: Harper and Row, 1951.

Old, Hughes Oliphant. *Themes & Variations for a Christian Doxology.* Grand Rapids, Mich.: Eerdmans, 1992.

_____. *Worship (That Is Reformed According to Scripture).* Atlanta, Ga.: John Knox, 1984.

Ortlund, Anne. *Up with Worship.* Glendale, Calif.: Regal, 1975.

Otto, Rudolf. *The Idea of the Holy.* Trans. by John W. Harvey. London: Oxford, 1950.

Paquier, Richard. *Dynamics of Worship: Foundations and Uses of Liturgy.* Trans. by Donald Macleod. Philadelphia, Pa.: Fortress, 1967.

Pass, David B. *Music and the Church.* Nashville, Tenn.: Broadman, 1989.

Petersen, Randy. *Giving to the Giver: Worship That Pleases God.* Wheaton, Ill.: Tyndale, 1990.

Phifer, Kenneth G. *A Protestant Case for Liturgical Renewal.* Philadelphia, Pa.: Westminster, 1965.

Pittenger, Norman. *Life As Eucharist.* Grand Rapids, Mich.: Eerdmans, 1973.

Pottie, Charles S. *A More Profound Alleluia!* Washington, D.C.: Pastoral Press, 1984.

Pritchard, G. A. *Willow Creek Seeker Services: Evaluating a New Way of Doing Church.* Grand Rapids, Mich.: Baker, 1996.

Randolph, David James. *God's Party.* Nashville, Tenn.: Abingdon, 1975.

Rayburn, Robert G. *O Come, Let Us Worship.* Grand Rapids, Mich.: Baker, 1980.

Regele, Mike. *Death of the Church.* Grand Rapids, Mich.: Zondervan, 1995.

Robinson, John A. T. *Liturgy Coming to Life.* London: A. W. Mowbray & Co., 1963.

Rookmaaker, H. R. *Modern Art and the Death of a Culture.* London: InterVarsity, 1970.

Routley, Erik. *Church Music and the Christian Faith.* Carol Stream, Ill.: Agape, 1978.

_____. *The Divine Formula.* Princeton, N. J.: Prestige Publications, 1986.

_____. *Words, Music and the Church.* Nashville, Tenn.: Abingdon, 1968.

Saliers, Don E. *Worship As Theology.* Nashville, Tenn.: Abingdon, 1994.

_____. *Worship Come to Its Senses.* Nashville, Tenn.: Abingdon, 1996.

Schalk, Carl, ed. *Key Words in Church Music*. St. Louis, Mo.: Concordia, 1978.

Schaper, Robert N. *In His Presence: Appreciating Your Worship Tradition*. Nashville, Tenn.: Thomas Nelson, 1984.

Schmidt, Herman. *Liturgy: Self-Expression of the Church*. New York: Herder and Herder, 1972.

Schoedel, Walter M. and David W. Christian. *Worship Is Celebrating as Lutherans*. St. Louis, Mo.: Concordia, 1990.

Segler, Franklin M. *Christian Worship, Its Theology and Practice*. Nashville, Tenn.: Broadman, 1967.

Sendrey, Alfred. *Music in Ancient Israel*. New York: Philosophical Library, 1969.

Shepherd, Massey H., Jr. *The Worship of the Church*. New York: Seabury, 1952.

Skoglund, John E. *Worship in the Free Churches*. Valley Forge, Penn.: Judson, 1965.

Thompson, Bard, ed. *Liturgies of the Western Church*. Cleveland, Ohio: World Publishing Co., 1961.

Torrance, James B. *Worship, Community and the Triune God of Grace*. Downers Grove, Ill.: InterVarsity, 1996.

Towns, Elmer. *Putting an End to Worship Wars*. Nashville, Tenn.: Broadman & Holman, 1997.

Underhill, Evelyn. *Worship*. Rev. ed. Guildford, U.K.: Eagle, 1991.

Van der Leeuw, Gerardus. *Sacred and Profane Beauty: The Holy in Art*. Trans. by David E. Green. Nashville, Tenn.: Abingdon, 1963.

Van Olst, E. H. *The Bible and Liturgy*. Trans. by John Vriend. Grand Rapids, Mich.: Eerdmans, 1991.

Verghese, Paul. *The Joy of Freedom: Eastern Worship and Modern Man*. Richmond, Va.: John Knox, 1967.

Von Allmen, Jean-Jacques. *Worship: Its Theology and Practice*. New York: Oxford, 1965.

Wainwright, Geoffrey. *Doxology—The Praise of God in Worship, Doctrine, and Life*. New York: Oxford, 1980.

_____. *Eucharist and Eschatology*. New York: Oxford, 1981.

Webber, Robert E., ed. *The Complete Library of Christian Worship*, 8 vols. Nashville, Tenn.: Star Song, 1993.

Webber, Robert E. *Worship Is a Verb*. Grand Rapids, Mich.: Zondervan, 1985.

_____. *Worship Old and New*. Grand Rapids, Mich.: Zondervan, 1982.

Werner, Eric. *The Sacred Bridge*. New York: Schocken, 1970.

Westerhoff, John H. *Liturgy and Learning through the Life Cycle*. New York: Seabury, 1980.

Westermeyer, Paul. *The Church Musician*. Rev. ed. Minneapolis, Minn.: Augsburg Fortress, 1997.

White, James F. *Introduction to Christian Worship*. Nashville, Tenn.: Abingdon, 1980.

_____. *New Forms of Worship*. Nashville, Tenn.: Abingdon, 1971.

White, Susan J. *Christian Worship and Technological Change*. Nashville, Tenn.: Abingdon, 1994.

Wiersbe, Warren W. *Real Worship*. Nashville, Tenn.: Oliver Nelson, 1986.

Willimon, William H. *The Service of God*. Nashville, Tenn.: Abingdon, 1983.

_____. *Sunday Dinner: The Lord's Supper and the Christian Life*. Nashville, Tenn.: The Upper Room, 1981.

_____. *Word, Water, Wine and Bread*. Valley Forge, Penn.: Judson, 1980.

_____. *Worship As Pastoral Care*. Nashville, Tenn.: Abingdon, 1979.

Winward, Stephen F. *The Reformation of Our Worship*. London: Carey Kingsgate, 1964.

Wolterstorff, Nicholas. *Art in Action*. Grand Rapids, Mich.: Eerdmans, 1980.

Woodson, Leslie H. *The Swinging Church: A Study in Extremes*. New York: Vantage, 1970.

Index

Speaking in tongues, *see* Glossalalia
Spectatorism vs. participation, 95-97,
    154-155, 200, 277
Spiritual gifts, 87, 88, 91, 101
Stott, John, 59
Styles of worship, 32
Surprise worship, 23, 234 (*see also*
    Improvising)
Sursum Corda, 33, 237, 241, 245
Symbolism, 48, 56, 66, 67, 98, 108,
    110, 164, 234
Synagogue worship, 16, 109, 222

Taizé music, 23, 32, 202, 242
Theological truth, 59, 71, 81-84
Theology
    differing, 83, 146
    in worship, 83-84
    house cleaning, 71
Tongues (*see* Charismatic; Glossolalia)
Traditional worship, 32 (*see also*
    Nonliturgical worship)
Transcendence-immanence, 48, 52
Trinitarian worship, 32, 39, 51-55, 94
Trinity, the, *see* Trinitarian worship
True worship, 32, 35-36, 51, 56, 59,
    219 (*see also* Full worship)
Truth, 45, 59

Unity, 135-137, 152-153, 157

Webber, Robert, 94, 243, 273
Wesley, Charles, 64, 73, 82
Whole person worship, 36, 59-62, 97,
    249, 268
Willow Creek Community Church, 29,
    139, 181, 230-235, 276

Words in worship, 59-64, 67, 69-70,
    73-79, 82
Worship,
    actions, 217, 226, 228, 243, 245,
        252
    arts in, 67, 191, 195, 253
    as a ministry, 33-34, 135, 227
    as work of believer, 34, 51, 94,
        104, 180
    beauty in, 191-195
    biblical rubrics, 112, 130, 156,
        221-230
    definitions of, 51, 56, 59, 120,
        123-124, 150, 180, 245-246,
        272-273
    essentials of, 104-106, 156, 221-
        227, 229-230, 236, 245-246
    for edification, 246-247
    in spirit, 25-27, 35-37
    in truth, 24-27, 37-38
    order, 228-230, 236-238, 266
    reverence in, 73-74, 115, 124
    styles, 32, 138, 141, 173
    (*see also* Full worship, Liturgical
        worship, New Testament, Old
        Testament, True worship)
Worship committee, 158
Worship leaders, 32, 52, 232, 242
Worship vs. entertainment, 143, 179-
    186, 274, 277 (*see also* Entertain-
    ment)
Worship wars, 7, 42, 133-134, 138-139
Worthship of God, 93-94

Youth for Christ, 18, 144, 187

DATE DUE